D0879558

PERCEPTUAL ACQUAINTANCE
FROM DESCARTES TO REID

PERCEPTUAL ACQUAINTANCE FROM DESCARTES TO REID

John W. Yolton

University of Minnesota Press, *Minneapolis*

Copyright © 1984 by the University of Minnesota
All rights reserved.
Published by the University of Minnesota Press,
2037 University Avenue Southeast, Minneapolis MN 55414
Printed in the United States of America

Library of Congress Cataloging in Publication Data

Yolton, John W.
Perceptual acquaintance from Descartes to Reid.
Bibliography: p.
Includes index.
1. Perception (Philosophy) — History.
2. Knowledge, Theory of — History.
3. Philosophy, Modern.
B828.45.Y64 1984   121'.3   83-16718
ISBN 0-8166-1162-9
ISBN 0-8166-1163-7 (pbk.)

The University of Minnesota
is an equal-opportunity educator
and employer.

852548

LIBRARY
ALMA COLLEGE
ALMA, MICHIGAN

To

John Wright

Sylvana Tomaselli

Stephen Ford

Shadia Drury

21692

Contents

Preface ix

Introduction 3

Chapter I. Perceptual Cognition of Body in Descartes 18

Chapter II. Malebranche on Perception and Knowledge 42

Chapter III. Direct Presence among the Cartesians 58

Chapter IV. British Presence 76

Chapter V. Locke and Malebranche: Two Concepts of Idea 88

Chapter VI. Ideas in Logic and Psychology 105

Chapter VII. Perceptual Optics 124

Chapter VIII. Hume on Single and Double Existence 147

Chapter IX. Hume on Imagination: A Magical Faculty of the Soul 165

Chapter X. Hume's Ideas 181

Chapter XI. Sense and Meaning 204

Bibliography 227

Index 241

Preface

Seventeenth- and eighteenth-century philosophers, whether on the continent or in Britain, were much concerned with sense perception as a means of access to physical objects. How does our sensory equipment interact with objects in the world to give us an awareness of that world? 'How do we know body?', or even, 'can we know body?', were questions dealt with by most writers. Such questions and their answers did not arise for the first time during these centuries, but the terminology employed, especially the terminology of 'ideas', *was* new. An examination of accounts of perceptual acquaintance during this period is, in large part, a study of the way of ideas.

In tracing the use of the term 'idea' during these two centuries, we discover the pervasiveness of spatial language at a time when there was not a well-developed psychological vocabulary for talking about awareness and knowledge. A principle and a phrase used throughout this period focus attention on that spatial or physical-object language. The principle is usually formulated as 'no thing can be or act where it is not', the notion of location being applied to mind as well as to body. The phrase is 'presence to or with the mind', the assumption being that the mind can only know objects that are near to and present with it. Analyses of perceptual acquaintance show that various attempts were made to modify a literal interpretation of the phrase and the principle, with varying success and differing awareness of the control this principle and this phrase exerted.

The principle and the phrase also play an important role in a fascinating debate in eighteenth-century Britain concerning the possibility that matter can be made to think. I have examined that debate in my *Thinking Matter: Materialism in Eighteenth-Century Britain*. That study grew out of the same research program as this work on perception. These two books are closely related; many of the same writers are discussed in both volumes. Although each stands on its own and can be read independently of the other, *Thinking Matter* is recommended reading for some of the background issues and concepts for *Perceptual Acquaintance*. The details of the physiology of the body used in both the materialism-immaterialism debate and in theories of perception can be found in chapter VIII of *Thinking Matter*. That book is also useful for giving an account of the different views about space and extension, as well as about the nature of matter (chapters IV and V).

The early research for *Perceptual Acquaintance* was presented in two articles: "On Being Present to the Mind, a Sketch for the History of an Idea" (*Dialogue* 14 [1975]:373-88), and "Ideas and Knowledge in Seventeenth-Century Philosophy" (*Journal of the History of Philosophy* 13 [1975]:145-66). A more recent article contains other material for the book: "As in a Looking-Glass: Perceptual Acquaintance in Eighteenth-Century Britain" (*Journal of the History of Ideas* 40 [1979]:207-34). Chapter X forms the basis for an article with the same title in *Hume Studies* 6 (1980):1-25. An early version of part of chapter V appeared in *John Locke: Symposium Wolfenbüttel 1979*, ed. Reinhard Brandt (1981). Portions of chapters VII and VIII have been read to the Washington Philosophy Club in Washington, D.C., to the Fullerton Club of Philadelphia, and to the Philosophy Club at Rutgers University in New Brunswick. A version of chapter I was read to the Philosophy Club at the University of Pennsylvania in the spring of 1982.

For works in French and Latin, I have used standard English translations, where they exist. Other translations are my own or those of my wife.

Besides thanking my wife, Jean, for her expert help in researching the text and bibliography, I want to thank my research assistant, James G. Buickerood, for his help in checking references. The dedication to this, as to my *Thinking Matter* volume, recognizes the role played in my research and thinking by four of my former graduate students at York University in Toronto, Canada. Their names will soon become known for their own contributions to the history of philosophy.

PERCEPTUAL ACQUAINTANCE
FROM DESCARTES TO REID

Introduction

Early in his survey of accounts of perception and our knowledge of objects, Thomas Reid (*Essays on the Intellectual Powers of Man*, 1785) echoes a theme found in other writers before him: the conflict between the philosopher's account of our world and the ordinary person's beliefs about that world.

An object placed at a proper distance, and in a good light, while the eyes are shut, is not perceived at all; but no sooner do we open our eyes upon it, than we have, as it were by inspiration, a certain knowledge of its existence, of its colour, figure, and distance. This is a fact which every one knows. The vulgar are satisfied with knowing the fact, and give themselves no trouble about the cause of it: But a philosopher is impatient to know how this event is produced, to account for it, or assign its cause. (p. 128)

Reid points out that philosophers were puzzled about the correspondence between "the thinking principle within us, and the material world without us" (p. 132). Despite some differences, he thinks there was great uniformity in the accounts given of our knowledge of objects from Plato to his own time: "For they all suppose that we perceive not external objects immediately, and that the immediate objects of perception are only certain shadows of the external objects" (p. 133). Reid suggests that philosophers go astray when they try to account for all phenomena, the phenomenon of seeing objects being

3

obvious and in need of no explanation. It is with the many accounts of seeing objects that this study is concerned. Most of the accounts in the two centuries we are examining used the terminology of 'ideas', a terminology not invented but greatly popularized by Locke.

From the very beginning readers of Locke's *Essay concerning Human Understanding* viewed his account of ideas as making our knowledge of the world indirect, representative, and uncertain. Many of the critics of his *Essay* charged that knowledge of the world was even rendered impossible by the new 'way of ideas'. Locke was not the first to use the term 'idea' as whatsoever is the object of the mind when we think: Descartes and the Cartesians employed the same term, albeit with some variations. But it was Locke's pervasive use of that term, in the course of attacking many traditional concepts and doctrines, which focused attention in Britain on the skeptical question. If ideas and their relations constitute knowledge and what is present with or to the mind, what are the guarantees that those ideas and relations do inform us about the world? A realm of ideas threatened to supplant, in our knowledge, the world of physical objects and events.

Locke's account, it is commonly said, embodies a 'representative theory of perception and knowledge'. A few brief references to some recent commentators on Locke, Berkeley, and Hume will give us a quick characterization of that theory, a characterization to be found in many histories of philosophy and in most textbooks. While insisting that Locke modified some features of the 'representative theory of perception and knowledge', R. I. Aaron formulated that theory as follows:

Knowledge of the real, the theory asserts, need[s] an intermediary object between the knowing mind and the ultimate object. This intermediary object is the one immediately given or thought and represents the ultimate object. The immediate object when I look at this table is no physical entity but an idea which represents the table.[1]

The modifications Aaron finds in Locke's account of that theory includes a rejection of the notion that *all* ideas copy objects and the treatment of some ideas as 'logical meanings'. But Aaron insists that, despite these modifications, "Locke thought . . . that some sort of representationalism and dualism was inevitable."[2] Two important features of the representative theory are captured by Aaron's formulation: ideas (at least *some* ideas) as special *objects*, and the 'double' existence of idea-objects and physical (Aaron's ultimate) objects. Jonathan Bennett identifies a third feature usually assigned to this theory: "Locke puts the objective world, the world of 'real things', beyond our reach on the other side of the veil of perception."[3] Richard Rorty accepts Bennett's tracing of "the veil of ideas" to the seventeenth century, finding in Descartes and Locke the inward turning to the ideas of the mind, away from outward objects.[4] On this reading, the problem of knowledge became one of discovering some features among our ideas which might inform us about the world of nonideas. Skepticism, Rorty thinks, is inevitable on this view of knowledge.

The seventeenth century gave skepticism a new lease on life because of its epistemology, not its philosophy of mind. Any theory which views knowledge as accuracy of representation, and which holds that certainty can only be rationally had about representations, will make skepticism inevitable.[5]

There is ample textual support for applying to Locke, and to other writers in the way-of-ideas tradition, this standard interpretation: talk of ideas as objects; talk of the indirectness of our knowledge of body; offer resemblance as the relation between ideas and things; characterize knowledge itself as the perception of the relation of ideas. At the same time, a careful examination of the writings of Locke, Descartes and his followers, and of many others in eighteenth-century Britain down to Reid, reveals other aspects of ideas and of the analyses of perceptual acquaintance that suggest an alternate interpretation of those texts. We shall find reasons to cast considerable doubt on Reid's historical accuracy. Whether Reid is responsible for the subsequent stereotype of the 'representative theory of perception and knowledge' and of its skepticism, his interpretation has survived. Reid should not, however, take all the blame for what I think are misreadings of these writers; for Locke, Berkeley, and Hume were generally characterized by their contemporaries in the way Reid does at the end of the century. If the standard reading *is* incorrect, it can only be corrected by going back to the original texts, including many little-known works in which the language and doctrines of the more well-known writers are found. Placing Descartes, Locke, Berkeley, and Hume in the context of the debates of their day—debates reflected in and commented upon by many writers in religion, natural philosophy, medicine, and optics—will help us understand the issues without being influenced by more recent labels and categories.

To set the stage for our study of these texts, we need to have (a) an outline of some of the antecedent accounts of perceptual acquaintance among scholastic writers; (b) some preliminary indication of ways in which optical treatises, which focused attention on images and their location, influenced the accounts of perception; (c) an introduction to a widely accepted principle that applied the notion of no action at a distance to cognition; and finally (d) some brief indication of attempts to replace a literal interpretation of that principle with a psychological or cognitive reading. An underlying theme in many of the texts to be examined is that perceiving is understanding, that to have objects present to the mind is simply to be aware of them, to apprehend them, to know them.

Scholastic Theory

The pivotal concept for the accounts of perceptual acquaintance in the seventeenth and eighteenth centuries is that of objects present to the mind. Depending upon how that concept was interpreted, those accounts moved between an indirectness of knowledge (because only a representative, proxy object can be present to the mind) and a strong direct realism where the object known was, in some way, itself present to or in the mind. By examining the writings in the following chapters, the importance of this concept will be revealed. Descartes's objective reality of ideas (which is the *being* of objects in the mind) set the terms for much subsequent discussion, both on the continent and in Britain. But that concept of objective reality, with its impetus toward direct realism , has its roots in scholastic doctrine.

Although there is no single theory of perception held by all scholastics, there are some features common to most versions after St. Thomas, features which are useful for setting the context for perception theories in the seventeenth and eighteenth centuries. Most versions of scholastic accounts are a mixture of literalness and abstraction, of the notion that some features of objects must be transmitted to the perceiver, together with the notion that cognition occurs in the category of the knower, not in that of the object. The category for knowing is immateriality, not materiality. Some scholastic philosophers accepted Aristotle's account of objects as matter and form, where the form of objects is that feature which can be transmitted to perceivers, just because it is indifferent to the medium of its instantiation. The Aristotelian form is clearly the ancestor of the seventeenth- and eighteenth-century concept of ideas, certainly of the Cartesian version. Descartes's notion of the objective reality of ideas is a direct descendent of St. Thomas's account, with borrowings from Aristotle.

Aristotle took as a general principle that the "actuality of any given thing can only be realized in what is already potentially that thing, i.e. in a matter of its own appropriate to it" (*De Anima*, 414a, 25-28).

The last clause of this quotation indicates that for one thing to *be* another thing is not a question of identity, at least not if the matter of both is taken into account. The being of a thing is matter-independent. Without this stipulation, cognition of objects would only be possible if, in cognizing the stone, I materially became the stone. "The thinking part of the soul must therefore be, while impassible, capable of receiving the form of an object; that is, must be potentially identical in character with its object without being the object" (429a,14-17). Thus, "actual knowledge is identical with its object" (430a,20), "the mind which is actively thinking is the object which it thinks" (431b,17-18); but we are to read these remarks only after we have made the distinction between *being identical in character with* and *being* the object. Material identity with the object is not what Aristotle means; it is formal identity alone. The succinct way of making this distinction is to say it is the *form* of the object, not the *object*, that is in the soul (431b,30), but we must be careful not to give a spatial connotation to the word 'in'. Aristotle drew a distinction between sensing and knowing: we sense individuals but know universals (417b,21); and he was careful to point out that whereas "to the thinking soul images serve as if they were contents of perception," the real contents, what is cognized, are the things whose form is in the soul (431a,14-15; cf. 432b,7-10). It is the role of the form in the soul which is especially relevant to understanding the Cartesian sense of 'idea'. This feature of our knowledge of objects was further developed by St. Thomas.

St. Thomas opens his account of cognition in the *Summa Theologica* by criticizing Plato for saying "the form of the thing known must of necessity be in the knower in the same manner as in the thing known itself" (Ia,84,1). Thus, the sensible form "is in one way in the thing which is external to the soul, and in another way in the senses" (ibid.). Similarly), the intellect, "according to its own mode, receives under conditions of immateriality and immobility the species of material and movable bodies; for the received is in the receiver according to the mode of the receiver" (ibid., cf. Ia,85,1). The intellect knows bodies through immaterial and intelligible species that not only are derived from things themselves (not from separate forms), but *are* the things themselves in the understanding. The agent intellect abstracts the intelligible species from the phantasms of sense. Abstraction in this way is the basis for knowledge: the sensible phantasms represent the individual material thing, and the intellect abstracts the form of the thing from the phantasms. These phantasms are "images of individuals, and exist in corporeal organs" (Ia,85,1,Art.3). But just as Aristotle had said that, while the images serve as the means of sensing and knowing, they are not what is known or sensed, so St. Thomas says "the intelligible species is not what is actually understood, but that by which the intellect understands" (Ia,85,2). In this respect, both Aristotle and St. Thomas anticipate a fundamental issue between Arnauld and Malebranche: whether ideas as the means of knowing can represent, without themselves being the objects of knowledge. And the difference between Arnauld and Malebranche is the same as that between St. Thomas and Plato regarding the following question: are the ideas, the forms that are the means of knowing, separate existences? For St. Thomas, what is "primarily understood is the thing, of which the species [which is secondarily understood] is the likeness" (ibid.). However—and it is at this point that St. Thomas's theory may open the way for divergent versions—the intellect "knows directly only universals"; it knows indirectly the particulars represented by the phantasm and the abstracted species (Ia,86,1).

The precise nature of our knowledge of particles did divide some of the subsequent scholastics. Picard[6] speaks of Thomists and Suarezians: the former characterize knowledge of objects by the metaphor of 'seizing of an object in a conscious way', the latter employ the stronger metaphor of 'vital assimilation'. The assimilation of knower and object does not avoid the function of representation: to know is formally to represent to oneself the object. The representation is sometimes referred to by Suarezians as the *esse objectivum*. Duns Scotus, Dalbiez tells us, called ideas 'objective beings'.[7] Durand of Saint Pourçain talked of a mental verb, referring to it as "a third thing between the formal concept and the thing."[8] In turn, Suarez criticized Durand for turning the objective concept into a special entity. Tolet seems to have sided with Suarez, for he denied, Picard tells us, the need for an intentional image and insisted on intentional assimilation being the conformity of the act with its object.[9] Tolet denied the need for talking of the intentional, objective presence of the object in the faculty.

However, for the Thomists and for most Suarezians, the object must be *present to* the faculty (of sense), either by itself or by means of an intentional species. Picard's analysis of the intentional species (he refers to it as "that mysterious scholastic entity," p. 15) is important for our understanding of the nature of ideas in seventeenth- and eighteenth-century writers. The intentional species is a *form*, in the sense of the actualization of a power. That form is not, however, a complete reality: it depends upon constant reinforcement from the object. The intentional species as form is, Picard says, neither corporeal nor spiritual: it is accordingly "outside of the categories of being" (ibid.). At the same time, Picard thinks the species, especially when it functions in sensible knowledge, became rather like those in-between agents in seventeenth-century physiology, animal spirits: more material than spiritual. The *intentio* of St. Thomas lends itself, Picard believes, both to a materialization and to being treated as a simple formula or way of speaking (a being of reason).

The resort to intentional species, when these are more than just a way of speaking, occurs when the object is not materially present to the sense organ, or when there is some intervening medium (p. 24). When "the sensible is united to the apprehensive faculty, the intentional species becomes useless," Picard reports Tolet as saying (pp. 26-27). For those Suarezians who retained the intentional species, those species were said to be emitted by the object. They were not similitudes of the object, only determinants of the faculty, producing the reaction the Suarezians called "vital assimilation by the act of knowing of the known," the latter being the expressed species which, for the Suarezians, was "the act of knowing" (p. 40). Representation of the object is contained in the act of knowing, not, as for the Thomists, in the species itself. The expressed species produced by the faculty simply is the act by which the object is known (p. 42).[10]

This opposition between the Thomists, who insisted on the intentional species as that which carries the information of the object, and the Suarezians, who settled for the act of knowing as putting us in *cognitive* contact (they spoke of 'cognitive assimilation') with the object, is a striking foreshadowing of the controversy Arnauld had with Malebranche. The struggles the scholastics had with the notion of the presence of objects to the knower are also precursors of problems that reappear in the seventeenth and eighteenth centuries. How can material presence give rise to immaterial, i.e. cognitive, understanding? The Thomists held tightly to the notion that "the object must be united to the faculty in order to provoke knowledge," but since material cannot be united to immaterial, "the external material object is replaced by an intentional species which presents the object to the faculty" (Picard, p. 55). The resulting *species vicaria objecti* performs as if it were the immediate object. Such was the path followed by Malebranche. Arnauld was much closer to the Suarezians in stressing the cognitive nature of knowing and in identifying ideas with acts of perception.

This Suarezian solution would seem to hold more promise than the adherence to intervening species, if we are to appreciate the nature of perceptual awareness. Of course, as Picard points out, the vital assimilation of knower and object through cognitive acts does not take us to the object itself. That assimilation is still "an intentional transportation of the object in the knowing act, according to certain aspects only and in a mode of being different from the real mode" of the object (p. 87). But this way of analyzing perception should not fall into the mistake, which Picard says some modern scholastics make, of believing that all will be lost "if they do not affirm that the sensible faculty absorbs the object itself in its numerically identical reality" (p. 88).[11]

The Language of Optics

It is not surprising that optics should have influenced the way in which perceptual acquaintance was analyzed in the two centuries. Descartes wrote a *Dioptrique*; Malebranche asked readers of his *Recherche de la verité* to acquaint themselves with his essay on vision; and Berkeley addressed some of the relevant optical problems in his *New Theory of Vision*. We shall discover that the language of images, of mirrors, of perspectives, and of the geometry of vision surfaces in many eighteenth-century accounts not specifically addressed to optics. A passing remark by Hume is a good example: "But my senses convey to me only the impressions of colour'd points, dispos'd in a certain manner."[12] While Hume talks of physical and mathematical points (he rejects the latter for perception) in the rest of that section, he makes no attempt to explain this remark about the senses and colored points. We can, of course, recall Berkeley's discussion of perceptual minima, of seeing visible points, in his *An Essay Towards a New Theory of Vision*, §82. Berkeley also mentions that Issac Barrow cited Tacquet's language of visible points (§30). Much of the discussion of vision in optical treatises in both centuries is in terms of the geometry of vision, of rays of light and of points on the retina. According to Newton's axiom 6 in his *Opticks*, the rays flowing from all the points of the object meet again after converging by reflection or refraction. They make "a Picture of the Object upon any white Body on which they fall." Each point of the object illuminates "a correspondent Point of the Picture." Thus, in the eye, light is conveyed "in so many Points in the bottom of the Eye, and there to paint the Picture of the Object upon that skin." These pictures, "propagated by Motion along the fibres of the Optick Nerves into the Brain, are the cause of Vision."

The suspicion that optical theories (not just Berkeley's) play some role in Hume's reference to colored points is further supported by the recognition that earlier writers on geometric optics (in particular,

Maurolico and Kepler) used the same language. In his account of these early writers, Vasco Ronchi describes the way in which it was said that an extended object reflects rays on to the retina, there producing a "system of points," from which is derived "a luminous and colored figure."[13] The problem for Kepler then was, how do we locate this figure or image where the object is? Ronchi's fascinating account of optical theory sketches some of the ways in which the apparent world, built from the details supplied by the sense organs, can supply us with information about the object world. What we see is the apparent world, Hobbes's phantasms (perhaps, we might suggest, Hume's perceptions). Sometimes, under certain conditions, we locate the phantasm or perception where the object is. What is present to us are our perceptions, our phantasms, but we normally take these to be the objects. "In effect, seeing the table means creating a phantasm, identical to the material table, and localizing it exactly where it is, so as to be able to put objects on it, and by touching find its dimensions and its position which sight gives it."[14] Ronchi remarks that seeing (for Kepler; Ronchi himself is very sympathetic to this analysis) is the result of a physical agent (rays of light), a physiological process (formation of retinal image, impulses along the optic nerve), and a psychic or psychological representation (the apparent world).[15] "The apparent world, the one we see, with its shapes, its luminous quality, its colors, is thus a psychic product, a creation of its observer, a collection of phantasms, that is, of shapes which have no body but only an appearance."[16] A collection of phantasms, a psychic entity of light and colors—for Ronchi, this feature of Kepler's theory is most important for understanding perception.

In developing the notion that what we see is the apparent world, Ronchi makes effective use of the photographic picture. The action of the rays of light on the camera and on the film or plate are well known. When this film is developed and then projected onto a screen, what is on the screen is the image of the building we photographed, having many details similar to those of the building. No one, Ronchi remarks, would think of saying the image on the screen *is* the building. "Why, on the contrary, when it is a question of vision, do we say the image seen *is* the object?" He draws out the similarities between the eye and film.

If the objective used to define the image is of poor quality, or if the optical adjustment has been poorly done, the picture on the film will be out of focus; the image projected on the screen will be out of focus too; but if by some optical or mechanical trick, for example, by adjusting the aperture, regulating the focus or adding an additional lens, you can improve the clarity of the image on the negative, the image projected on the screen will become clearer. An analogous phenomenon is produced for the eyes: if they are altered [e.g. by contact lenses] or if the dimensions of the eyeball don't allow the formation, on the retina, of a clear image of external objects, the observer sees fuzzy shapes instead of objects; but these shapes become clearer immediately if, by use of additional lenses, for example, eyeglasses, you improve the clarity of the retinal image. (p. 41)

One other example from Ronchi's book is useful for fixing in our minds how, from facts about vision, we might be led to formulate a problem of perception in the way Hume did, in terms of a double (phantasm and real object) or a single (real object only) existence. When we look up at the sky, we find a kind of screen or plane. On that background plane we see clouds, sun, moon, stars, planets. These objects are in fact at varying distances from us and from each other, some of them at immensely different distances. Nevertheless, we see all these objects on the same surface; they appear to be on a common plane, the surface of the sky as seen. From these facts about vision and about the distances of sun, moon, and stars, Ronchi concludes that

the seen shapes under the canopy of heaven are not celestial bodies, nor real clouds nor shooting stars. They are only the *phantasms* which the mind of the observer creates and locates where and as it wishes. Since the mind has no way of calculating such great distances, even when they are varying distances, it places them all at the greatest distance possible, that is, at that distance beyond which it lacks information. (p. 45)

No Cognition at a Distance

Many essays, treatises, and tracts contain the dictum that 'no thing can be or act where it is not'. The notion of 'present to mind' is familiar from Hume's repeated appeal to it. When he says, "'tis universally allow'd by philosophers, and is besides pretty obvious of itself, that nothing is ever really present with the mind but its perceptions,"[17] we may think of Malebranche's remark: "I believe that everyone agrees that we do not perceive objects external to us by themselves."[18] Malebranche reached this conclusion (as we shall see in chapters II and III) by an elaborate appeal to the dictum about 'no cognition at a distance'. When Hume links the notion of what is present with the mind to the further claim that "the very being, which is intimately present with the mind, is the real body or material existence,"[19] we may think we hear an echo of Descartes's doctrine of the objective reality of ideas, a doctrine which like the scholastic theory, tried to find a way of having objects present with the mind. Hume's struggles with the single and double existence views (examined in chapter VIII of this book) may be seen as an eighteenth-century British version of Cartesianism, of the notion that ideas have a dual reality, as modes of mind and as bearers of the reality of objects.

That Hume's discussion does reflect this Cartesian doctrine is, I think, clear, but not quite in the way in which Arnauld and Malebranche (who were much closer in time to Descartes) reflected Descartes's formulation of the same doctrine. Much additional discussion and transformation of the doctrine had occurred before Hume wrote his analysis. Philosophical theories hardly ever stand still. They are absorbed but modified almost as soon as the next writer focuses on the problems that the theory was meant to solve. But Hume's use of the phrase 'present with the mind' is a significant indication of one of the ingredients in his thought about perception and our knowledge of external objects. The fact that that phrase runs throughout the *Treatise* (it occurs also in the *Enquiry*), that it is invoked almost as a litany, suggests that it may have been frequently used by the writers Hume was reading. In fact, that phrase has a long and interesting history from the Cartesians, right through the eighteenth and into the twentieth century. It still appears in very recent writing.[20] By tracing some of the appeals made to this notion (and some of its rejections; see chapters III and IV), we can shed light upon perception theories in the eighteenth century and better understand the nature and role of ideas in these theories.

Meaning and Understanding

Along with the physical and optical languages used in talking about mind and perceptual acquaintance, we shall find writers in both the Cartesian and Lockean traditions who begin to draw away from the literalness of 'present to the mind'. (1) Many stress the meaning or significance of ideas, rather than any resemblance they may have. Linguistic comparisons are made, rather than optical ones. (2) A few contrast the physical responses of the body to stimuli from objects with the significatory responses of the perceiver. This contrast is found in Descartes, though more hinted at than developed in detail. I offer in chapter I a reconstruction of his theory of the perception of bodies, using this suggestion and relating to it the distinction between the formal and objective reality of ideas. This suggestion of a significatory response that accompanies the physical reactions in the physiological mechanisms of the body is more explicit in Cudworth and in the eighteenth-century Swiss doctor Charles Bonnet. One can also hear echoes of this notion in Reid's talk of signs and in Berkeley's language of God. (3) Another aspect of the stress upon meaning and significance, both for ideas and for our cognitive responses, is the cashing by Arnauld and Locke of the metaphor of ideas being *in* the mind. Both writers insist that 'to be in the mind' just means 'to be understood'. Arnauld elaborated this translation in his long exchange with Malebranche (chapter III). Locke borrowed from Arnauld in several passages of his *Essay*. The same reading of 'present with the mind' or of 'being in the mind' is found, though less clearly, in Berkeley, in Hume, and in many of the new logic books of the eighteenth century. Many works of psychology (treatises on the soul) also follow this reading of those metaphors (chapter VI). (4) Still another aspect of the way of ideas, which shows the movement away from the literalness of the language, is the firm distinction drawn by the majority of writers between ideas as objects or entities, and ideas as perceptions, as acts with contents. Arnauld and Locke drew this distinction in their attacks on Malebranche (chapters III and V); but this distinction is also recognized by many other writers in the eighteenth century, as well as by several eighteenth-century and early nineteenth-century historians of the way of ideas. In these accounts, Malebranche's conception of ideas as things is always ranged against the other, more common notion of ideas as perceptions. These two concepts of ideas are discussed in chapters V and VI.

Once we become sensitive to these significatory features of the way of ideas, a revision of the standard interpretation is required. It is not at all easy to shake ourselves loose from established readings; stereotypes in philosophy are no less difficult to correct or replace than those in other areas, particularly when there are so many supporting features for that stereotype in the language about ideas and knowledge found in the writers we are to examine. None of these writers fully articulated the perceptual theory required by the revision I am suggesting; none has entirely freed himself from the optical analogies and the spatial metaphors. The same sort of tension, found in scholastic theories, between literalness and cognitivity reappears in the two centuries we are studying. On occasion, the acceptance of the notion that what is known must be intimately present to the mind leads writers into saying that the mind does go to the place where objects are located. Not just the phantasm, image, or perception is seen as being where the object is; the mind is there instead. Such writers are not as sophisticated as those we normally read, but they do reveal one of the puzzles of explaining how mind can know body without intervening mental entities. It was difficult to understand the nature of cognition, to appreciate the possibility that we can know body directly, that direct knowledge of body need not be construed on the model of touching, of spatial contiguity.

There were a variety of attempts to articulate the difference between what Arnauld identified as *spatial* and *cognitive* presence. The spatiality of mind and the extensionality of space were two concepts affecting the discussion of matter and thought in that related debate over thinking matter. That principle, that no thing can be or act where it is not, was at work in that debate as well. Many writers did manage to free themselves from the literal application of space and place to mind. There was a growing recognition of the psychological aspect of thought, of what one writer in England called the "Apprehension of the Thing seen or heard."[21] This writer carefully distinguished between the physical and the physiological aspects of perception and what he nicely characterized as *"that Acquaintance which I have with an Object, in what I call an Act of Perception."*

When the accounts of perceptual acquaintance from Descartes to Reid are carefully examined, when we read the tracts and pamphlets of lesser-known writers who entered the debates and commented on these accounts, when we trace the history of the concept 'present with the mind', and when we pay close attention to the use of the term 'idea', certain revisions in the standard interpretation of the way of ideas are required.

(1) We must correct Reid's interpretation of Descartes, Arnauld, Locke, and others. He ascribed the wrong concept of ideas to most of those in the tradition of the way of ideas. The representationalism and the consequent skepticism that he found in that tradition more nearly fit Malebranche and his few British followers, for whom ideas are special objects that could be viewed as intervening between objects and perceivers.

(2) If ideas are not themselves entities, if to have ideas and to be perceptually aware are one and the same (as Arnauld and Locke explicitly said), the way is left open for an account of perceptual acquaintance that asserts we see objects, even that we see objects directly.

(3) One important barrier to such a reading of Descartes, Arnauld, Locke, and others in Britain has been a curious notion that cognitive directness requires some sort of literal joining of mind and object. The heavy use of optical language, the pervasive acceptance of the principle of no cognition at a distance, and the mistaking of the use by these writers of ideas as objects, has led philosophers, even in our own time, to reject direct realism because it is impossible. On this

reading of directness, it is incoherent. But it was not this incoherent version of directness that the way-of-ideas philosophers accepted. Direct acquaintance is not the scholastic's assimilation of objects by the mind, nor the formal being of objects in the mind. Representation of objects by ideas is not a distancing of objects from our awareness.

(4) Appreciation of the above should enable us to understand that Descartes, Arnauld, and Locke, and the tradition stemming from their writings, were developing a psychological account of perceptual awareness, a cognitive psychology. The more important part of that cognitive psychology was the elaborate analysis of the workings of the mind, of faculties and mental acts, to be found in Locke and Hume in particular (but present also in many other writers). When that psychology treats ideas *and* perception, we must recognize it as a way of distinguishing the act of being perceptually aware from the content or meaning of that act. It is the role of meaning in perceptual acquaintance that has been overlooked in the standard discussions and histories of the way of ideas.

Notes

1. Richard I. Aaron, *John Locke*, 3rd ed. (Oxford, 1971), pp. 101-2.

2. Ibid., p. 105.

3. Jonathan Bennett, *Locke, Berkeley, Hume: Central Themes* (Oxford, 1971), p. 69.

4. Richard Rorty, *Philosophy and the Mirror of Nature* (Princeton, 1979), pp. 50-51.

5. Ibid., p. 113.

6. Gabriel Picard, "Essai sur la connaissance sensible d'après les scolastiques," in *Archives de philosophie* 4, Cahier 1 (1926).

7. R. Dalbiez, "Les sources scolastiques de la théorie cartésienne de l'être objectif à propos du 'Descartes' de M. Gilson," in *Revue d'histoire de la philosophie* 3 (1929): 466.

8. Ibid., p. 468.

9. Picard, "Essai," pp. 10-11.

10. Ibid., p. 42. The scholastics asked themselves about the status of mirror images, as a way of explicating knowledge by means of the intentional species. Typically, Suarez insisted that the mirror "in no way prevents our looking at the object: it does not put between us and the object any real image. By means of the mirror we reach directly the object itself: the object itself is the term of knowledge, the 'objective concept'; the intentional similitude, insofar as it is preserved in this system, is the act itself of knowing, it is in no sense said [to be] the term of knowledge." (Picard, "Essai," p. 53)

11. L. Noel (*Notes d'epistémologie thomiste*, 1925) confirms Picard's remarks about the literalness of some modern Thomists. In dealing with the question "How can the object be present to awareness?" they work, Noel says, with spatial concepts and end with indirect realism (pp. 33; cf. pp. 73-75, 82-84, 117-20). Pierre Garin (*La théorie de l'idée suivant l'école thomiste*, 1937) warns against confusing St. Thomas's notion of the form of the object being in the knower with *physical* assimilation. *Cognitive* assimilation involves the form, not the mode of being of the object known (pp. 53, 57). C. Boyer ("Réflexions sur la connaissance sensible selon Saint Thomas," in *Archives de philosophie* 3, cahier 2 [1925]) also points out the same distinction: "Knowing the other is having in one's self besides one's

own being, the being of the other. It is not finding oneself opposite the other, or touching it, it is becoming the other." (p. 108).

12. Hume, *Treatise*, p. 34.

13. See his Preface to Paul-Marie Maurin's French translation of Hobbes's *De Homine* (1974), pp. 15-16. Also, his *L'Optique science de la vision* (1966). Further support for tracing Hume's remark to optical theories is found in an essay by John Stuart Mill: "Bailey on Berkeley's Theory of Vision," in *Essays on Philosophy and the Classics*, ed. J. M. Robson, vol. XI of the *Works* (1978), p. 248. In characterizing "The theory of vision, commonly designated as Berkeley's, but in fact the received doctrine of modern metaphysicians," Mill writes: "The sense of sight informs us of nothing originally, except light and colours, and a certain arrangement of coloured lines and points. This arrangement constitutes what are called by opticians and astronomers apparent figure, apparent position, and apparent magnitude."

14. *L'Optique*, p. 49.

15. Ibid., p. 37.

16. Ibid.

17. Hume, *Treatise*, p. 67.

18. Malebranche, *De la recherche de la vérité*, ed. Geneviève Rodis-Lewis, vols. I and II of the *Oeuvres complètes* (Paris, 1972). The passage cited is from vol. I, p. 413 (bk. III, pt. II, chap. I). The English translation used is that of T. M. Lennon and Paul J. Olscamp (1980), p. 217.

19. Hume, *Treatise*, p. 206.

20. See, e.g., N. Rescher's *Conceptual Idealism* (1973), p. 101. For a discussion of this aspect of Professor Rescher, see my "Pragmatism Revisited: An Examination of Professor Rescher's Conceptual Idealism," in *Idealistic Studies* 6, no. 3 (1976): 218-38.

21. Humphrey Ditton, *A Discourse concerning the Resurrection of Jesus Christ* (1712), p. 497.

Chapter I

Perceptual Cognition
of
Body in Descartes

That observation and experimentation are important for our knowledge of the world about us is a truth amply illustrated by Descartes's scientific work. There is, however, no systematic account of the nature of observation in his writings. There is a detailed physiology in *La Dioptrique, Le Monde ou Traité de la lumière*, and *Traité de l'homme*. The sixth of his *Meditations* contains an elaborate argument for the conclusion that body exists, even though body may not be as it seems. There is also the doctrine of the objective reality of ideas, a doctrine which tantalizes by its brevity and metaphor, but which is part of a general theory of knowledge assumed rather than elaborated. There is no theory of perception, no account of perceptual cognition. There are materials in his works for constructing some account of perceptual cognition: we can extract a coherent theory of perception from his sketch of a physiology and a psychology in the *Regulae*, from his proof for body in the sixth *Meditation*, from his semantic or epistemic account of signs and ideas, and, of course, from his account of the objective reality of ideas.

In examining the various components of this theory, we should pay special attention to Descartes's rejection of any causal relation between the physical activity of objects on our sense and the perceptual ideas in our minds. He does not always take care to deny such causal connections, but it is, when properly considered, his mature view. Ideas are not formed at random, however; there is a definite correspondence, even response, between ideas and objects. The correspondence is, in one respect, occasionalist: on the occasion of certain physical motions caused in nerves and brain by the motion of body, the mind by a natural faculty forms ideas.[1] The response of the mind to such motions is, however, more than occasionalist: ideas are not causal effects of motion but semantic and epistemic responses to it. This particular part of Descartes's theory of perception is a bit obscure and is not fully developed. An equally puzzling and important component of his theory is the doctrine of the objective reality of ideas, especially when there is no causation between things and ideas. The doctrine of objective reality can be read, as I shall do here, as an epistemic one. But such a reading appears less than Descartes meant when he introduced the doctrine at the beginning of his proof for God's existence. That God exists in the mind of the believer—not just the *idea* of God—appears to be an integral part of that and all similar proofs. Do adventitious ideas, or true adventitious ideas, also have an ontic aspect? Or does the objective reality of infinite substances differ from that of finite, created substances in this one essential? Are there two doctrines of objective reality in Descartes?

We may not be able to resolve all these questions and problems, but I think we can come close to articulating a theory of perceptual cognition that brings together a number of the strands in Descartes's account of ideas and knowledge.

The Psychology of Perception

Rule 12 of the *Regulae* sketches a theory of perception and an account of the origin of ideas. In talking of knowledge of things, Descartes points out that we must give some analysis of our cognitive faculty, as well as some account of the nature of the objects of knowledge. He identifies four faculties, all of which are involved in knowledge, especially in cognition of body. The understanding alone is capable of apprehending truth; but the imagination, the senses, and the memory are relevant to our knowledge and perceptual cognition of things.[2] He does not wish, in the *Regulae*, to give a detailed and precise account of our knowledge of body, but he offers a quick sketch of a likely hypothesis.

The senses are passive when receiving the modifications generated by physical contact with external bodies. Descartes uses the model of wax receiving an impression. This model is not meant as an analogy.

The reception of the stimulus by the sense organs is exactly the same as the reception by the wax of some figure impressed on it:

In this way, the first opaque structure in the eye receives the figure impressed upon it by the light with its various colours; and the first membrane in the ears, the nose, and the tongue that resists the farther passage of the object, thus acquires a new figure from the sound, the odour, and the savour, as the case may be. (H and R, vol. I, p. 37)

When any external sense is stimulated by an object (i.e., when it is moved by an object), the figure or shape that it receives is transmitted to the common sense. This transmission takes place in an instant, without any entity being passed along. The nature of this instantaneous transmission is like that of the movement of the lower and upper portions of my pen when I write: all parts move at the same time. In its turn, the common sense functions like a seal on the fantasy or imagination: it impresses the figures it has recieved from the senses on the imagination. He refers to what the common sense transmits to the imagination as "figures or ideas," and says that they come to the common sense in a pure and incorporeal form. The imagination or fantasy is still part of the body. It is not clear, then, why the physical forms in the external sense organs have to be incorporealized, especially since he is emphatic in saying they are impressed on the fantasy as impressions are on wax.

The fantasy is located in the brain, where the motor nerves for our sense organs originate (or teminate). The fantasy in turn moves these nerves. The movement is the same as occurs between external sense and common sense: instantaneous and continuous, as in the pen example. These movements of nerves by the fantasy are sufficient to move our limbs. The movement of animals is of this form also: they have no knowledge of objects, but by this physiology the stimuli from objects can have the result that animals move. Animation in animals requires only a corporeal fantasy. The motive power of animals and of many of our actions is thus located in the brain.[3] Such motive power is matched in humans by a cognitive power that is purely spiritual. This cognitive power receives impressions at the same time as the fantasy receives figures from the common sense.[4] The same cognitive power attends to the impressions in the memory. In his attempt to characterize this cognitive power, Descartes says it is sometimes passive, at other times active; sometimes it can be compared with the seal, at other times with the wax. But in this last comparison, he is careful to say that here the seal-wax example is only an analogy. Strictly, there is nothing comparable in bodily things to this cognitive power (H and R, p. 39). When the cognitive power attends to the common sense, with the help of the imagination, we can say that that power sees, touches, and so on. If it applies to the imagination alone—that is, to the figures inscribed there—we can say that it remembers. It also understands and senses, and is capable of forming new ideas in the fantasy.

The linear progression of the first stages in this process of receiving figures or ideas in the fantasy is displaced by a reciprocal interaction, once the account is completed by the activity of the cognitive faculty. The pure understanding can be moved by the imagination, but the understanding can also act on the imagination. The imagination can act on the senses by means of the motor force of the brain, as when it applies the senses to objects; or the senses themselves can act on the understanding, when it paints there images of bodies (p. 39).[5] When dealing with questions that have nothing to do with body, or with anything that resembles body, the senses, the imagination, and the memory are not useful for our cognitive power. But Descartes insists, in this theory about our knowledge of body, that if the understanding considers any object connected with body, "we must form the idea of that thing as distinctly as possible in the imagination" (p. 40). He goes on to say, however, that what the understanding needs from the senses is not the things themselves; rather, it needs schematic figures of things that are in some way faithful to the things or to the impressions of things in the fantasy. What he has in mind are the simple natures, which in the case of body are geometrical figures or the components of such figures.

Descartes's brief account of the psychology of perception (for that is what this account of the cognitive power is) quickly gives way to a question that is of more interest to him: how the understanding can best apprehend the truths of body.[6] Because he sketches only briefly a psychology, even because he calls it an hypothesis, we should not forget that he outlines a psychology to link cognition with physiology. When the physiological processes are informed by the understanding attending to the imagination or the senses, sensation as cognitive activity occurs. The same psychology is present throughout his argument for the existence of body in the sixth *Meditation*. In that argument, his objective is not to produce a proof that establishes schematic, geometrical objects (despite some remarks about body and mathematical objects), but one that articulates the reality of the bodies that surround and affect our own, those that are linked causally with our body according to the brief physiology of the *Regulae* (whose details are in the *Traité de l'homme*). In characterizing the faculties of sense and imagination as cognitive when informed by the understanding, Descartes was confronted with the difficulty of how causation could work across categories, between body and mind, from physiology to psychology. There can in fact be no causal relation between such diverse substances, but the relation is nonetheless intimate. The occasionalist alternative to causation is not only found in his remarks on Regius's program: it appears also in *Traité de l'homme.*[7] The rejection of causation between brain and cognitive activity is aided by two other doctrines: the clear distinction between sensation and its cause, and the theory of natural signs.

Signs and Ideas

Walking at night along an uneven path without a light, you need to use a stick to guide your way. If you have had this experience, Descartes remarks, you will know that you are able, by means of the stick, to feel the differences in objects that lie along the path around you. You can distinguish trees, sand, rocks, water, grass, mud, and other objects. For sighted persons, such distinctions in the dark by means of a stick may be a bit unsteady and unsure, but blind people, who are accustomed to being guided by a stick, would find distinguishing objects this way to be natural and easy, so much so that "we would almost be able to say that they see with their hands, or that the stick is the organ of some sixth sense."[8] The combination of the resistance of bodies and of the sensations we receive through the stick enables us to identify specific objects. In the same way, Descartes suggests, light, which in bodies is nothing other than a quick and lively motion, acts on the air and transparent bodies between our eyes and the body we see, enabling us to identify objects in the environment.[9] Moreover, just as the combination of hands, sensations, and stick enables the blind person to discriminate different kinds of objects, so we, with the combination of eyes, sensations, and motion of air are able to discriminate red, yellow, green, and other colors. Descartes sees no need, in the case of light- and color-discrimination, to talk, as did the scholastics, of intentional species, 'little flying images'. Just as nothing passes from the object to the blind man through his stick, so no particles or images or anything else pass from objects through the air to our eyes.

Besides the elimination of intentional species as unnecessary entities, Descartes uses the example of the blind man and his stick to assert an additional truth about perception: there is nothing in these objects that is similar to the ideas or sensations we have when we make these perceptual discriminations of colors or of kinds of objects. The two examples (of colors and of objects) are not quite similar, of course, but in both cases Descartes wants to say that there is nothing in the objects as we perceive them other than different motions. The *Traité de la lumière* begins by drawing a distinction between the sensations ('sentiments') we have of light and the cause of these sensations. The latter are identified with "the idea which is formed in our imagination by means of our eyes" (A, vol. I, p. 315; A and T, vol. XI, p. 3). Other examples of the dissimilarity between sensation and physical counterpart are cited. A man opens his mouth, moves his tongue and speaks: there is in these physical actions nothing similar to the idea of sound which those movements generate (or to which they correlate). The idea that an infant has when a feather is passed gently over his or her lips while sleeping in no way resembles the feather. A soldier, after battle, thinks he has been wounded but, after calling a doctor, discovers that it was only a buckle that caused the sensation he mistook for a wound. Had there been a similarity between cause and sensation, the soldier would have known it was not a wound. Other examples can be found in the *Principles*. Writing on paper with a pen, by moving the pen in one way, we can trace letters that make us imagine battles and storms; but by moving the pen in other ways, we can cause quite different thoughts, e.g., of peace or rest, even though the movement of the pen in both cases is similar. Another example: the pain arising from the cut of a sword is neither like the sword nor like the movement it makes in cutting.

In all these examples, not only is Descartes concerned to establish or illustrate the lack of similarity between felt experience and physical causes; he is concerned as well to suggest that, even though there is no similarity between ideas and their causes (or their physical correlates), the former give us information about the world. It would seem that the relation envisaged by Descartes is that of sign to signified. In explicating the sign relation, he again resorts to examples. Words have no similarity to the things they signify. The word-thing signification relation is conventional and instituted by humans, but Descartes thinks there are some natural sign relations, as tears signify sadness and smiles, joy. We as it were read the joy and the sadness in the face of the person (A, vol. I, p. 316; A and T, vol. XI, p. 4). Descartes suggests that nature has perhaps established certain other signs that give us the sensations of light. This kind of sign, too, is totally dissimilar to that which it signifies.

This last suggestion should be examined carefully It is a reversal of what we might expect. The expectation from what Descartes has been saying is, I think, that ideas or sensations are going to be signs; thus, the sensation of light would be a sign of specific motions in the object and air. His problem would accordingly seem to be to explain how we can get information about the world from our ideas and sensations. *But* the sign relation here suggested is the other way around: the physical motion is the sign *of* or *for* the sensation. In a passage from *Le Monde, ou Traité de la lumière*, Descartes writes:

But, if words, which signify nothing except by the convention of men, are sufficient to make us conceive of things with which they have no resemblance, why is Nature not able to have also established a certain sign which makes us have the sensation of light, even though this sign has no feature which is similar to that sensation. (A, vol. I, p. 316; A and T, vol. XI, p. 4)

It is clear, as Alquié notes in his edition of this text, that Descartes's suggestion is that "the physical action of light signifies to us the sensation that we feel. "In other words, that which we habitually consider as the signified (the physical action) becomes here that which signifies" (ibid., n. 2). A few sentences further on, Descartes appears to distinguish *signifying* from *representing*. It is the mind that *represents* to us the idea of light when the action that *signifies* light touches our eyes. Again, it is the physical action of light (of light corpuscles) that signifies the idea we have of light. The 'sentiment' of the previous sentence becomes explicitly 'idée'. The physical stimulus signifies the idea.

There is one passage in the sixth *Meditation* where Descartes uses 'sign' in this way. He has been discussing those errors in sense perception that we make, e.g., mislocating pain. He indicates the physiology of pain sensations, saying that when the movement of the impulses reaches the brain, it excites there "a certain movement which nature has established in order to cause the mind to be affected by a sensation of pain" (H and R, p. 197). Similarly, in *Les Passions de l'âme*, Descartes explains how the passions are excited in the soul: the animal spirits enter certain pores in the brain and there excite "a particular movement in this gland which is instituted by nature in order to cause the soul to be sensible of this passion" (H and R, p. 348). The notion of what is instituted by nature reminds us of his discussion of natural signs. In the Latin version of the same passage from the *Meditations* as cited above, the reference to natural signs is explicit: "Ita, exempli causâ, cùm nervi qui sunt in pede vehementer et praeter consuetudinem moventur, ille eorum motus, per spinae dorsi medullam ad intima cerebri pertingens, ibi menti signum dat ad aliquid sentiendum."[10]

The stress upon meaning in perception, especially the suggestion of motion being a natural sign for the mind, enables Descartes to replace the causal connection between felt experience and physical motion; motion in body does not cause but it signifies our sensations. Is there more to this distinction than just the convenience of a substitute relation for causation? Is there in these treatises, or elsewhere in the texts of Descartes, an explication of natural signification?

In the *Traité de l'homme*, Descartes speaks of the figures traced on the brain by animal spirits as representing in some way the lines and surfaces of the objects seen. He extends this relation of representation also to those figures on the brain that give occasion to the mind to sense or to experience movement, size, distance, color, sounds, and so on. Do the tracings on the brain *represent* the sensed color, size, etc.? He recognizes that for figures correlated with color, size, etc., the figures on the brain do not have corresponding figures on the relevant sense-organ, as is the case with the retina of the eye. In these cases, there are only the figures traced on the surface of the pineal gland. It is these forms or images that the rational mind immediately considers. In his account of sensing, then, there is the motion of object and nerves, the brain impression, and conscious sensation. If the motion signifies the sensation (as that passage in the treatise on light seemed to say), does the sensation represent the qualities of the object? Or does the representative relation hold only between brain impression and object quality?

We get some help in answering these questions by looking first at the *Dioptrics* and then at the doctrine of the objective reality of ideas. Discourses 4, 5, and 6 in the *Dioptrics* seem to be referring to representation, not to signifying. There, Descartes criticizes the theory that images come from the object to the brain. First of all, he says that writers espousing such a theory have no way of explaining how such images can be carried from the object to the brain.[11] Second, these writers forget that there are other ways in which thought can be excited or stimulated, e.g., by signs or speech, neither of which resembles in any way the things that they signify. Third, even if we accept the suggestion of images coming from objects to the brain, there are no images that resemble their objects completely. If there were such images, we could not distinguish the images from the objects. Moreover, representation usually requires only a partial resemblance. For example, the marks on a map represent forests, villages, humans, etc., but the only resemblance they have to such objects is in their figure. Because of the laws of perspective, circles are often represented better by ovals than by other circles, squares are often better represented by diamond shapes than by squares. The best representation is frequently unlike that which it represents. If there are images in the brain when we sense, it is not any resemblance they may have to objects that constitutes their representative function. To understand representation, we must ask ourselves how these images enable the mind to sense all the qualities of objects. Descartes recalls at this point the blind-man example. When the blind man touches bodies with his stick, the stick is variously moved according to the different qualities of the bodies. The nerves of his hand are moved in the same way, and that motion is carried to the brain. It is the motion from bodies to stick, to nerves, to brain that gives the mind the occasion to sense the qualities of objects.

In his notes to this treatise, Alquié writes that it is clear from these passages that Descartes wants to substitute signs for the notion of resembling images. "The sign is able, in effect, to provide the means for knowing that which it signifies without necessarily resembling it" (A, vol. I, p. 685). But I do not think it clear that Descartes means to treat the *impressions* on the brain as signs, especially if there is a difference between *signifying* and *representing*. It is the *motion* in the brain, "acting immediately against the mind," that gives us the sensations that we have. This link between sensations and motion in the brain is instituted by nature (A, vol. I, p. 699; A and T, vol. VI, p. 130).[12] It is the nature of our mind to be so made that, when movements of a certain sort occur in the nerves and brain, we have specific sensations. There are specific changes in the brain (changes of movement, of force, and of manner) that enable the mind to know. But knowing (perceiving) is not reading off from our sensations properties of the world. Perceptual knowing is the having of these sensations. This is the point of the reverse-sign relation: ideas are not signs of things, they are the interpretations of physical motion (of things), the cognitive counterpart of things and their physical features. Interpretation is not signification; it is representation.

In her explication of this part of Descartes's account of perceptual knowledge of body, Geneviève Rodis-Lewis ("Langage humain et signes naturels dans le cartésianisme," in *Le Language*, 1966, pp. 132-36) cites the passage from *Le Monde* (see above, p. 24) as an illustration of the way in which Descartes compares "the extrinsic association between words and things signified" with the correlation between "the quantitative modifications which diversify bodies and the qualitative sensation felt on this occasion" (p. 132). Rodis-Lewis considers as a metaphor the notion of "the external action which causes light" being a sign. It is for her a metaphor that catches the fact that the 'material sign' gives rise to the interpretation by the mind. She compares this interpretation to our response to language, when we understand the meaning of what we hear even though we are not conscious of the sounds we hear. She does not go on to draw out the comparison; she is, in this article, more interested in those natural signs that are related to the passions, both in humans and in animals. She gives a somewhat more extensive discussion of some of these natural-sign passages in another article, "Le domaine propre de l'homme chez les cartésiens" (*Journal of the History of Philosophy*, 1964, pp. 157-88), but her main concern in this article is also with other aspects of Descartes's thought. There are, however, one or two hints in this second article of how we might interpret physical motions as signs. One suggestion is to link the mind's responses to the movements in the brain with the notion of natural geometry. More generally,

Man is distinguished from animals because he alone is capable of freely imposing a meaning on figures or sounds which animals by their nature lack. But it is in that way also that man can interpret the language inherent in nature, and he by dominating it can use it, instead of simply obeying it instinctively. (p. 179).

Man discovers, prior to reflection, that there is meaning "in natural data" (p. 182).

Louis Marin (*La Critique du discours sur la "Logique de Port-Royal" et les "Pensées" de Pascal*, 1975) also uses the notion of a natural geometry to explicate Descartes's account of motion as a natural sign.

Descartes shows that there is, latent, unconscious, a geometry of signs in Nature, in the world and in the body, thanks to which, spontaneously and instinctively [these] signs give to us, but uncertainly, in the form of a schema and not of an image, of an analogy and not of a mimesis, the things themselves which become visible in the signs which they represent and do not resemble. (p. 91)

More briefly, "Knowing naturally is this deciphering of the signs that Nature produces in a geometrically structured convention, but in an uncertain manner."[13]

Aside from a brief discussion in the Port Royal logic, there is very little discussion or use made of this notion of natural signs. It is the sort of notion we would expect to find in the works of subsequent writers, even though it does not have great prominence in Descartes's own work. There is, as we shall see later, a hint of this doctrine in Reid's notion of natural signs, but between Descartes and Reid I have found only three writers who explicitly use this notion. In his *The Vanity of Dogmatizing* (1661), Joseph Glanvill refers to the account of matter and motion as the cause of sensation: "Sense is made by motion, caus'd by bodily impressions on the organ; and continued to the brain, and centre of perception" (p. 8). Glanvill wants to know "how the pure mind can receive information from that, which is not in the least like it self" (p. 28). He thinks the reception of information from objects is 'inexplicable', but he refers to some unnamed writers who say that "the soul indeed is not passive under the material phantasms; but doth only intuitively view them by the necessity of her Nature, and so observes other things in these their representatives." The 'other things' in these material impressions are their meanings.

But how is it, and by what Art doth the soul read that such an image or stroke in matter (whether that of her vehicle, or of the Brain, the case is the same) signifies such an object? Did we learn such an Alphabet in our Embryo-state? And how comes it to pass, that we are not aware of any such congenite apprehensions? . . . That by diversity of motions we should spell out figures, distances, magnitudes, colours, things not resembled by them; we must attribute to some secret deductions. (pp. 29-30)

He also speaks of an "implicit inference" and, in the later revision of this work, *Essays on Several Subjects* (1676), of "some kind of Mathematicks in the Soul." In the same later work, the comparison with understanding a language is made more explicit: without "some unknown way of learning by them [the motions of the filaments of nerves] the quality of the Objects," the soul would be like an infant who hears sounds or sees lips move but has no understanding of what the sounds or movements signify, or like an illiterate person who sees letters but "knows not what they mean" (p. 6). Glanvill does not seem to take from Descartes this suggestion of an interpretation of brain impressions made by means of a 'congenite' code or alphabet, because he remarks: "Nor will the Philosophy of the most ingenious *Des-Cartes* help us out," i.e. help us understand how from diversity of motions we are able to acquire information about the distance, size, or color of objects. I suspect this suggestion may have reached Glanvill from the Cambridge Platonists.

In his posthumously published *A Treatise concerning Eternal and Immutable Morality* (1731), Cudworth follows Descartes's account of this doctrine, without mentioning Descartes. Noting that nothing is "Communicated in Sensation from the Material Objects without, but only Certain Motions, that are propagated from them by the Nerves into the Brain," Cudworth goes on to make the comparison with language or speech. "Wherefore the Truth is, that Sense, if we well consider it, is but a kind of *Speech* (if I may so call it), Nature as it were talking to us in the Sensible Objects Without, by certain

Motions as Signs from thence Communicated to the Brain" (pp. 214-15). While the connection between the sounds in speech and ideas is conventional, 'Nature's Law' establishes a natural connection between certain motions and sensible ideas.

> Just in the same manner Nature doth as it were talk to us in the Outward Objects of Sense, and import Various Sentiments, Ideas, Phantasms, and Cogitations not by stamping or impressing them passively upon the Soul from without, but only by certain Local Motions from them, as it were dumb Signs made in the Brain; It having been first Constituted and Appointed by Nature's Law, that such Local Motions shall signify such Sensible Ideas and Phantasms, though there be no Similitude at all betwixt any Local Motions and the Senses of Pain or Hunger and the like . . . (p. 216)

Cudworth continues by speaking of the soul "as by a certain secret Instinct, *and as it were by Compact*, understanding Nature's Language, as soon as these Local Motions are made in the Brain, doth not fix its Attention immediately upon those Motions themselves . . . but presently exerts such Sensible Ideas, Phantasms, and Cogitations, as Nature hath made them to be Signs of" (pp. 216-17).

An even more explicit statement of this doctrine is made later by Charles Bonnet, a Swiss scientist who wrote on the mind and its faculties. He published an *Essai de psychologie* at Leyden in 1754. The physiological basis for perception is elaborated by Bonnet: motions imprinted on the brain give rise to ideas in the mind. Those brain motions are, he says, "species of natural signs of ideas which they excite." Ideas "are only clothed in *natural* signs, and these signs are the images which the objects trace in the Brain" (p. 17). When thinking of anything—whether it be in recollection, imagination, or association—the mind acts on the brain by stimulating the same motions as the object did originally, or by calling to mind the words for that object (the words then excite the appropriate brain motions). Words are artificial signs; brain motions, natural signs (pp. 39-40). Bonnet rejects the notion of any similarity between the perception of an external object and the movement occasioned by that object. He then draws an interesting comparison between the relation of words to ideas and the relation of brain motions to ideas: "What a word is to an idea which it represents, motion is, so to speak, to perception which it causes. It is a kind of sign used by the CREATOR to arouse in the Soul a certain perception, and to arouse there only that perception" (p. 135). In his *Essai analytique sur les facultés de l'ame* (1760), Bonnet remarks that he does not understand how the fibers of the nerves and brain produce ideas in the mind, but it is clear that ideas do result from such movement. He then offers a conjecture: "I consider them [the movements of the fibers] as natural Signs of Ideas; I study these Signs, and the results of their possible combinations" (p. xxi). Later, in chapter IV of the same book, he says of abstract ideas—which are also caused by corporeal movements—that "we only have these ideas by means of these *Signs*, which represent them; and these *signs* are figures, sounds, motions, *body*" (p. 13).

With these later uses of the natural-sign doctrine by Cudworth and Bonnet, with the suggestions made by Marin and Rodis-Lewis, and with the examination we have made of Descartes's treatises, I think we can say that the relation that gives the mind the occasion to form ideas or to have sensations is what I have called the reverse-sign relation. What we normally call 'signs' are words and ideas or thoughts. A sign stands for something else. It requires an interpreter; that is, a sign is a sign *of* something *for* someone. Physical motions, as signs, can be understood when those motions are movements of hands and arms (signals), or even facial movements that stand for or indicate moods or intentions. But physical motions in nerves and brain are not motions of which we are aware. We do not read consciously from the physiological impulses any referent of these impulses. Nevertheless, in these passages, Descartes is trying to assimilate physiological motions to natural signs, even though the signification relation in this case is not one of which we are aware. He is searching for an alternative to a causal relation. There is a relation, not just a coincidence, between motion in nerves or brain and the ideas we have. Thus, what could that relation be other than semantic? The mind can be activated in two ways: causally and semantically. The mind reads the physical motions, as it does the tears and smiles of a face. The difference is that with natural signs, such as the motion and force that activates nerves and brain, the mind does not consciously have the signs and then move to the signified. The suggestion is that the mind's reaction is a significatory reaction to specific physical activities in nerves and brain. The mind is so created by God that it has the semantic reaction of sense and idea. There is no preestablished harmony, if that means the mind does not respond to physical activity. The mind *does* respond to what happens in nerves and brain (and hence to what happens in its environment), but this is not a response *caused by* physical events; rather, physical events are *interpreted by* the mind. Descartes has this interpretation in mind when he speaks of the mind attending to or studying the figures on the pineal gland. Mind and cognition are thus connected with the world, but the connection is precisely that which is proper to cognition: significatory, not resemblance or causal. The doctrine of signification only briefly adumbrated by Descartes is far from clear. It may, however, give us some hint of how to interpret the doctrine of the objective reality of ideas. For we shall see that that doctrine leans on scholastic theory but offers 'being understood' as the mode of being for objects in the mind.

Objective Reality

Formal reality is the actual reality any given kind of thing has. The formal reality of my desk is that it exists in space and time, is extended, is a substance. The formal reality of ideas is that they are modes of thought, exist in minds, are not caused by corporeal objects. Formal reality is being in its own kind. Ideas have an additional kind of reality. They represent objects; this representing function is their objective reality. In the third *Meditation*, Descartes introduces the terminology of 'objective and formal reality' *en route* to a demonstration of God's existence. In the case of the idea of God, there is some kind of causal connection between idea and object. Descartes also talks of causal relations between my idea of heat or of a stone and the cause of those ideas. Such causal relations do not, apparently, come into play for the formal reality of those ideas: being entirely a work of the mind, the idea of heat or of a stone does not require or indeed acquire its formal reality from anything other than the mind. It is only with respect to the objective reality of these ideas that the relation with heat or a stone is said to be causal: "in order for an idea to contain one specific objective reality rather than another, it must without a doubt receive that reality from some cause, in which there is at least as much formal reality as the idea contains of objective reality" (H and R, p. 163). Axiom 5, in his proof for God where he replies to the second set of objections, states that the objective reality of an idea requires a cause that has formally as much reality as our idea has objectively. Moreover, "this axiom is highly necessary for the reason that we must account for our knowledge of all things, both of sensuous and of non-sensuous objects" (H and R, vol. II, p. 56). We can, he goes on to say, judge that the sky exists when we see it (i.e., when we have an idea of it) only if we suppose that "every idea needs to have some really existing cause of its objective reality." The causal link, for any idea other than that of God, is difficult to understand. Part of what Descartes wants to say is that, e.g., an idea of heat cannot represent a substance, because a substance has more actual or formal reality than does a quality such as heat. The representation in idea cannot go from a lower to a higher order of reality. Ideas as ideas have only the mind as their cause, with the exception of the idea of God which has God as its cause.[14] Ideas in their representing role, however, have causes: their causes are what they represent. Is it possible that this causal relation between formal and objective reality is the sign-signified relation suggested in the treatises? This would be a relation that was not really causal but which was more than occasionalist. There is a response by the perceiver to the stimuli.

The difficulty with accepting this semantic relation alone is that Descartes does not just mark the *representative* function of ideas by the phrase 'objective reality'; he links this function with the *being* of *objects* in the understanding. In the restatement of the proof for God, at the end of the replies to the second set of objections, "the objective reality of an idea" is defined as the being of the thing represented by the idea, in so far as that object is in the idea (H and R, vol. II, p. 52). The most detailed statement of this doctrine is found in his reply to the first set of objections. Caterus raised the question, "what is it to be objectively in the understanding?" (H and R, vol. II, p. 2). Caterus argues that this notion of objective existence is a mere name, an extrinsic denomination which adds nothing to the reality of the object. In his reply, Descartes says that to be objective signifies nothing other than "existing in the mind . . . in the way in which objects are wont to exist in the mind" (p. 10). This explanation is not, it must be confessed, a very enlightening one, but it does indicate that 'objective reality' refers to the *being* of *objects* in the mind. What is the idea of the sun? It is, he says, "the thing thought, in so far as it is objectively in the understanding." The sun as an object external to my mind is obviously not in my mind. The phrase "to be objectively in the understanding" does not signify the sun's action on me but only the being of the object in my understanding. The idea of the sun "is the sun itself existing in the understanding."

How can we interpret this ontic notion, with respect to the ideas of physical objects? Quite clearly, Descartes does not mean that the object in its own formal reality is in the understanding. Equally clearly, he rejects a skeptical reading, where no connection at all is allowed between ideas and physical things. Ideas represent physical things, not by some arbitrary relation but by a natural relation in which physical motions are translated into cognitive form. If this is the only alternative to literal presence of objects in the mind, Descartes is specifying a cognitive presence of objects as the only way in which objects can be present to minds, i.e., meaningfully. Are there any passages where Descartes discusses objective reality which enable us to determine what he intended by the doctrine, when applied to our perceptual cognition of body?

In an attempt to go beyond these bald statements, Descartes cites a number of points where he agrees with Caterus. (1) An object existing in the understanding is not a real or actual being, "i.e., is nothing situated outside the intellect" (H and R, vol. II, p. 10). Existence outside the understanding should not be confused with existence in the understanding; formal differs from objective reality. (2) Descartes also agrees with Caterus that the object existing in the understanding is not made by the mind, is not a being of reason, is only a real object conceived; but from that fact Caterus concluded that it was real in the understanding. Caterus does not believe that thinking or perceiving involves any ontology in thought. (3) Descartes agrees that the thinking or perceiving does not affect the object perceived, that we do not need to find a cause for the object's formal existence. What needs to be explained is how this object rather than some other object is perceived or thought by me. For this explanation, we need to know "what is the cause of that idea."

Alquié thinks that Caterus and Descartes are not understanding each other, that Descartes is trying to say something new with an old, indeed a scholastic, vocabulary. For Caterus, a Thomist, Alquié says "there is no place in knowledge for what Descartes calls an idea" (A, vol. II, p. 509n). We know things, not ideas, and there is no need for any intermediary. Alquié reads Descartes as saying we are unable to have a direct presence of things to our mind: "The thing is never known except by the intermediary of an idea" as the representative or image of things (ibid., p. 520n). Alquié does not say what such presence of objects to a mind would be. It sounds as if he is suggesting the literalist alternative that Descartes was careful to avoid. Alquié might, however, have in mind the Thomist notion of the intelligible species. He points out that this species is not "an image or substitute for the real object, but the object itself considered in the action which it exerts on the subject." The key phrase is "in the action which the object exerts on the subject." What is the nature of that action? Is it causal or perhaps only semantic?

That Descartes knew the Thomist doctrine is clear, for he tried formulating his concept of objective reality in the scholastic vocabulary. In his replies to the fourth set of objections (those of Arnauld), he says that ideas are nothing but *forms*, when they are taken as representing things. Alquié admits that in this passage, Descartes is forcing himself to follow the vocabulary of the Schools, where "ideas retain the forms of things independently of their matter" (ibid., p. 674n). The being of objects is captured by the form in the understanding. Ideas as the forms of objects are hardly intermediaries.

They are, as Alquié remarks for the Thomist, the things themselves in the understanding. But we still have no clear conception of what the being of objects is in the understanding. What we can say is that Descartes was conscious of the very close similarities between his talk of the objective reality of ideas and the scholastic talk of the form of objects in the understanding.[15] Both the scholastics and Descartes offered this account as a way of characterizing our cognition of objects. That characterization was made by reference to (a) the object perceived or thought about, (b) the intellect which does the thinking or perceiving, and (c) the form of the object in the understanding. As another attempt to throw light on (c), we need to see whether we can say something definite about the status and nature of ideas for Descartes.

Ideas and Perception

To the three parts of the characterization of our knowledge of objects given above, Descartes adds a fourth, (d) the idea as an entity, according to the standard reading of Descartes. "But for Descartes, the *res cogitata* that exists in my mind when I think of the sun is not the sun itself, but some proxy for the sun."[16] Gilson also says that between the thought and the object, Descartes introduces an entity: "Being a representative form, the idea is a thing thought, and in that way, a reality."[17] Gilson echoes here the phrase "the thing thought" from Descartes's reply to Caterus. He supports his reading of that phrase as applying to the idea (instead of to the object that is thought about) by a marginal note added by Descartes in the Latin edition of the *Discourse*: "Note here and everywhere in what follows that the name Idea is generally used for everything thought, insofar as there is something objective in the mind."[18] There may be some ambiguity in this note, but it appears to mean that the word 'idea' designates the things thought of, insofar as those things are objectively in the mind, Alquié also speaks of ideas for Descartes having a *nature* of their own, a reality different from the things they represent.[19] Even though Descartes writes "objectively *or* by representation" (the Latin text has only ('objectivum'), Alquié separates the *representative content* of an idea from its *objective reality*.[20] Descartes speaks of only two ways in which ideas are real: *formally* as modes of thought, and *objectively*, as representing something other than themselves. Alquié draws a distinction in the latter which I do not think possible on Descartes's account.

Brian O'Neil, in *Epistemological Direct Realism in Descartes'*

Philosophy, agrees with Gilson that Descartes "frequently reifies *esse objectivum,*" although O'Neil rejects the claim that the *esse objectivum* becomes a *tertium quid* (p. 85). How it can be reified but fail to become a third sort of thing is far from clear. O'Neil's view arises from his belief that Descartes distinguishes the *content* of an idea from the idea as a mental event (p. 5). Consequently, O'Neil suggests, Descartes needs to ask for the cause of the content as well as the cause of the idea. The content of the idea is, O'Neil says, also real; hence the search for its cause. We must, I think, be very careful here. Is not the reality, which the content of an idea has, precisely the reality of the *object?* The content has a borrowed reality, a reality fetched from the object itself. As O'Neil remarks, there are three realities "to be taken into account: the object, the idea of the object, and the object as it exists in the idea" (p. 5). But the idea of the object is not *two* realities; it is one reality with a double cause. An idea cannot be identified without its content. Even if ideas were entities for Descartes, they would not be two entities. If ideas are in fact activities, the temptation to take the content of these activities as an entity may fade. And if, as I have suggested, the causation of the *esse objectivum* is semantic, this temptation may disappear entirely. The reality of the object in the idea is the *meaning,* the cognitive meaning, of the object.

There are other passages in Descartes that speak against ideas being *res cogitatae.* In his objections, Gassendi had suggested that the formal reality of ideas for Descartes was the idea "not as representative but as an actual entity."[21] Descartes did not respond to this suggestion in his replies to Gassendi's objections, other than to remark that he did not take ideas, as Gassendi did, as images depicted on the fantasy. But in his letter to Clerselier of January 1646, where he comments on Gassendi's objections, Descartes writes that "if we take the word idea in the way in which I expressly said I took it," the only way one could deny having an idea of God is if one does not understand what these words signify: "that thing which is the most perfect that we can conceive" (H and R, vol. II, p. 129). He then equates 'not having any idea of God' with 'having no perception' which responds to "the signification of that word, God." Arnauld was later to cite this passage against Malebranche in support of his (Arnauld's) equation of ideas with perceptions. Arnauld was emphatic in his interpretation of Descartes on this point: "it is without question that the word 'idea' must be taken for 'perception', as has M. Descartes in that demonstration of the existence of God."[22] We might add as well, "and note the stress Descartes places upon linking the having of ideas with understanding and signification."[23]

In his "Preface to the Reader" of his *Meditations*, Descartes speaks to an objection: from the fact that I have in me an idea of a thing more perfect than I am, it does not follow that that idea is more perfect than I am. To this, Descartes responds that there is an equivocation in the word 'idea'. (1) It can be taken *materially* for an operation of my understanding, in which case the idea could not be more perfect than I. (2) It can be taken *objectively* for the thing represented by that operation of the understanding, and the thing can of course be more perfect than I. The term 'materially' is the same as 'formally' in the *Meditations*: the formal reality of ideas is that of modes or operations of the mind. Thus acts of the mind do the representing. Descartes's switch in vocabulary can be confusing, but it does indicate a concern on his part to explain his doctrine to different writers by trying different terms. Another switch occurs in his reply to Arnauld's objections, in the passage where he uses the scholastic term 'form' for 'objective reality'. As forms, ideas have no matter. Thus, he says to Arnauld, when we take ideas as representing something, "they are not taken *materially*, but *formally*." If instead of taking ideas as representing something, we take them as being *operations* of the understanding, we can speak of taking ideas materially; but we must remember that to speak thus is not to consider them as having any connections with truth or falsity of objects, that is, with representing objects. Arnauld was raising questions about privative ideas, ideas of hot and cold. Cold is a privation of heat, hence is not something on its own. Thus, if our idea of cold is taken as representing something, it is false. Ideas can be materially but not formally false. The idea of cold is what it is, whether cold is a privation or not, but this idea can be the occasion of or can give me the basis for error. Thus, a materially false idea is an idea that leads me to draw a false conclusion or that gives me the occasion for or the material for drawing a false conclusion. A *materially false* idea is not the same as *taking ideas materially*. To do the latter is just to take them as acts of mind. Arnauld's reading of 'ideas' seems justified.

There is still one difficulty with this interpretation. The problem can be stated in terms of the passage from the "Preface to the Reader" of the *Meditations*. There, the contrast to *materially* is *objectively*: the taking of an idea objectively is to take *it* as *the thing that is represented*. That thing as represented, as existing in my mind, can be more perfect than I, whereas my act cannot be more perfect than I. The problem is still how to understand the being of the object in my understanding. This problem is closely related to that of making sense of the 'causal' connection between formal and objective. The *thing* represented by the idea (and hence the thing *in* my mind) is different from my idea. Thus, by Descartes's interpretation, do we not have (a) the object or thing in the world and (b) the idea of that thing in my understanding? The latter will be an idea distinct from an act only if ideas are themselves entities, or if, as Aquila recently suggests, the *natures* of objects are in our minds.[24] That is, ideas seem to be the very objects in the mind, different from the acts whereby I apprehend those objects. The objects exist in the act, Aquila wants to say. Besides the act of the mind and the transcendent object that exists external to the mind, there is (this line of reasoning says) "an *immanent* object which will exist, at least in the mind, whether or not the object which it represents exist in the external world."[25] Moreover, only if there is such an immanent object can the idea that represents God, infinite perfection, be itself infinitely perfect. The distinction between transcendent and immanent object is one between "two different ways in which one and the same entity might exist. It might exist apart from the mind, or it might exist within the mind. The view with which we are left, then, is the view that the mind contains two very different sorts of things. It contains its own mental activity, and it also contains all the proper objects of that activity."[26]

Aquila's reasoning is forceful, especially for the objective reality of the idea of God; the being of God, it would seem, is in our minds. The objective reality of ideas is not only epistemic or semantic in God's case: there is a suggestion that there is a transference of the being of the object to the mind. Is the being of physical objects in my mind when, under conditions of perception, I have ideas of such objects? Although in having the idea of God the being of God is somehow present in my mind or heart, I do not find Descartes saying that in having the idea of any particular body, the being of that body is present in my mind. The line between an epistemic-ontic reading of 'objective reality' is thin and delicate. Moreover, in employing the ontic language in talking about the way such objects exist in the mind, Descartes is echoing older doctrines of an Aristotelian and scholastic kind which tried, as we saw in the Introduction, to find a way in which some feature of perceptual objects, e.g., their form, did exist in the mind of the perceiver. Within those echoes, however, there is a new doctrine: to *be* in the understanding for physical objects just is to *be understood*. The ontic being has been transformed into an epistemic reality; but that translation occurs through the mind's reactions to the significatory motions in sense organs and brain. Descartes's stress upon signification, his insistence in a number of passages that by ideas he means acts of the mind, and Arnauld's confidence that his interpretation of Descartes is correct—all of these support the reading of ideas as acts of the mind, acts of understanding, reactions to the meaning of the world.

Conclusion

For a seventeenth-century philosopher, there were four possible interpretations for the notion of *being* of objects in the understanding. (1) According to the scholastic interpretation, the *form* of the object exists in corporeal as well as in incorporeal substances. One frequently finds quasi-literal talk of objects penetrating the mind, of the mind assimilating the object, of intimate union. (2) A wildly impossible view, but one in the background (sometimes quite explicitly) in many discussions, is that the object itself is *literally* present to or in the mind. (3) Another interpretation holds that the object is present in the mind by proxy, by representation. The object cannot be in the mind, but ideas can. Ideas, then, in some way (resemblance is frequently suggested) represent objects. This view, in one strongly stated version, makes ideas third things between knower and object. (4) Finally, it is maintained that to be in the understanding is simply to be understood. This view goes along with treating ideas as identical to perceptions: to have an idea just is to perceive.

The second interpretation was considered by Malebranche as the alternative to ideas as separately existing entities. Since that alternative is absurd, the third interpretation, Malebranche argued, is true: he went on to give Platonic status to ideas in the mind of God. God puts ideas in our minds at the appropriate time to represent objects that can never be present to the mind. There is no reason to think Descartes ever entertained the second interpretation, and there are good reasons for saying he rejected it: the formal reality of objects is not in the mind. The first interpretation is ambiguous. It can, under a careless account (and there were several eighteenth-century writers who took this direction), lead to the second interpretation. Under a different rendering of 'form', the first interpretation might lead to the fourth. Descartes is clearly in the tradition of the first interpretation; but for a variety of reasons, instead of the ambiguity of the term 'form', he tried to offer a cognitive or semantic interpretation of the being of objects in the mind. Interpretation three is the position Descartes (as well as Locke) is most usually assigned by commentators (Malebranche thought this to be his view). Descartes's text (like that of Locke's) is not unsupportive of that assignment. But it is the fourth interpretation which I have suggested is Descartes's view. I support Arnauld over Malebranche.

It is the stress upon understanding as the basic feature of cognition, including perception, that marks Descartes's departure from the scholastic theory, the departure from the ontology of objects—their pictures or forms being in the understanding. It is this substitution of an epistemic or psychological operation for ontology which both Arnauld and Locke pursued. Once that shift was made, it was natural to develop a doctrine of signs as a way of capturing the significatory nature of understanding. The steps in Descartes's move toward a doctrine of signs were the following:

1. Perceptual consciousness is a result of the cognitive activity of the mind working in conjunction with (even attending to) physiological processes in the brain.

2. The sixth *Meditation* reaffirms the close interrelations of cognition and bodily activity; the close intermingling of mind and body makes perceptual awareness possible.

3. Perceptual discriminations (a) do not require any entities (particles or images) to be transmitted from object to perceiver; (b) do not require any similarities between idea and object; (c) are made on the basis of sensations felt by the perceiver; and (d) those sensations are a response to or an interpretation of natural signs, i.e., motions in the environment that are duplicated in nerves and brain.

4. (a) The 'causal relation' between formal and objective reality is replaced by (or just is) the relation of sign to signified. (b) The formal reality of ideas is that of a mode of mind: ideas and perceptions are the same. (c) The being of objects in the understanding is just their being understood, apprehended, cognized, or perceived.

Notes

1. For one forceful statement of this view, see his "Notes Directed Against a Certain Programme," in *The Philosophical Works of Descartes*, translated by Elizabeth S. Haldane and G. R. T. Ross, volume I. This edition will be referred to as "H and R."

2. H and R, vol. I, p. 35. The Latin edition of the *Regulae* is in the Adam and Tannery (A and T) edition, volume X. The relevant passages from Rule 12 are on pp. 411ff. A useful edition of Descartes in French is *Oeuvres philosophiques*, edited by F. Alquié. The *Regulae* is in Volume I. Where I cite material from writings of Descartes not translated in standard editions, I will usually give the A and T reference as well as a reference to its location in Alquié's edition. The latter will be cited as "A."

3. Cf. *Traité de l'homme*, A, vol. I, p. 390; A and T, vol. XI, p. 131. This work is translated by T. S. Hall as *Treatise of Man* (1972), p. 22: "External objects which merely by their presence act on the organs of sense and by this means force them to move in several different ways . . ."

4. Elsewhere, Descartes locates the reasonable mind in the brain. See *Treatise of Man*, p. 22. Like many writers, Descartes accepted the notion of the instantaneous propagation of light. For a discussion of this notion, see A. I. Sabra, *Theories of Light; from Descartes to Newton* (1967), pp. 46-47.

5. The *Treatise of Man* locates the place of the imagination and the common sense as the pineal gland. It is the images or forms traced on the gland which the reasonable mind is said to consider immediately or directly (p. 86).

6. Even with the apprehension of truth, there are many truths taught us by nature. These truths are acquired through experience and observation; the nature that teaches them is my nature as a whole of mind and body. For learning these truths, the faculty of imagination is very important; this is the faculty that 'turns toward the body' (as stated in the sixth *Mediation*), the faculty that works with those impressions coming to us from external objects. The truths taught me by nature in this way differ from the truths about body that the understanding discovers. Our perceptual knowledge of body gives us scientific, not metaphysical truths. What the wax example reveals is that the metaphysical truth about body — that a body is a thing, a substance, which is capable of many different shapes — is a product of understanding when we reflect on our perceptual experiences.

7. Certain movements of nerves cause movements in the brain, and these latter give occasion to the mind to have a specific feeling (*Treatise of Man*, pp. 37-38).

8. *La Dioptrique*, in A, vol. I, p. 654; A and T, vol. VI, p. 84.

9. Descartes is not suggesting, as some ancient theories of vision did, that anything goes out from our eyes to the objects seen. This theory was not dead in the early eighteenth century, however. Chambers, in his *Cyclopaedia: Or, An Universal Dictionary of Arts and Science* (1728), observes that LeClerc reintroduced the term 'expressed species'. According to Chambers, LeClerc said that " 'tis not by Species or Images empress'd on the optic Nerve, that the Soul sees Objects, but by Rays, which she herself directs to them, and which she uses as a Blind Man does his staff, to grope out Objects." (Entry under 'Species'.) For Descartes, the staff enabled tactual-muscular sensations to be felt by the blind man, just as the open eyes are the avenue for other sensations. In both cases, it is what is felt which gives us knowledge of the objects, not the mode of access.

10. A and T, vol. VII, p. 88. Haldane and Ross follow the Latin version: "Thus, for example, when the nerves which are in the feet are violently or more than usually moved, their movement, passing through the medulla of the spine to the inmost parts of the brain, gives a sign to the mind which makes it feel somewhat, to wit, pain . . ." (vol. I, p. 197).

11. A, vol. I, p. 684; A and T, vol. VI, p. 112.

12. A somewhat similar doctrine is found in Malebranche's talk of natural connections between the brain traces produced by or correlated with the objects which we see, e.g., between a tree or a mountain and the ideas of trees and mountains. Malebranche does not use the language of signs, however. Such ideas, as well as the ideas associated with the cries of humans and animals, or with the threatening gestures of humans, and the corresponding ideas of pain and fear, are natural and independent of our will. These ideas are shared by all humans and necessary for the preservation of life. (See his *Recherche*, edited by Rodis-Lewis, vol. I, pp. 216-17; Lennon and Olscamp's translation, pp. 102-3.)

13. See also p. 88 in Marin: "Sensible quality is a sign which signifies the sensation or idea we have of light; its physical action signifies the idea it represents; it is the signifier of which the signified is the representative idea of light." There is a brief mention of the passage on natural signs in two recent essays: "Descartes' Empirical Epistemology," by Charles Larmore, and "Cartesian Optics and the Geometrization of Nature," by Nancy L. Maull, both in *Descartes: Philosophy, Mathematics, and Physics*, edited by Stephen Gaukroger, 1980.

14. Descartes clearly says that *all* ideas are the work of the mind in their formal being.

This remark presumably includes the idea of God as well. There may be a problem with this particular idea, however. If the idea of God is innate, am I the cause of this particular idea? Can an idea be a mode of my thought but not caused by me? In the case of this idea, does the causality of the objective reality control the causality of its formal reality?

15. In an important book, *Epistemological Direct Realism in Descartes' Philosophy* (New Mexico, 1974), Brian O'Neil argues persuasively and with textual support for these close similarities. O'Neil believes, though, that Descartes ran into difficulties in trying to modify the scholastic account, difficulties which led him gradually toward a representative realism. O'Neil and Alquié point out the direct realism in the scholastic doctrine.

16. A. J. P. Kenny, *Descartes, A Study of His Philosophy* (New York, 1968), p. 114. The term 'entity' or 'thing' designates 'substance'. The substance-quality metaphysic forced writers to classify what there is either as a substance or as a quality, property, or mode of a substance. A good example of a philosopher who treated ideas as things in this sense is Malebranche. Malebranche talked of ideas as 'real beings', or as 'real spiritual beings'. The controversy between Arnauld and Malebranche over the nature of ideas involved Arnauld's asserting that ideas are not things, but acts of the mind. For a good discussion of Descartes's account of ideas, with a corrective to Kenny's reading, see "The Inherence Pattern and Descartes' Ideas," by Thomas A. Lennon, in *Journal of the History of Philosophy* 3 (1974): 43-52.

17. E. Gilson, *Etudes sur la role de la pensée médiévale dans la formation du système cartésien* (Paris, 1967), p. 206.

18. E. Gilson's edition of *Discours de la méthode* (Paris, 1947), p. 320. The Latin is as follows: "Nota hoc in loco et ubique in sequentibus, nomen ideae generaliter sum pro omni re cogitata, quatenus habet tantum esse quoddam objectivum in intellectu."

19. *Le Découverte métaphysique de l'homme chez Descartes* (Paris, 1950), p. 202.

20. Ibid., p. 208.

21. A and T, vol. VII, p. 285; H and R, vol. II, p. 157.

22. *Des vraies et des fausses idées* (1683); vol. XXXVIII of his collected works, p. 339.

23. I do not want to assimilate the understanding of the meaning of 'God' to that of physical-object words and ideas. There is an obvious difference in the signification. In the case of 'God', the signification is fully conscious, but Descartes's appeal to the meaning of the word 'God' as a way of indicating the having of the idea *is* a semantic move.

24. Richard E. Aquila, "Brentano, Descartes, and Hume on Awareness," *Philosophy and Phenomenological Research* 35 (1974-75):223-39.

25. Ibid., p. 236.

26. Ibid., pp. 236-37.

Chapter II

Malebranche

on

Perception and Knowledge

Any discussion of Malebranche's theory of perception and of the role of ideas in that theory must take account of a number of other doctrines held by him. (1) His view of matter makes matter infinitely divisible and limits its properties to motion, figure, and extension. (2) His view of causation limits it to God; second causes are *mobile* but not *self-moving*. The first of these doctrines has the consequence that most of the properties we think we see as properties of bodies cannot be the properties of bodies. Malebranche does not appear to want to say that perceived motion is the real motion of matter because (a) the activity of matter is a result of little 'tourbillons' which are invisible and (b) motion is normally linked with experienced colors and sounds. Extension or matter has two sorts of figures or shapes. The one is external to matter, as the perceived roundness of a piece of wax. The other, and for Malebranche the proper, shape-property of matter, is internal to matter: the configurations of the little parts of wax.[1] Matter is infinitely divisible, but its inner source of activity is the 'petits tourbillons' of subtle or ethereal parts.[2] This subtle matter moves very rapidly and in vortexes. Perceived qualities are explained in terms of vibrations *"more or less frequent . . . of the subtle matter."*[3]

The second of the above doctrines has the consequence that the activity of matter cannot cause activity in nerves and brain; hence

42

there is no real causal connection between bodies in the environment and my body, even though the motions of the former are transferred to the latter. Animal spirits in my body also play a transfer role from senses to brain. In strictness, the transfer does not occur either: there is instead an established correlation of the motion in the one and the motion in the others, established by God, reflected in the laws of the order of nature. Similarly, the psychological components—sensations and ideas—are only concomitant events because of the laws of the union of mind and body, also established by God.

A third factor important to his theory of perception is his view of science. Scientists do not observe the properties of bodies: they cannot do so because of the first two doctrines described above. Science discovers the relations or connections of bodies. Just how this is done or what the status of relations is for Malebranche is not entirely clear. There are recognized problems about the possibility, for Malebranche, of scientific knowledge, since it would seem to rest upon sensations. However these problems may be resolved, it is important to note that Malebranche held that bodies have only relational properties. Sometimes he talks as if the relations that science discovers are only perceived relations, but at other times he says about some qualities, e.g., size, that "nothing is either large or small in itself" (L-O, p. 31; R, vol. I, p. 91). We cannot discover the size bodies have, "only the relations they have with one another" (L-O, p. 38; R, vol. I, p. 102). It is not clear whether he would really go so far as to say that all the properties of bodies are relations, but he is clear about scientific truth being the relations we can discover to hold between bodies: "Yet it is certain that all knowledge consists only in the clear perceptions of the relations objects have with each other" (L-O, p. 213; R, vol. I, p. 407). It may also be relevant to our understanding of his philosophy of science that relations of the sort that interest scientists can probably be assimilated to mathematical and geometrical relations.

A closely related (fourth) feature, affecting his philosophy of science, is Malebranche's view of knowledge as requiring understanding in terms of universals. Behind both his stress upon relations and his stress upon universals lies some ideal of deductive knowledge, or of a derivation of certainty from general or universal concepts.

In approaching his dictum about seeing all things in the mind of God, we need to keep these four doctrines firmly in mind, but we need especially to see his theory of perception as an attempt to link the third with the fourth. The union of body and mind is some kind of analogue or mirror of the relation between science and metaphysics. The theological parallel is the relation between man and God. The bodily seeing required for science has to be assisted and guided by the intellectual understanding of the mind. But it is in the attempt to combine both seeing with the senses and understanding or intellectual seeing that ambiguities in his theory begin to appear.

In extracting his theory of perception from his writings, we must examine closely a number of terms used by Malebranche: see (voir), perceive, 'apperceive' (apercevoir), visible-invisible, look at (regarder). Two of these terms, 'voir' and 'regarder', intellectual and bodily seeing, are used with some precision in the *Eclaircissements* to his *Recherche*. He is not entirely consistent there in limiting the use of 'voir' to intellectual seeing, i.e., understanding, and bodily seeing to looking, 'regarder'; but by and large he persists in that distinction in those essays. It becomes clear, then, that seeing things in the mind of God is not in fact a theory of perception but a theory of knowledge or of understanding. He made some additions to the sixth edition of the *Recherche* in keeping with this distinction in the *Eclaircissements*; but on the whole the ambiguity between perception and knowledge remains in the *Recherche*. It is useful, for understanding Malebranche and for understanding the history of the term 'idea', to outline what Malebranche has to say in the *Recherche* on ideas and seeing.

In the Preface to the *Recherche*, Malebranche accepts the notion that the mind is united with the body and that the mind is the form of the body. But he calls attention to a much more important union, that of the mind with God: this union is closer and more essential (L-O, p. xix; R, vol. I, p. 10). Although the relation of mind to body is natural, it is not, as is its union with God, necessary and indispensable. Before giving details on how the mind works, Malebranche adds, in the sixth edition, a note about his essay on optics, *Eclaircissement* XVII. He urges the reader to read that essay first, for if the reader is to follow Malebranche's argument about errors of sight, it is necessary to know "how the eyes are constructed or how they function in seeing objects" (L-O, p. xxxi; R, vol. I, p. 28).

The human mind, which is a simple, indivisible substance, has two faculties. The first of these faculties is the understanding, which he defines as the faculty of receiving ideas. He also explicitly states that this faculty is the same as the faculty of "perceiving various things" (L-O, p. 2; R, vol. I, p. 41).[4] To receive ideas and to perceive things is the same. Ideas are of two sorts, pure and sensible. Examples of the latter are pleasure, pain, light, colors, smells, and so on. Sensations are said to be only ways of being of the mind. They can exist even if there are no bodies outside the mind that we take to be their causes. In the first edition Malebranche had drawn the same distinction in a different vocabulary. Some ideas represent to us something outside us, e.g., the idea of a square, a triangle. Other ideas represent to us that which occurs in us, e.g., sensations of pain and pleasure. There is in this distinction no idea that represents to us bodies outside our minds.

It is the understanding that perceives or, as he sometimes writes, that knows, because it is the faculty that receives ideas; and, he repeats, to receive or have an idea is the same as to perceive ('apercevoir') an object. Sense and imagination are only the understanding becoming aware of objects by the organs of the body. There are in fact three ways of perceiving, of becoming aware: through the understanding, the imagination, and the senses. The pure, i.e., nonsensory, understanding perceives universals, common notions, the idea of perfection, the idea of an infinite being. Malebranche even claims that by the pure understanding we also perceive, apprehend material things, by which he explains he means "extension with its properties" (L-O, p. 16; R, vol. I, p. 66). With strong echoes of Descartes, he offers, as an example of perceiving or being aware of material things, our perceiving a circle, a perfect square. The mind works in these instances without images in the brain.

By the senses, the mind perceives sensible and gross objects, when those objects are present to the sense organs and form impressions on those organs. Those impressions are then carried to the brain by the animal spirits. But the presence of the objects is not necessary, since the mind can have the same perceptions or awarenesses without the objects. 'Voir', as well as 'apercevoir', is used in these passages. After giving the brief physiology of stimulus, animal spirits, and brain activity, Malebranche says it is in this way that the mind "sees [voit] plains and rocks before [present to] its eyes," but he then switches in mid-sentence to 'knows': "It knows the hardness of iron" (L-O, p. 17; R, vol. I, p. 67). Later on, he speaks of seeing light, along with feeling heat. It is clear that in these passages, 'voir' is a sensation word. As did Descartes, Malebranche also makes the point that we cannot be wrong about our sensations. Deception comes in with the representation of our sensations, when we take them to tell us about objects. Following Descartes again, he maintains that we do not *see* objects as they are, since our sensations are not at all like any properties of body (L-O, p. 25; R, vol. I, p. 79).

In the light of Malebranche's later attempt at a distinction between seeing and looking, it may be helpful to collect a few passages from the *Recherche* in which these terms are used. The sensation use of 'voir' may be its ordinary use; its distinction from 'regarder' and its limitation to intellectual seeing (understanding) may be Malebranche's philosophical clarification. But it is just this slide from the sensory use to the nonsensory use of 'voir' that is both important and ambiguous. In the *Recherche*, the nonsensory use occurs in a sufficient number of passages to warrant saying that the distinction in the *Eclaircissements* is present in the *Recherche*; but the distinction between 'voir' and 'regarder' is not singled out for emphasis in the latter, except in one or two additions to the sixth edition, after the publication of the *Eclaircissements*. There is ground for saying, as Arnauld did, that Malebranche changes his mind about the nature of ideas between the early and later books of the *Recherche*, and that Malebranche confused sensory with non-sensory perceptual vocabulary.[5]

In talking in the *Recherche* of his belief that there are an infinity of worlds, an infinity of organisms inside organisms, Malebranche says "an entire tulip is seen [on voit] in the seed of a tulip bulb. Likewise, a chicken that is perhaps entirely formed is seen in the seed of a fresh egg" (L-O, p. 27; R, vol. I, pp. 82-83). With microscopic eyes, we could go even farther. Our eyes are in effect only natural glasses: depending upon the situation and upon the figure on the cystalline lens and its extension to the retina, "we see [voyons] objects differently" (L-O, p. 28; R, vol. I, p. 84). In a later discussion of our perception of distance, he observes that the image on the eye is different or will vary "with the distance of objects we see" (L-O, p. 42; R, vol. I, p. 111). In order to see an object close-up, "his [a man's] eyes are necessarily longer, or the crystalline lens is farther from the retina" (ibid.). He also speaks of seeing (voir) the object whose image is on our retina, and he writes easily of seeing a man or a tree. In chapter XII of Book I, he says that "it can be seen that colors are almost as strong and vivid on the fundus of the optic nerve as on visible objects" (L-O, p. 56; R, vol. I, p. 136). He reports that there are people who see certain bodies as yellow with one eye, green and blue with the other eye (L-O, p. 66; R, vol. I, p. 153).

Earlier in book I, Malebranche talks of "la vue de l'esprit" (the mind's eye) as well as of "la vue du corps" (the body's eye), and he insists that it is a prejudice and wrong to believe that "we see [on voit] objects as they are in themselves" (L-O, p. 25; R, vol. I, p. 87). In certain places he uses 'regarder' and 'voir' as he does in the *Eclaircissements*. For example, "When we look at [regardons] a cube . . . it is certain that the sides of it that we see [voyons] never project an image of equal size in the fundus of the eye" (L-O, p. 34, cf. p. 221; R, vol. I, p. 96, cf. p. 420). We use our eyes to look at physical objects: "When, for example, we look at a sufficiently remote bell tower, we ordinarily see at the same time several fields and houses between us and it" (L-O, p. 44; R, vol. I, p. 115). We also look at the sun (L-O, p. 71; R, vol. I, p. 162).

In these passages in the *Recherche*, there is no systematic contrast between the sensation use of 'voir' and its use in conjunction with 'regarder'. We both see and look at objects. But some of the additions made to the sixth edition show that Malebranche tried to clarify his view by using 'regarder' for turning the eyes toward some object and 'voir' for our judgments or our understanding. The perception of distance becomes a natural judgment when I open my eyes and look in a certain direction (L-O, p. 46; R, vol. I, pp. 119-20). Another addition at the end of Chapter XI of Book I reminds us that as yet he has neither proved "that objects are not seen in themselves nor explained what is seen when one looks at them," and he hints at a clarification of the role of ideas for "the mind's eyes when those of the body are opened" (L-O, p. 55; R, vol. I, p. 134).[6]

In declaring that we do not see bodies as they are in themselves, Malebranche was following Descartes in distinguishing the *motion* in the nerves from the *sensations* that we feel. The heat that we feel is not identical with motion. To make correct judgments about light, colors, and all sensible qualities, "the sensation of color must be carefully distinguished from the movement of the optic nerve, and reason must make it clear that motion and impulse are properties of bodies" (L-O, p. 59; R, vol. I, p. 141). We find here the familiar account given by Descartes in his *Dioptrique* and the *Traité de l'homme*. As with some passages in Descartes also, Malebranche replaces the causal connection between the motion of bodies and nerves with the finely tuned correlation set up by God. But there is another, and for Malebranche stronger, reason why we do not see bodies as they are in themselves. This reason sounds bizarre to us, but it is in fact used by a number of writers, both before and after Malebranche. As a proof that we have no sensations that do not contain some false judgments, Malebranche offers the following argument.

It is indubitable, he says, that our minds do not fill spaces as vast as those between us and the stars. Thus it is unreasonable to believe that our minds are in the sky when we see the stars in the sky. Nor is it believable that our minds leave our bodies in order to see (voir) houses at a distance. It follows that our minds "must see stars and houses where they are not, since the soul does not leave the body where it is located, and yet sees them outside it" (L-O, p. 67; R, vol. I, p. 156). There are a number of premises at work in this amazing argument. One premise (often used by eighteenth-century writers in

England) is that there can be no action at a distance, including cognitive action. A variant of this premise (a variant that also has a long history) is that the mind can perceive only that which is intimately united with the mind, present to the mind. Our mind is in our body; it does not leave the body when it sees stars and houses; it does see stars and houses; thus the stars and houses it sees are not the stars in the sky or the houses along the road. Besides the stars in the sky, there are those that are "immediately joined to the soul." These are the only stars that we are able to see. (L-O, pp. 67-68; R, vol. I, p. 156).

Later in the same chapter, he is even more explicit. There are two kinds of beings relevant to our cognition: "those our soul sees [voit] immediately, and those it knows only by means of the former" (L-O, p. 69; R, vol. I, p. 159). He is using 'voir' for the sun that is immediately united to our mind. When I perceive the rising sun, and assuming a causal connection (or, really, a correlation)[7] between my sensations and something external, I judge that this sun that is in my mind is also external to me. 'Immediate', 'intimately', 'see' go together and contrast with 'regarder', turning my eyes. We *see* a sun in our mind; we *look at* the sun on the horizon. The sun on the horizon is not larger than it is when it is high above the horizon. It is the sun in my mind, the one intimately united to my mind, that is larger when the other sun is rising. Those things that we see immediately are always just as we see them.

These passages read like a mixture of several points from Descartes. Descartes had talked of the sun as seen normally and as judged by science. He had also used some scholastic vocabulary (modified slightly) to refer to the sun existing in my understanding. Malebranche appears to combine these two points, without explicating existence in the mind, other than to say it involves intimate union with the mind. The intimate union requires that the two entities so united be of the same kind, or that one of them be able to traverse categories. The Aristotelian doctrine said that the form of matter can exist in immaterial minds during cognition. Some of the scholastics gave to the active intellect the ability of subtilizing matter, of transforming sensible into intelligible species.[8] Descartes's doctrine of the objective reality of ideas in the mind is a combination of these two doctrines: the sun as known exists in the understanding. In these chapters of book I of his *Recherche*, Malebranche produces a literalized version of Descartes's objective reality, adding this strange denial of the walking mind. When he moves to the second part of book III ("The Pure Understanding"), the walking mind argument is retained, but ideas are substituted for the sun and stars in the mind. He begins book III by declaring he is going to consider the mind by itself, in abstraction from any connection with the body. This announcement gives us a clue about the role and nature of ideas for Malebranche, since ideas are what the mind by itself uses in its cognition of nonimmediate objects. He distinguishes intellectual ideas from sensory ones, and he defines the pure understanding as the faculty of the mind "knowing external objects without forming corporeal images of them in the brain" (L-O, p. 198; R, vol. I, p. 381). We know objects without images but not without ideas.

In showing the need for ideas in our knowledge of body, Malebranche remarks, at the start of the second part of book III, that everyone agrees we do not perceive external objects by themselves. He now uses 'see' (voir) for seeing objects: "the sun, the stars, and an infinity of objects external to us" (L-O, p. 217; R, vol. I, p. 413). Instead of two suns, we now have the sun and the idea of the sun. The walking-mind argument in this section is as follows:

We see the sun, the stars, and an infinity of objects external to us; and it is not likely that the soul should leave the body to stroll about the heavens, as it were, in order to behold [contempler] all these objects. Thus, it does not see them by themselves, and our mind's immediate object when it sees the sun, for example, is not the sun, but something that is intimately joined to our soul, and this is what I call an idea. (L-O, p. 217; R, vol. I, pp. 413-14)

The phrase "the immediate object" is also rendered in more spatial terms as "the closest to the mind." Ideas touch and modify the mind when it perceives or sees objects.

The seeing vocabulary is still not sorted out, for having just said that we see sun and stars, he speaks on the next page of seeing ideas. He also writes interchangeably of seeing body and of perceiving ('apercevoir') body. Nevertheless, it is clear that his account of perception of bodies is that we do not and cannot perceive them without having ideas. The phrase "by themselves" means "without ideas." When we perceive a sensible thing, we find in our perception both a feeling or sensation and a pure idea (L-O, p. 234; R, vol. I, p. 445). The sensation ('sentiment') is a modification of our mind. It is God who causes me to have that feeling; he joins the sensation to the idea when the objects are present to me.

With all causal links between objects and perceivers severed, with ideas as existing entities added by God to our sensations, and with the shift of emphasis from two suns in book I to ideas and objects in book III, one begins to suspect that Malebranche is developing a concept of knowledge rather than one of perception. The last few chapters of book III reinforce this suspicion. The section headings of chapter VII refer to four different ways of *seeing* things, but the chapter itself distinguishes ways of *knowing* (L-O, p. 236; R, vol. I, p. 448).[9] We know ('connaître') corporeal things by their ideas, by the ideas God gives us. We cannot *see* bodies by themselves because they are not *intelligible* by themselves. When we keep in mind that corporeal bodies have only the properties of figure, motion, and extension, and when we note that God has, with extension alone, been able to produce "everything admirable we see in nature," it is not too difficult to discern in Malebranche's doctrine of seeing all things in God a program for understanding the world in terms of geometrical properties. Descartes's simple natures have been reduced to one, extension.

In *Eclaircissement* VI (on the proof for body), Malebranche characterizes the ordinary person's attitudes: it is only necessary to open our eyes in order to assure ourselves that there is body. If we think we have an illusion, we need only get closer or use other sensory tests. The ordinary person has grounds for this view about perception of body: that is the way body does appear to our senses.[10] 'Opening our eyes' is for Malebranche looking ('regarder'). Our eyes represent to us colors as on the surfaces of bodies, light as in the air and in the sun. In short, our senses locate sensed qualities outside us. If "we look with the eyes of the body," no other conclusion is possible.

Malebranche's rejection of this ordinary view of perception is made on the basis of certain principles which he takes to be self-evident, e.g., only like can act on like, only spirit can be an active agent. Physiology is a phenomenon, a frequent concomitant for us, but all action is God's action in us. That brain activity is not necessary for perception is shown by asking: "how is it contradictory that our soul should have new ideas while our brain keeps the same motion?" (L-O, p. 572; E, p. 59). Since there is no contradiction, we can conclude that brain activity is not necessary. If brain movements are not necessary for perception, neither are those bodies that the ordinary person believes to be present in the environment. When we see bodies, we are in fact seeing *intelligible* bodies. The concept of an intelligible world is now used to articulate the talk of two suns from book I of the *Recherche* and that of object and idea from book III. The intelligible contrasts with the material. The bodies that we see (voir) are not those that we look at (regarder). To look is "turning the body's eyes toward" something, but to see is to apprehend the intelligible. Even the term 'visible' is associated with intelligible: "the material world is neither perceptible nor intelligible in itself" (L-O, p. 573; E, p. 61). He talks of intelligible bodies and of intelligible spaces and extension. Just as there are material spaces between our body and the sun, so there are intelligible spaces between the intelligible bodies that we see.[11]

One of the models for perception used by Malebranche is God's perception. God *sees that* there are spaces between the bodies that he has created, but he does not see those bodies or their spaces by themselves: "he sees [voit] the material world only in the intelligible world He contains" (ibid.). The same model is used in *Eclaircissement* X (on the nature of ideas). God knows all things only because he includes ('renferme') in his nature, in an intelligible way, the perfections ('essences') of all things. In the same way, it is only by cognizing such intelligible perfections that humans can know anything. Ideas are such perfections; we see them; they are necessary and imitable; we acquire them from God (L-O, p. 617; E, p. 136).

There are, in a stretched sense of 'know', two ways in which we know things: "through illumination and through sensation" (L-O, p. 621; E, p. 141). We know or see by feeling, by the senses, only in a confused way. To know things properly is to see them by the light of reason or the illumination of God. The secular translation of this theological metaphor is that knowledge proper results when we are able to make the kind of comparisons and derivations of properties typical of geometry, derivations which rest upon the inclusion of one property in another.[12] 'Voir' is used in the *Eclaircissements* for the apprehension of the truths of mathematics and geometry (L-O, p. 613; E, p. 129). We also see moral truths (L-O, p. 614; E, p. 131). Similarly, we see the rule, order, and reason of God. If we had proper knowledge of bodies, we would be able to compare heat with tastes, smells, and colors, and discern some relations between them. With geometrical figures, we can make precise and certain relations. Knowledge requires such comparisons of necessarily related terms; it is the movement by inclusion from one step to the next (L-O, pp. 635-36; E, pp. 167-68). We can come to know the nature and properties of matter only by acquiring the clear idea of extension. We acquire this idea by participation in God's nature. His nature includes an idea of intelligible extension. Only as we are able to perceive a part of this extension are we able to see bodies (L-O, p. 626; E, p. 151). From an understanding of this intelligible extension, we are able to derive the space and motion of bodies, since intelligible extension represents and includes all kinds of relations of distance. From this idea of extension we can, Malebranche thinks, derive the notion that the parts of body have different relations and locations to each other (L-O, p. 627; E, p. 153).[13] We can even, by means of this idea of extension, "see or imagine bodies in motion." We experience bodies in motion because the sensations of color appear successively to us. In these successive colored extensions, we see (understand) different parts of the intelligible extension, the idea of extension. Thus in the example of the sun on the horizon looking larger than the sun at high noon, we see now a greater, now a lesser part of the intelligible extension.

Malebranche explicitly denies that the intelligible world duplicates the material and sensible world. There is not an intelligible horse, sun, or tree that represents to us the material horse, sun or tree. Intelligible extension alone can represent any sensible object. The representation could only be effective, as Descartes would say, insofar as bodies have geometrical properties. It could not be the particularity of bodies that intelligible extension represents: we cannot derive the sensory qualities of the sun, the tree, or the horse from that idea of extension: only the essential properties of these bodies *qua* extended objects can be so derived or comprehended. Malebranche has helped strengthen this conclusion by excluding from the nature of body any sensible quality. This 'deperceptualizing' of body finds its extreme form when he *identifies* the sun, the horse, the tree with the intelligible extension. He even tries to identify the intelligible extension with the *sensible* sun, horse, or tree. Intelligible extension *represents* the intelligible, but it *is* those objects, and it *becomes* the sensible objects when we have sensations linked to the idea of intelligible extension. The disappearance of the paticular in the universal is complete: so is the absorption of the sensible and the visible into the intelligible. For Malebranche, this absorption is a making visible. Normal perceptual vocabulary is transferred to cognition. 'Visible' becomes an epistemic, not a sensory word.[14]

There are many passages in which Malebranche is close to following up what is implicit in his theory of knowledge, that we know only to the extent that we ignore or are free from the senses. But he was concerned to account for the possibility of knowledge of particulars. It is the addition of sensations to ideas that particularizes body (L-O, p. 625; E, p. 149).[15] When we are in the presence of body, God excites in us sensations (L-O, p. 621; E, p. 142). Moreover, sensations are necessary before intelligible extension can become the sensible object. It is on the occasion of objects being present to us that we have sensations and that we can know body through the general concept or idea of extension. One of the tensions in Malebranche's philosophy is that between knowledge of essence and knowledge of particulars.

The tension arises in part because sensations for Malebranche have no truth value; they reveal nothing about the properties of objects in our environment. They are, however, useful in alerting us to that which is useful or dangerous. Even so, as Alquié points out,[16] Malebranche presupposes some truth about the world contained in our senses. The tension arises mainly from Malebranche's allocating knowledge to essences and to intellect alone. But he had to recognize, for his own scientific observations at least, that sense perception has some relation to truth, that the senses play an indispensable role in our knowledge of the world in which we live. God of course has a nonsensible knowledge of our world; but being embodied, we can see only actual, particular objects "by the impressions they make on our senses,"[17] or more exactly, by the impressions that arise in our mind, according to the established laws of the union of mind and body. Sense impressions by themselves would yield no information about the world; they would be, as supposed sources of information, totally confused and misleading. Correspondingly, ideas of essences would be nonspecific without sense impressions. In order to apprehend a particular object, e.g., the sun, a tree, a horse, two conditions are necessary: (1) a sense impression, e.g., of a color, and (2) a pure idea of intelligible extension.[18] If I perceive a column of marble, I have a clear idea of extension, but a confused idea of the marble. The reason that the particular is confused is that we do not know the internal configurations of the parts of marble: "that which makes marble what it is and not a brick or lead."[19]

The sense impressions are not, of course, in God any more than they are in or on bodies. Malebranche does speak of seeing bodies in God, but he is careful to remind us that, speaking more exactly, "we see in God only their essences. . . . One sees in God . . . only that which makes them intelligible or known."[20] Even more emphatically, he clarifies the difference of precisely what is in God and what is in me, in another reply to Arnauld in the same letter:

For having in God, by means of the intelligible extension which he contains, the idea, e.g., of this paper, and relating to it the whiteness which it does not have, I am able to see this paper in God. Thus this white paper, this *sensible* body that I see—that is, that which modifies my mind by a sensible perception of white— is not in God that which I see with my eyes. For the intelligible extension which enables me to see this paper is not white; for whiteness is a mode of mind. . . . Thus *sensible* bodies taken in this sense, and as the locus of sensible qualities, are not in God.[21]

Even with this careful allocation, in our particular knowledge, of what is in God and what is in us, knowledge proper is restricted to what we can derive from the universal ideas in God's mind. Our knowledge falls far short of God's knowledge. We can make some geometrical deductions from the idea of extension. God can derive knowledge of body from his idea because he contains those ideas from which he has formed the world. The model in the background for human knowledge is that of deduction or containment of concepts. This model of inclusion of concepts, taken from the theological doctrine of essential inclusion in God's nature, rests uneasily alongside Malebranche's recognition of the role of sense perception in our knowledge. It is especially difficult to determine how he thought his detailed account of the workings of the eye (*Eclaircissement* XVII) was relevant to this ideal of knowledge.

The *Eclaircissement* on optics is written without any careful attention to the 'voir-regarder' distinction. His announced purpose is to show us how we see objects. He speaks of seeing in an instant the light of a candle: one sees it the moment one looks at it (L-O, pp. 723-24; E, p. 312). From the construction of the eye and from the nature of light, it is clear that "we see objects distinctly only when their images are distinct" (L-O, p. 731; E, p. 323). Even when he pauses to remind us that strictly it is not the eye that sees but the mind, Malebranche continues to use the sensory sense of 'voir' for seeing objects (L-O, pp. 732-33; E, pp. 325-27). We see objects "at a glance." He even says that the eyes are made to see the objects around us. The sensory sense of 'voir' is also used as he describes the workings of the eye, what the eye does when we see objects near or far (L-O, pp. 736-39; E, pp. 331-34). To explain how it happens that when I open my eyes in the middle of a field in the country I see in an instant an infinity of objects, he cites details of the physiology of vision, the images on the retina, and the way light moves. In all this descriptive detail, however, he is talking of second or occasional causes and of natural judgments, not the judgments informed by the light of reason. In this account of optics he says that he is speaking imprecisely and nonphilosophically. He then ends this *Eclaircissement* by rehearsing his philosophical account: that it is God alone who is active in our perception; that God works through second causes and general laws; and that we do not see bodies by themselves but only that which is immediately and directly united to our minds, i.e., ideas or intelligible objects (L-O, pp. 745-46; E, pp. 346-47).[22]

In one frame of mind, Malebranche found it tempting to speak of knowledge and truth being acquired only in the next world, when we have left our body.

We must, therefore, wish for the death that unites us with God, or at least for the image of this death, the mysterious sleep during which all our external senses are deadened and we can listen to the voice of inner truth, which is heard only in the silence of night, when darkness hides sensible objects from us, and, as far as we are concerned, the world is, as it were, dead. (L-O, p. 632; E, pp. 160-61)

Equally attractive of course was a detailed natural science, enlightened by the proper metaphysic. Just as the general metaphysical claim about God's will being the only actual cause in nature does not undermine a careful observational science, so his optics does not run counter to his metaphysical claims about perception and seeing. Perception of body involves physical processes in material space and in our own body; but if we base our beliefs about the material world on our sense perceptions, not only will we hold incorrect beliefs about the properties of body, we will also easily reach conclusions about active matter. Malebranche's metaphysics tells us that matter has only the properties of figure, extension, and motion; that matter cannot initiate action and cannot act on minds; that every sensory experience is accompanied by nonsensory ideas given to us by God. To go this far in a theory of perception does not give Malebranche a theory different in any essentials from many other accounts that combined cognition with sensation in our awareness of objects. What changes Malebranche's theory of perception from these sorts of theories is the geometrical, possibly deductive, model that was the secular translation of God's inclusion of the essences of all things in his nature. Malebranche's theory is also different from most other theories because of the nature and status of his ideas, as entities in God's mind.

Notes

1. *Recherche de la verité*, ed. G. Rodis-Lewis, in *Oeuvres de Malebranche*, ed. A. Robinet, volume I, pp. 41-42. Future references to this work will be indicated by 'R'. References to the English translation by Lennon and Olscamp will be cited as 'L-O'.

2. *Eclaircissement sur la lumière* (XVI), in *Oeuvres de Malebranche*, volume III, pp. 270ff. The various clarifications of 'difficult principles' in the *Recherche* are also translated by Lennon-Olscamp. References to the French text will be indicated by 'E'.

3. Ibid., p. 260; L-O, p. 690.

4. The French uses 'apercevoir'. Although I constructed an English equivalent—'apperceive'—earlier in this chapter, there really is no such word. In French, the meanings of 'apercevoir', 'voir', and 'percevoir' are similar, but 'apercevoir' perhaps carries more the sense of 'apprehend' or 'comprehend' than does either of the others. In the following discussion, I will follow the English translators' usage by employing 'perceive' even when the text reads 'apercevoir'. It is the distinction between 'voir' and 'regarder' that is more important.

5. See his *Des vraies et des fausses idées* (1683), chapter III, in volume XXXVIII of his collected works. This important work has, to my knowledge, been reprinted only once, in an edition of *Oeuvres philosophiques de Antoine Arnauld* (1843), by Jules Simon.

6. The distinction is used fairly consistently in the *Entretiens sur la métaphysique et sur la religion* (vol. XII of the *Oeuvres*). For example, "the world that we look at or that we consider in turning our head on all sides, is only a material world invisible in itself" (p. 38). Or, "it is not strictly your room that I see [voi], when I look at it [regarde]" (p. 39). Or again, "the spaces that you see [voiez] are quite different from the material spaces which you look at [regardez]" (p. 95).

7. Malebranche does use causal language here: what is external to me *produces* certain motions in my eyes and in my brain. But it is clear that he would want to replace such language by occasionalist correlations.

8. Picard, in "Essai sur la connaissance sensible d'après les scolastiques," *Archives de philosophie 4*, cahier 1(1926), refers to the opinion of some scholastics which attributes to the sensible object "a mysterious power of self-dematerialization which it manifests in giving off the no less mysterious intentional species" (pp. 25-26).

9. Cf. his *Réponse . . . au livre des vraies et des fausses idées*, volume VI of the *Oeuvres*, p. 94, where he equates 'voir', 'connoître', and 'apercevoir', and p. 108 where he writes "voit, ou connoît." These are just two examples of what is found throughout his *Réponses* to Arnauld.

10. In *Oeuvres*, vol. III, p. 55; L-O, p. 569.

11. The full passage in *Eclaircissement* VI is as follows: "the material world we animate is not the one we see when we look at it, i.e., when we turn the body's eyes toward it. The body we see is an intelligible body and there are intelligible spaces between this intelligible body and the intelligible sun we see, just as there are material spaces between our body and the sun we look at" (L-O, p. 573; E, p. 61). The material world is neither visible nor intelligible by itself. There are many other passages that make the same point and that carefully distinguish 'voir' from 'regarder'. For example: "For it should be noted that the sun that we see, for example, is not the one we look at. The sun, and everything else in the material world, is not visible by itself" (L-O, p. 625; E, p. 149). The *Entretiens* also makes the same distinction. The chapter heading to the first *Entretien* reads: "the world where our bodies live, and which we look at [regardons], is quite different from the one we see [voions]." And in the text of that chapter he writes: "if our bodies walk in a corporeal world, our mind transports itself without ceasing in an intelligible world which touches it, and which by means of that world becomes sensible of the body" (p. 36). In his *Réponse* to Arnauld, he says: "For the bodies which we see are not those which we look at. We often see them without looking at them . . ." (*Oeuvres*, vol. VI, p. 69).

12. Alquié (*Le Cartésianisme de Malebranche*, 1974) seems to reject the geometrical model as being what Malebranche had in mind. "We do not believe it useful to recall here the thesis held by Brunschvicg, invoking analytic geometry in order to explain intelligible extension. Never, in his explications, does Malebranche make appeal to such a solution." (p. 213, n. 7) But later in the same book, Alquié says: "Intelligible extension is not a collection of ideas: it is the principle from which one is able to construct geometrical figures" (p. 222).

13. There is an interesting similarity between Malebranche's linking of a knowledge of intelligible extension with a deductive knowledge of nature and Locke's talk of a knowledge of nature independent of experience, were we able to know real essences. Hume also speaks of a deductive knowledge of the secret springs of nature and real causes.

14. Alquié does not systematically track this reversal of our normal perceptual vocabulary in Malebranche, does not note the attempt by Malebranche to distinguish between 'voir' and 'regarder'. After repeatedly following Malebranche's talk of the intelligible world being visible, Alquié does finally remark that "intelligible signifies, then, to be comprehensible, extension becomes knowable extension, it is explicable" (*Le Cartésianisme de Malebranche*,

p. 216; cf. p. 188: "The theory of vision in God is thus, before all else, a response to the question of the possibility of our knowledge, an explication of its universality and its truth"). In *Berkeley, the Philosophy of Immaterialism* (1974), I. C. Tipton notes on page 22 Malebranche's distinction between "the external objects which we behold (regarder) and mental entities which we *see* (voir)."

15. The *Réponse* draws a distinction between seeing or knowing body (where the existence of a body is not necessary for my seeing) and seeing (still using 'voir') bodies "as actual existents" (where sensations of color, heat, etc., are necessary). See volume VI, p. 108. Also, *Trois Lettres touchant la défense de M. Arnauld*, vol. VI, p. 200.

16. *Le Cartésianisme de Malebranche*, pp. 159-73.

17. *Réponse*, vol. VI, p. 108.

18. Ibid., p. 55.

19. Ibid., p. 98. Cf. again Locke's example of why we do not know the real essence of body: because we do not know the internal arrangement of the insensible particles.

20. *Trois lettres*, vol. VI, p. 201.

21. Ibid., p. 221. In this passage, the same verb, 'voir', is used for sensible and intelligible seeing, but the difference in the seeing is clear.

22. Rodis-Lewis suggests that vision was for Malebranche a *symbol* of "pure intellectual receptivity," due in part to "the intervention of our body's appearing more reduced" (*Nicolas Malebranche*, 1963, p. 115).

Chapter III

Direct Presence
among the Cartesians

One of the assumptions at work in Malebranche's account of perceptual knowledge is that what we know, certainly what we know without inference (i.e., what we are acquainted with), must be intimately present to or united with the mind. The direct presence to the mind of the object known was a prevalent demand in accounts of perception in both centuries. It is a concept plagued with ambiguities, however. If it is meant as a metaphor, the metaphor must be interpreted. If that concept is taken literally, the sense in which two immaterial beings—minds and ideas or objects—can be joined, united, or near to each other needs explication. We noted in chapter I that Alquié reads Descartes as ruling out a direct presence of things to our minds; hence the need for intermediary objects (ideas) representing external objects. In a similar vein, we noted Gilson saying that whereas 'objective being' for a Thomist indicates the seizing by thought of an external essence, Descartes introduces an entity—an idea—in between the seizing and the essence. Is Gilson suggesting that if we translate the metaphor of thought seizing an essence, we would have some literal grasping? What is the way in which thought can seize an essence, how can an object be directly present to mind?

That a concept of literal presence to mind was tempting to some writers—at least as an alternative that had to be raised if only to be rejected—is indicated by Marin Cureau de La Chambre's open appeal to the walking-mind argument, prior to Malebranche. In his *Le Système de l'ame* (1665), La Chambre says that the understanding is active in knowing. The objects that the understanding knows are most often external to it. Since no action can be taken on distant objects, "it is necessary either that the understanding be near the objects, or that the objects be near it" (p. 7). As Malebranche did later, so La Chambre rejects the first alternative: the understanding "is not able to leave the body in order to find" objects. But since objects are not able to move to the mind, to join themselves to the mind, the second alternative is also not possible. La Chambre follows the Epicurean route: "Nature, by means of images which leave objects and which represent the objects, aids our perceptual acquaintance" (ibid.). These images pass through the sense organs and unite themselves to the imagination. The interaction of the imagination and these images enables the imagination to know the images, which are called 'Phantasmes'. This is, I believe, a case of sensitive knowledge, not the knowledge of the understanding. As La Chambre says later in his work, the senses know "in the place where they sense" (p. 158). The phantasm is essentially material; it cannot be an accident of the understanding, which is immaterial. But instead of following the scholastics who talk of the spiritualizing of material phantasms, La Chambre says—and here is his literalness—the understanding works on or with these phantasms. In fact, the understanding unites itself to the phantasms, "for every active power must be united to the subject on which it acts" (p. 8). There is no need, he says, to object that the understanding cannot unite with the material phantasm, since the mind unites itself or is united to the body. He does not explain this union, but he insists that the understanding knows that which is represented in the phantasm, not the phantasm itself (p. 9). Union is not yet knowledge, edge, only a necessary condition for knowledge.

He now wants to know what the action of the understanding is. The common opinion is, he tells us, that the understanding illumines the phantasm and renders it intelligible, that is, spiritual. La Chambre does not think this step is helpful. His own account is that the understanding forms portraits and images of objects, on the model of phantasms. He calls these images *ideas* in order to distinguish them from the phantasms in the imagination: a parallel with Hume's later distinction between impressions and ideas. The ideas represent to the understanding the objects that it knows. He uses the language of the understanding *becoming* that which it knows, i.e., it becomes the image of the idea that it forms. The presence of phantasms in the imagination is the occasion for the understanding to know by forming ideas. He talks literally here: the understanding, in an instant, "becomes . . . an animal, a star, a stone" (p. 17). The understanding is potentially the things that it can know. It transforms itself into that which it knows, the transformation being in terms of the ideas which, very much after the fashion of Malebranche, are said to be other objects. "For it is necessary that the understanding in knowing the sun forms itself another sun; it is necessary that it form stars, elements, in a word, all that is in the Universe" (p. 22).

There were other writers during that time who attempted to avoid any literal union of mind and object, while using spatial metaphors of objects being in the mind or grasped by the mind. I have suggested that Arnauld's reading of 'objective reality' as 'understood' is a proper explanation of these metaphors, one that fits Descartes as well. There was another writer, closer to the scholastics than either Descartes or Arnauld, but contemporary with them, who rejected any literal reading of these metaphors. His name was Pierre Chanet. He also sets the walking mind firmly aside. In his *Traité de l'esprit de l'homme et de ses fonctions* (1649), Chanet writes:

Knowledge does not consist properly in the union of the object with the faculty which knows. . . . But as experience tells us that the external object does not enter our body in order to join itself to the powers of the soul; and since we know besides that the powers of our soul do not leave their organs to unite themselves with the external object, it is necessary to say that that union is not immediate, but rather that it is accomplished by means of that which is called the sensible or intentional species. (pp. 1-2).

Later, he argues that if this notion of union of object with faculty was true, we would also have to say that insensible faculties would have sensations and "that our passive faculties would know their object when they would be united locally [spatially] with it" (p. 52). All natural causes would know the objects on which they act immediately, if union was sufficient for knowledge. Union of object with faculty could yield knowledge only in the case of faculties that are capable of knowledge. But Chanet thinks the union metaphor is misleading and false. He follows the scholastics in giving to the species the cognitive-carrying role.

He remarks that some moderns say that these species are not real, that they are "nothing other than what they call 'representative'" (p. 3). Real is contrasted with representative. Chanet thinks we can be convinced of the reality of such species or images if we consider mirrors in which images of bodies are reflected. Some mirrors even enable us to see images more clearly. Also, different uses of lenses give us other arguments in favor of these images or species. He also cites the *camera obscura*. Suppose you were inside a room that had only a small slit for seeing outside. Here you see pass by the slit a great number of species "which are united without being confounded, and which imprint themselves on white paper or on some other body" (pp. 3-4). The senses are, he suggests, like windows for the mind to consider what goes on outside (p. 51). The species are perhaps best termed 'appearances' on Chanet's view, for he rejects representation: to know or perceive is to look out of our sense organs at the objects passing by. Direct realism would seem to be a label we could use to characterize Chanet's view: the species are the things themselves as they pass by or come into contact with our senses.[1] Species as entities that represent, as opposed to being, the things themselves are rejected. He cites a modern writer (undoubtedly Descartes) who says that "it is not necessary that the image of external objects be conserved in the memory, nor that they have any resemblance of the things which they represent" (p. 150). He agrees with the nonresemblance nature of species because resemblance leads to representation, not to direct perception. In another work, *Eclaircissement de quelques difficultez touchant la connoissance de l'imagination* (1648), he says that either images are like the species that come from the object, in which case they are redundant; or they are not similar to the species, in which case they cannot represent objects (p. 30). Thus the term 'image' can be used to characterize the species of objects, so long as we do not take that to mean that images are pictures of things that then need to be compared with that of which they are pictures.

Chanet rejects both the demand for union of object and knower *and* the representative role for species. Descartes retained the scholastic notion that the object is somehow in or present to the mind; but instead of talking of the senses as windows open to the world, Descartes's concept of objective reality stressed the semantic and cognitive nature of the presence to mind of the object. It was Arnauld who worked out more of the details of this approach to perceptual knowledge. The stimulus for Arnauld was Malebranche, who he thought not only misread Descartes but erred by playing upon several ambiguities. The exchanges between Arnauld and Malebranche were extensive.[2] Arnauld's *Des vraies et des fausses idées* (1683) is the best place to go for his corrections to Malebranche. It is also a good piece of philosophy on its own.

Arnauld discusses a number of issues in that work; for his analysis of perception and ideas, we can examine a set of definitions he gives early in the work. He accepts that mind is a substance that thinks. He equates 'penser', 'connoître', and 'apercevoir'; they are "the same thing." He also takes for the same, "the *idea* of an object and the *perception* of an object" (Def. 3). It is from this definition that Arnauld rejects Malebranche's entity-ideas, Arnauld's perception-ideas do stand in two relations. One relation is to the mind which they modify; the other is to the thing perceived, insofar as that thing is objectively in the mind. The word 'perception' designates the first relation; 'idea' marks the second. When I speak of the perception of a square, I am indicating that my mind is perceiving a square. When I speak of the idea of a square, I am indicating the square as the object in my mind, the object to which I am attending or which I am perceiving. In drawing out this dual relation that our perception-ideas have, Arnauld explicitly seeks to combat Malebranche's move of separating the perceiving and the ideas as two different entities. Perception and ideas are rather "a single modification of our mind, which contains essentially two relations" (Def. 6).

To be objectively in the mind for Arnauld is simply to be conceived (Def. 5). He is careful not to confuse idea with object, objective with formal existence of objects, "*the idea of an object*" with "*the object conceived*" (Def. 10). He repeats some of the reply Descartes gave to Caterus about the difference between the extrinsic relation that being conceived has to the sun and the intrinsic relation that the sun has to our mind as it is conceived, i.e., as it is objectively in my mind. He does not view the senses as windows on the world for passing objects, nor does he put ideas between perceiver and the world. Arnauld recognized that our perceptual relations with the world are cognitive. There is a difference between our perception-ideas and the objects in the world. In cognition, the former are representative of the latter, but representation does not in this case include entities that do the representing. Arnauld insists that "all our perceptions are essentially representative modalities" (Def. 7). This representativeness of our perceptions is unlike the way a picture represents its original, or the way words are images of our thoughts. The representativeness of perception-ideas is unique: they represent because they are our conceptions of things. To be conceived, to be objectively in the mind, is to represent: "that way of *being objectively in the mind* is so particular to mind and thought, as being that which specifically contributes to the nature of it, that we will seek in vain for something similar in that which is not mind or thought" (Def. 8).[3]

Not only does Arnauld accept this special kind of representativeness for perception-ideas, he also agrees with the claim that we do not know things immediately. He is prepared to follow Malebranche's formulation, that it is *"the ideas of things which we see immediately, or that which is the immediate object of our thought"* (pp. 206-7). Arnauld follows this formulation, once we understand 'idea' as 'perception-ideas'. His argument in defense of Malebranche's formulation contains several parts. (1) Thought or perception is reflective or reflexive, i.e., I do not think except that I know that I think; I do not know a square except that I know that I know it. (2) We are able to examine our perceptions by another perception, e.g., a geometer, having conceived of a triangle as a figure terminated by three straight lines, then discovers, by examining his perception of the triangle, that it must have three angles, that its three angles equal two right angles, and so on. (3) Thus, since all perception is representative of something, and since it must be reflexive on itself, its immediate object must be itself as idea, as objective reality. It is the objective reality that is immediately perceived, that is what perception is reflexive on: "If I think of the sun, the objective reality of the sun, which is present to my mind, is the immediate object of that perception, and the possible or existing sun, which is outside my mind, is the mediate object of the mind" (p. 204).

Arnauld is thus prepared to accept Malebranche's formulation, without idea-entities: it is our ideas which "we see *immediately*." But Arnauld insists that this does not prevent us from also seeing things by these idea-perceptions; the object that contains formally that which is only objectively in the idea is seen. We see both idea and thing. If we take seriously the equation of idea with perception, then to say we see or conceive the sun mediately just is to say we see, perceive, or know the sun only by the perception that we have of it (p. 210). If anyone means by 'immediate perception', seeing or perceiving in a way opposed to this sense of 'perception' as equated wth 'idea', then Arnauld rejects that reading. The same holds for our knowledge of God and of our own minds: we know them only through our perceptions, through our awareness. If anyone means by not knowing these objects immediately, that we know them only through ideas as distinct, representative *beings*, then Arnauld is prepared to say we know all these objects immediately as well as mediately, because we are able to know them without there being "any medium between our perceptions and the object."

Arnauld's remarks for this conclusion are reinforced by the clarification, in his next chapter, of Malebranche's claim that everyone agrees that we do not perceive external objects by themselves, but only by means of ideas. Arnauld finds an equivocation in the phrase "by themselves." If this phrase means that objects are not the cause of our perceptions of them, that the objects do not produce perceptions in us, Malebranche is right, but this is a point about the origin of perception-ideas, not about their nature or status. From the fact that there is no causal connection between physical object and idea, it does not follow that ideas are entities distinct from perception (p. 212). If 'being known by itself' is opposed to 'being known by representative beings' distinct from perceptions, then, Arnauld says, Malebranche has begged the question in saying we do not know objects by themselves. Had Malebranche only consulted his own experience, Arnauld suggests, he would have discovered easily that he knows bodies, that when he turns toward the sun, "he sees the sun." Arnauld agrees that it is not our eyes that see the sun, but our mind, "on the occasion of our eyes giving the sun to the mind."

Arnauld suggests that philosophers reach the view of ideas as distinct from perceptions by accepting uncritically three notions: (1) that "it is necessary that the object be before our eyes, in order that we are able to see it; this is what they call *presence*"; (2) that, having seen sensible objects reflected in mirrors and in water, they come to believe that they never see bodies themselves but only their images; and (3) that we know many sensible things that we are not able to see with our eyes, e.g., things too small, insensible things such as air, things very far off: "This is what obliges them to believe that there are things that we see by the mind, and not by our eyes" (p. 190). It is the first of these notions in particular that Arnauld thinks Malebranche accepted: in order for our minds to know objects, the objects must be *present to* the mind. But objects such as the sun are distant from the place where our mind is; thus the need for proxy, representative ideas of the sun (pp. 214-15). Arnauld remarks on the mistake of applying bodily words to mind. "Thus, the word *presence* [signifies] with respect to bodies, a *local presence*, and with respect to minds, an *objective presence*, according to which objects are said to be in our mind when they are there objectively, i.e., when they are known by the mind" (p. 216).

Seeing the sun for Malebranche is having certain sensations and having an idea that represents the sun but which is causally independent of the sun. To see, for Arnauld, is not a matter of spatial distance, of being near to an object: it is to have the object in the mind cognitively. What is present to the mind on Arnauld's analysis is the object itself, though of course not the object in its physicality. If the notion we have of direct knowledge is copied from an object being directly in front of me or touching my body, not only is direct realism ruled out, but knowledge becomes impossible.

For, in speaking in the ordinary way, we say that the object must be present to our eyes if we are to see it . . . nevertheless, in speaking exactly and philosophically, it is quite the opposite. Objects must be absent, since they must be distant from the mind; whatever would be in the eye, or very near to it, would not be seen. (p. 194)

Spatial or local presence has nothing to do with cognition. Were God to allow our mind to leave our body and to travel to the sun in order to see it, our mind would have made, Arnauld says, "a great, very useless voyage" (p. 217). We cannot even see our own body, on Malebranche's account. It makes no difference whether bodies are present or distant: "it is for it [the mind] the same thing, and that which is condemned by an irrevocable sentence of that philosophy of false ideas, of never seeing bodies by themselves, present or absent, near or distant," must be rejected. Objective presence is not spatial proximity, nor does it require resemblance between perception-ideas and the object known. Both are irrelevant to knowledge and perception. Nor does representation by and the immediacy of perception-ideas lead to a denial that we perceive objects. 'Representation', Arnauld seems to be saying, is 'making known'. Since 'know' can mislead, especially among Cartesians where it is normally linked with intuition and demonstration, not perception, it may be better to say that 'representation' is 'making cognitive'. Arnauld is saying that just because an object is apprehended does not put that object at a distance from us, removed from access except by some other proxy objects.

In his first reply to Arnauld, Malebranche insists on his basic principle, that to know external objects, we need to have something united to our mind which is different from our mind, not different in kind but numerically different. A modality of mind, as all Cartesians agreed sensations are, cannot lead to knowledge of what is not mind. To represent is to give information about something other than that which does the representing. From a perception in our mind, we can only know that we are perceiving and that it is *our* perception.[4] Malebranche does not find any demonstration in Arnauld's Definition 3 that ideas and perceptions are the same. All Arnauld has done is to assert that they are the same. For Malebranche, Arnauld's perception-ideas are only modes of mind, as Arnauld said. From a mode of mind, from a perception, nothing follows. A perception-idea does not, for Malebranche, provide us with an object. By making ideas and perceptions the same, Arnauld has left us with only a perception, no object.[5]

To Arnauld's charge that according to Malebranche we cannot see objects that are distant from us, Malebranche replies that he does not say this at all. Since he thinks we sometimes see bodies that do not exist, obviously he thinks we can see distant bodies.[6] What Malebranche does not say is that his 'voir' is rather special, although in the same passage he does correctly use the 'voir-regarder' distinction. Clearly, if 'voir' is taken in Malebranche's sense, we do see objects distant from us, but Arnauld means to use 'voir' and 'apercevoir' in their sensory sense. Malebranche then goes on to say that his walking-mind remark is "a kind of raillery," rather than a serious principle on which he bases his theory. What he rails against is the notion that the mind can walk in material space; he is not objecting to the notion that the mind can be in a place. In fact, it is necessary for the mind to be where it sees objects; it is this that the walking-mind argument is meant to establish. The mind is not extended, Malebranche says in the first of his *Trois Lettres* (replying again to Arnauld). But the mind is "where you see colors, and where you feel the pain. For there is a contradiction if the modification of a substance is found where that substance is not located. Thus, the soul finds itself at the same time here and there, i.e., in several places."[7] The places where it is when it perceives are, however, only intelligible places. In other words, the walking-mind argument is used by Malebranche to deny that the immediate objects of the mind in perception are physical or material: "I wish to say, if the immediate object of the mind which sees the stars is not intelligible, but material, it is necessary to say that the mind is in the stars which it sees white and luminous." Even stronger and more absurd, because of illusions, would be our having to say that the mind is in objects that do not exist.[8] It is necessary, the *Entretien* insists also, that "the mind . . . is where the color is, where the pain is"; it is also "in the flower which it sees, it is in the fire which it feels"; it is also in the idea that "touches it and strikes it" or that penetrates the mind.[9] All these spatial terms are used by Malebranche but only in the intelligible (i.e., nonphysical) sense. "The true place of intellects ['intelligences'] is the intelligible world, as the true place of bodies is the material world."

The idea and the sensation are involved in apprehending particular bodies. The two ingredients—idea and sensation—are present to the mind. If we did see bodies by means of our sensations, we would be seeing them by qualities that bodies do not have, for even Arnauld accepts the view that colors, sounds, etc., are only sensations. Thus, for Malebranche we need to use the idea of extension, from which bodies have been formed by God and from which we can derive their geometrical properties. Both ideas and sensations have a locus, a place: sensations, being modes of mind, are located in the mind; ideas, being modes of God, are located in God. Whereas we see (regarder) the color of the rose where the color is (in our mind), we see (voir) the geometrical properties of the rose where those properties are (in God). We cannot look at or see things where they are not. What we look at is not seen where we ordinarily take those objects to be: they are not visible in themselves. Visibility as understanding, usurps sensory seeing. We cannot see (apprehend) the sun in material space because (a) our mind is not in *that* space, (b) the qualities of the sun that we think we sense are really only sensations in our mind, and (c) seeing requires, in addition to sensation, ideas that are located in God. Hence we see all things in the mind of God with which we are united.

In his *Défense* of his *Des vraies et des fausses idées*, against one of Malebranche's replies, Arnauld offered an explication of the concept of 'intelligible' as Malebranche used it. He suggests that "an intelligible sun is nothing other than, as we see in St. Thomas, the material sun which is in the understanding of those who know it: secundum esse quod habet in cognoscente."[10] Malebranche cannot accept this explication for two reasons: it makes the relation of the sun to God's mind epistemic only, and it confuses the way in which the sun is in God's mind with the way it is in our mind. Malebranche is prepared to say that we can have the sun in our minds *ideally*, that is, that we have the idea of the sun. This is how he reads Arnauld's attempted translation into the language of objective reality. But God does not have in his mind the idea of the idea of body: he really has intelligible extension in his mind. The distinction is obscure, but Malebranche wants to say that what is in God's mind is the ontological source of matter, not just the knowledge of matter. This ontological feature of the ideas in the mind of God enables those ideas to represent things. The ontic containment relation is the necessary condition for representation. Our ability to derive epistemically some truths of body from the idea of extension in God's mind is only an analogue of that more fundamental relation. Not only does representation require that that which represents be something other than the knower and his or her modification, it requires this ontic relation between thing and that which represents.

This firm conviction leads Malebranche into a misreading of Descartes on ideas and objective reality. When, in the third *Meditation*, Descartes says that some of his thoughts are images of things, to which alone is it proper to give the name 'idea', Malebranche sees this as distinguishing images as modes of mind from other thoughts that represents things to us.[11] Representative thoughts *contain* (Descartes uses 'contient', Malebranche likes to substitute 'enferme') an objective reality. Just as a purse that contains one hundred pieces of gold is a purse of one hundred pieces of gold, not just a purse, so a thought that represents to me a circle or infinity (the examples Malebranche uses now, instead of stars, sun, house) does so only because it contains "the *idea* or the *objective reality*" of a circle or of infinity, not just because it is a thought.[12] Without that objective reality, the mind would not be able to have a perception or thought of a circle or of infinity, no more than a purse could be a purse of one hundred pieces of gold if it did not contain that amount of gold. Thus, whereas Descartes claims that one and the same idea has the formal reality of a mode of mind as well as the objective reality of objects, Malebranche separates idea from objective reality, making the latter something that the mind contains. Once this separation is effected, it becomes easy for Malebranche to argue that the objective reality of infinity cannot be a mode of our mind, since a modality of mind cannot *be* that which it is not; especially, it cannot be infinite. The mind for Malebranche cannot contain infinity, but it can contain the objective reality of infinity, since the objective reality is the idea of infinity in God's mind. That idea in God's mind is more than an idea: it is infinity. Malebranche translates 'objective' as 'intelligible', giving to the intelligible an ontological status. Thus it is not ideas as modes of mind which lead me to a knowledge of things, it is only ideas as entities separate from me and as part of God which can yield knowledge. The presence required by Malebranche for knowledge is clearly ontic.

A few years before the first Arnauld-Malebranche exchange, another Cartesian, Simon Foucher (*Critique de la Recherche de la verité*, 1675), tried to develop a view of representation that made ideas stand proxy for the *presence* of things. He was careful not to make ideas into entities, they are only "ways of being of our mind," or "our mind disposed in a particular way or manner" (p. 44).[13] To represent is, he insists, "to make a thing *present*" (p. 52). To represent, our ideas must "dispose us just as if the thing was actually in us, and was *immediately* present to us" (p. 53). What would be the effect if the object was present to us? Foucher seems at first to say it would be an image. He cites an example of the word 'tree'; this word is not similar to trees, but yet it represents the tree. Strictly speaking, it is not the word, but the idea or image excited by the word which represents. When we pronounce the word 'tree', we imagine something similar to that which we see when a tree is actually present before our eyes (p. 57). But Foucher quickly makes two additional points which show that representation for him is not a matter of an image resembling an object. First, the image excited in us by the word 'tree' is not similar to the tree. Rather, the image is similar to that which the object produces in us by means of our senses. Second, we do not ever see trees directly. If we were able to know external objects "in themselves and by themselves," it would be because "they are able to pass the substance into our mind" (p. 60). Only if objects could substantially be in our mind, could we dispense with ideas or images in recognizing those objects. Our ideas represent objects by making the object present to us, in the sense that we have all the reactions the object would have caused in us had it been present. The object is not substantially present to us, but we possess it nevertheless because of this representative nature of ideas. Foucher goes all the way with the assimilation notion: "we become all things through our knowledge" (p. 61).

This last move by Foucher reveals his concern to retain union of object and knower. His ideas, like those of Descartes in their objective reality, bring the object within us, not substantially but effectively, in that all that the object could do were it present is done by the ideas. Foucher has not appreciated the point suggested by Chanet and developed later by Arnauld: that union with the object would not be cognition of the object; but Foucher was clearly trying to find a formulation that would protect the direct presence of objects to us, while recognizing the role that must be played by perception in cognition. Ideas are not entities, in Malebranche's sense. Foucher's modification of the scholastic theory is slight, but both theories come as close to direct realism as they can, given their shared belief that the object must be in the mind in some way if we are to cognize it. The form of the object, the intelligible species, or the idea is in the mind. Hence we do after all know the object, even possess it. Arnauld sought to cut through the ambiguities of place for cognition, but he recognized that of course we cognize objects by perceiving them, by being aware of them. Foucher tried to link representation and possession, Arnauld thought he had connected representation and immediacy of objects.

Commentators on Arnauld have not known how to take his attempts to achieve some form of realism. Lest we think the notion of a substantial presence too naive to take seriously, a controversy over Arnauld between John Laird and A. O. Lovejoy in 1923 is illuminating.[14] Laird characterized Arnauld's theory as realism. Morris Ginsberg, in the Introduction to his translation of Malebranche's *Dialogues on Metaphysics and on Religion* (1923) had similarly characterized

Arnauld: "Arnauld detects most of the vulnerable points of doctrine of representative perception, and furnishes a foundation for a thorough-going realistic theory of knowledge" (p. 39). Lovejoy argues that on Cartesian grounds "our apprehension of physical realities cannot be direct. Bits of matter cannot enter consciousness bodily."[15] Direct apprehension of objects requires that the object literally enter consciousness. Lovejoy goes on to state that one reason for maintaining Arnauld was not a realist is that a perception or an idea for Arnauld is a psychical mode of existence, "which implies that it cannot be existentially identical with any physical object."[16] Ginsberg had pointed out that for Arnauld, there is no "additional entity, forming part of the sum of existence" when we cognize an object. In an act of knowing, "there is only one thing to which existence ought to be ascribed, the modification, namely, of the soul, the process or event of knowing" (p. 42). There is the object and my awareness of the object. Of course, my awareness has a content; but that content, for Arnauld, is not reified. Lovejoy thinks that once a content is added to an act, there are two entities, or an entity and a process. For Arnauld, the two could not be separated. Lovejoy insists that the content of perception is "representative mental entities," whereas Arnauld sought to deny precisely that. Lovejoy assumes that either there is contentless perception or there is perception with content. Since the former is impossible (if not nonsense), the latter is the case, and therefore mental entities are real.

Malebranche believed that representation requires something distinct from ourselves to do the representing. Sensations cannot represent since they are modalities of mind. Thus ideas as entities distinct from us are required. Lovejoy seems to accept this doctrine of representation. His conclusion about Arnauld was reached both because of his notion that direct realism requires substantial presence and because of his acceptance of Malebranche's notion of representation. If knowledge is representative of things, it cannot be direct. Arnauld was trying to show that, as Laird remarked in replying to Lovejoy, the belief that "knowledge involves psychical processes which have a 'content' is not incompatible with realism" (p. 178).

Brian O'Neil finds in Descartes a tension between reified contents and a stress upon the act of perceiving (the opposition, in fact, between Arnauld and Malebranche). I have said that I think Arnauld's reading of Descartes fits the texts. Arnauld insisted that his reading of 'ideas' yields direct awareness of objects, but it is *awareness*, not *physical* contact. Lovejoy takes literal contact as his model of directness. Clearly, such a model will not suffice; it is the negation of awareness. One might ask, have Arnauld and Descartes done any bet-ter, by clinging to the scholastic tradition of the object being in the mind? O'Neil believes not, or at least, he believes there are problems in Descartes's account. O'Neil is aware of the dangers of the meta-phor of the knower "being in direct contact" with the object. At the same time, he defines direct realism as the view that there is no gap or intermediary between knower and known (*Epistemological Direct Realism in Descartes' Philosophy*, 1974, p. 7). What will count as the absence of a gap? One way to eliminate the gap, O'Neil says, is to fol-low the scholastic tradition in extending "the activity of the mind, in a sense, all the way to the fingertips" (p. 61). *Cognitive* contact for Aristotle and Aquinas "took place initially at the surface of the body, so to speak" (p. 64). Even "within the Cartesian system" there is a way in which the gap could be removed: "enlarge and 'elevate' the role of the animal spirits. Let the process of sensing end with them" (ibid.). In other words, the gap that worries O'Neil is the dif-ference between sensing and understanding, between sensible and in-telligible species, between knowing and being. The directness of St. Thomas's theory lies in the notion that the form of the object exists in the mind, but this existence occurs only because a transformation takes place from physical to incorporeal. O'Neil thinks, however, this transformation occurs at the point of sensing, not at a later stage of the process. The later stages are just refinements of cognition.

O'Neil recognizes (and this is part of the importance of his book) the closeness of Descartes to this theory.

The foundation of Descartes's physics and metaphysics is a theory of real es-sences. These constitute the world and are knowable; when they are known they exist in the mind as intentional reality (*esse objectivum*). Hence, it is not diffi-cult to see why *esse objectivum* often appears to be treated as a 'thing'. It *is* a thing in a way; if the intentional being in question is an essence, a 'simple na-ture', then it is a building block of the world. Yet it is known. So something which constitutes the world ontologically is possessed intentionally. (p. 87)

Yet O'Neil believes that Descartes has not explained *how* essences that are "formative of the world" are "present to and known by minds" (p. 88). There is, he says, "no argument for, nor explanation of, how that which is fundamentally formative of the world can also be directly present to a mind that knows" (p. 90; cf. p. 92). What is needed, O'Neil insists, for any direct realism is some justification "that at some point there be direct contact with the world" (p. 88).

'Present to mind', 'direct contact with the world'—these phrases are always used in discussions of perceptual knowledge, whether in the seventeenth or the twentieth century. What is unclear in most discussions is what would count as direct cognitive contact. O'Neil's discussion of Descartes is thorough and careful; he does not, of course, confuse physical with cognitive contact. It is the category difference between physical and mental, together with his belief that in some places Descartes reified the content of ideas, which leads O'Neil to find indirect realism in Descartes's account. Nevertheless, the concept of *direct contact* remains unclear in O'Neil's account.

The same concept plagues Alquié's recent study of Malebranche (*Le Cartésianisme de Malebranche*, 1974). Alquié sees Malebranche as starting from the conviction that being is unknowable (p. 73). More precisely, the being of body "is not able to be seized directly," is not "immediately present to us" (p. 82). We think we live in a world of bodies, but in fact we are in *contact* only with ideas. These spatial terms are not explicated by Alquié. Sometimes he is content to state that we do not perceive bodies, that bodies are invisible, that a profound impression pervades Malebranche's text of the "unreality of the physical universe" (pp. 82-83). Without marking the reversal of our normal perceptual vocabulary in Malebranche, Alquié maintains that extension (he means intelligible extension) is directly visible, that this extension is present to our thought (p. 84). Alquié does remark on the importance of studying the metaphors used by Malebranche, e.g. vision of God, the nourishing of our soul by the divine reason (pp. 113-14), but he does not attempt to analyze the metaphor of presence to mind. The notion of directly seizing the presence of God has a place in religious discourse, but the denial of the direct presence of body to our mind is hardly explicated by this religious usage. We need to have some notion of how bodies can be directly seized (p. 139). We are still inside a metaphor when we are told that Malebranche rejected the belief that "our mind would be able to extend itself externally in order to seize bodies where they are located" (p. 153).[17] Nor are we helped by being told that in order to know we must "leave our self" (p. 155). The notion of ideas being external to our minds (p. 185) makes use of the same ambiguity around the spatial talk, but Alquié does explain the metaphor of the place of ideas: "The space our mind perceives is less a reality than it is a matter of contemplating that by means of which . . . we are able to know and comprehend Nature" (p. 190). Are we then to infer that the denial of a direct seizing of objects is just a denial that we know or contemplate objects by themselves, as Malebranche maintains all along? But then Arnauld is right in saying that either Malebranche has begged the question or he has failed to explain what he is denying. For Malebranche argues that we know bodies through ideas because we do not directly apprehend them, and we do not directly apprehend them because they are not close to the mind. Alquié thinks there is a problem—indeed, a paradox, "the paradox of . . . objective interiority"—in Descartes's claim that ideas have an objective reality but yet are only modes of mind (p. 202). This seems to be a paradox because Cartesian dualism makes unintelligible the needed contact of the mind and its object (p. 204). The question for both Descartes and Malebranche is "of knowing how the mind of man is able to come into contact with that which is not mind" (p. 207). Bodies for Descartes, ideas for Malebranche, are 'outside' the mind, but in ways not, I think, clarified by Alquié. The ambiguity of presence and of contact, which Arnauld sought to eliminate from Malebranche's account, is still found in Alquié's commentary. He even says that Malebranche has introduced a new notion, that of proximity, although Alquié assures us that it is not a spatial proximity.[18] Alquié may have eliminated the spatial proximity for ideas by suggesting that 'nearness' means 'that by means of which we apprehend'.[19] In this, he is perhaps recognizing with Arnauld that being in the understanding or nearness to the mind just means 'understood by the mind'. Alquié does say that "the words 'immediately' and 'proximity' do not resolve the problem of knowledge" (p. 209).

What will resolve the problem of knowledge, the seventeenth-century problem of how what is mental can know what is physical? We have found in Descartes, and in a number of Cartesians, two useful suggestions which, if they do not resolve entirely the problem, do transform it: (1) ideas as our means of access to the physical world are not entities, proxy objects, but are the psychic contents of awareness; and (2) the being of objects in the mind is their being understood, known, apprehended. Both suggestions bring to the front the fact that perceptual acquaintance is a significatory response to meaning.[20]

Notes

1. Chanet's use of the *camera obscura* model is the reverse of its normal use. This model was frequently used in perception theories during the two centuries, but in most cases the model is compared with the mind or understanding and the images are inside the box. The *camera obscura*, that is, is usually used for some form of indirect realism.

2. The exchange over the issue raised by Arnauld in his 1683 work on ideas ranged through a variety of replies from both writers. They had a related dispute over theological doctrines, which gave the Arnauld-Malebranche controversy some prominence, both through their exchange of treatises and through journal exchanges and comments. The main publications about the nature of ideas and perception are, after Arnauld's *Des vraies et des fausses*

idées (1683), the following: *Réponse de l'auteur de la Recherche de la verité, au livre de Mr. Arnauld, Des vraies et des fausses idées* (1684); *Réponse de l'auteur de la Recherche de la verité, au livre de Mr. Arnauld* (1685, second edition of the previous item); *Défense de Mr. Arnauld . . . contre la Réponse au livre, Des Vraies et des fausses idées* (1684); and *Trois Lettres de l'auteur de la Recherche de la verité, touchant la défense de Mr. Arnauld* (1685). For a full bibliographical description of these and other items, see Robinet's Introduction to volume VI of Malebranche's *Oeuvres complètes* (1966).

3. These and other definitions and axioms are in chapter V of *Des vraies et des fausses idées*, pp. 198 et seq., in volume 38 of his collected works.

4. *Réponse de l'auteur de la Recherche de la verité*, vol. VI of the *Oeuvres complètes*, pp. 50-54, 58-60.

5. Ibid., pp. 83-84.

6. Ibid., p. 95.

7. *Trois Lettres*, in *Oeuvres complètes*, vol. VI, p. 211; cf. *Entretiens sur la métaphysique et sur la religion*, in *Oeuvres complétes*, vol. XII, p. 114.

8. Ibid., pp. 211-12.

9. *Entretiens*, p. 399.

10. Quoted by Malebranche in *Trois Lettres*, p. 205.

11. Ibid., p. 216.

12. Ibid., p. 217.

13. Robert Desgabets (*Critique de la Critique de la Recherche de la verité*, 1675), writing against Foucher, agrees with this concept of ideas: they are nothing other than our thoughts (p. 105). To think of something "and to have an idea are formally the same thing" (p. 203). René Fedé (*Méditation métaphysique*, 1683), who was very close to Malebranche in holding that God makes objects intelligible to me by containing them, and in holding that there is an interpenetration between God and me when I perceive objects, insists that "my ideas are nothing other than the ways in which I contemplate the divine power" (p. 29).

14. John Laird, "The 'Legend' of Arnauld's Realism," *Mind* 33, no. 130 (1924):176-79, and A. O. Lovejoy, "Representative Ideas in Malebranche and Arnauld," *Mind* 32, no. 128 (1923):449-61. In his *Studies in the Cartesian Philosophy* (1902; reprint 1962), N. Kemp Smith briefly discusses Arnauld's rejection of representative perception, noting Arnauld's saying there is no evidence that our subjective states act as intermediaries between mind and matter (pp. 115-16). Lovejoy must have missed Kemp Smith's reference to Arnauld's realism. Sir William Hamilton also understood Arnauld in this way (see his edition of Reid's *Works*, p. 296). Two recent discussions of Arnauld have captured the difference between Malebranche's object-ideas and Arnauld's act-ideas. See "Arnauld's Alleged Representationalism," by Monte Cook, *Journal of the History of Philosophy* 12, no. 1 (1974):53-62, and "Representationalism in Arnauld's Act Theory of Perception," by Daisie Radner, *Journal of the History of Philosophy* 14, no. 1 (1976):96-98.

15. Lovejoy, "Representative Ideas in Malebranche and Arnauld," p. 450.

16. Ibid., p. 454.

17. Alquié says that Malebranche followed Descartes in rejecting this belief (*Le Cartésianisme de Malebranche*, p. 153). There is a passing reference to this notion in *The Passions of the Soul*, I, XXXIII: "so that it is no more necessary that our soul should exercise its functions immediately in the heart, in order to feel its passions there, than it is necessary for the soul to be in the heavens in order to see the stars there." Both Alquié and Rodis-Lewis (*Nicolas Malebranche*, 1963, p. 57n) cite Plotinus (*Ennead*, IV.6.I): "In any perception we attain by sight, the object is grasped there where it lies in the direct line of vision; it is there that we attack it; there, then, the perception is formed."

18. That this is not new is shown by the various appeals to and debates over the notion of union of object with mind in previous accounts of knowledge and perception.

19. He tries to explicate Malebranche by drawing a distinction between two kinds of externality, that of 'proche' and that of 'lointain': "Things are at the same time external and distant, that is why they are inaccessible. Ideas are external to me but they are closely related: their proximity is immediate. They thus constitute the objects of my perception." (p. 208).

20. Louis Marin (*La Critique du discours*, 1975) provides a fascinating discussion of the presence of objects to the mind through meaning. He analyzes the notion of signs and of natural signs in the Port Royal logic. The comparisons he draws between the presence of objects in cognition and the real presence of Christ in the Eucharist are instructive, but somewhat difficult to follow. It is the linking of presence to signification which is important in Marin's account. See especially pp. 32-33, 41-42, 52-54, 56, 59-67, 76-77, and 87-92.

Chapter IV

British Presence

Arnauld may not have developed a full cognitive psychology, but he at least attempted to explain the metaphors. Commitment to the notion that the object known must be present to the mind, acceptance of the dictum of no action (including cognitive action) at a distance, led Malebranche to follow the way of ideas as entities in his theory of knowledge. The differences between Arnauld and Malebranche, over the nature of ideas and over the application of these principles of presence and no action at a distance, are repeated in eighteenth-century British philosophy. The most familiar British version of the notion of presence to mind is that found in Hume's writings. I examine in some detail Hume's use of this notion, as well as his discussion of our knowledge of body, in chapter VIII. It is helpful to sketch in first, in this chapter, the context around Hume. We need to appreciate the extent to which British writers appealed to and reacted against the notion of presence to mind.

Arthur Collier (*Clavis Universalis*, 1713) provides an appeal to the notion of presence to mind before Hume. One of the many remarks Collier makes, to support his denial of an independently existing world of material objects, contains this appeal:

For is there any other possible way of *seeing* a Thing than by having such or such a Thing *present* to our Minds? And can an Object be *present* to the Mind, or Visive Faculty, which is affirmed to be External to it? Then may we think,

76

without thinking on any Thing; or perceive, without having any Thing in our Mind. If then the Presentialness of the Object be necessary to the Act of Vision, the Object perceived cannot possibly be External to, at a *Distance* from, or *Independent* of us: And consequently, the only Sense in which an Object can be said to Exist *without* us, is its being *not Seen* or *perceived*. (p. 36)[1]

Writing late in the century, Dugald Stewart (*Elements of Philosophy of the Human Mind*, 1792) linked this notion of presence to the mind with that of no action at a distance. Stewart remarked that "in the case of the perception of distant objects, we are naturally inclined to suspect, either something to be emitted from the object to the organ of sense, or some medium to intervene between the object and organ by means of which the former may communicate an impulse to the latter" (p. 79). Stewart cites this notion in Newton. Newton, he says, plainly proceeded on the assumption that "no connection could be carried on between matter and mind, unless the mind were *present* . . . to the matter from which the last impression is communicated" (p. 81). Query 31 in Newton's *Opticks* spoke of the species of things being "carried through the organs of sense into the place" of the soul's sensation, the brain, "where it perceives them by means of its immediate presence, without the intervention of any third thing." Similarly, God is "every where present to the things themselves." The General Scholium at the end of book III of the *Principia* tried to characterize God's presence more precisely.

He is not eternity or infinity, but eternal and infinite; he is not duration or space, but he endures and is present. He endures for ever, and is every where present; and by existing always and every where, he constitutes duration and space. Since every particle of space is *always*, and every indivisible moment of duration is *every where*, certainly the Maker and Lord of all things cannot be *never* and *no where*.[2]

Nor is God's presence virtual only: "He is omnipresent not *virtually* only, but also *substantially*; for virtue cannot subsist without substance."[3] David Gregory, one of Newton's disciples, wrote in 1705 that

The plain truth is that he [Newton] believes God to be omnipresent in the literal sense; and that as we are sensible of objects when their images are brought home within the brain, so God must be sensible of every thing, being intimately present with every thing: for he supposes that as God is present in space where there is no body, he is present in space where a body is also present.[4]

The correspondence between Leibniz and Clarke (a defender of Newton) highlighted this eighteenth-century version of 'present to the mind'.[5] This exchange opened, on Clarke's side, with the correcting of a remark Leibniz made about Newton: "that space is an organ, which God makes use of to perceive things by" (p. 1). Newton's view is rather, Clarke assures Leibniz, that since God is omnipresent, he "perceives all things by his immediate presence to them" (p. 13). God has no need of any organ or medium. Clarke points out also that Newton illustrates his meaning by a similitude: "that as the mind of man, by its immediate presence to the pictures or images of things, form'd in the brain by the means of the organs of sensation, sees those pictures as if they were the things themselves; so God sees all things, by his immediate presence to them" (ibid.). Just as Newton does not consider the brain and sense organs "as the means by which the mind sees or perceives" the images on the brain, so God does not see all things by any organs. Newton meant nothing more than this, Clarke assures Leibniz, when he says that space was the sensorium of God.[6]

Leibniz replies by saying that Malebranche and the Cartesians deny that the mere presence of the soul to what passes in the brain accounts for perception. Leibniz does not object to the notion of presence, only that presence is not sufficient. If it were, space, which is "intimately present to the body contained in it," would perceive the body. He says the soul is indivisible and hence can only be immediately present at one point in the body. Hence, how could it perceive "what happens out of that point"? Clarke replies by saying the word 'sensory' signifies the place of sensation, not the organ of sensation. Moreover, Newton said space is *as it were* the sensorium of God: an analogy only. Clarke admits that bare presence is insufficient for perception, but "without being present to the images of the things perceived, [the soul] could not possibly perceive them." He generalizes the principle to living substances: "a living substance can only there perceive where it is present either to the things themselves . . . or to the images of things" (p. 21). Clarke then formulates a principle that is repeated throughout the century: "Nothing can any more act, or be acted upon, where it is not present; than it can be, where it is not" (pp. 20-21). It is not simple presence, Clarke admits, that enables God to perceive things or the soul to perceive images; it is by God being a living and intelligent substance and by the soul being a living substance that things can be perceived when they are present.

Leibniz responds that the presence of an animated substance is not sufficient for perception, hence Clarke has still not explained perception: "The author must explain, how the soul perceives what is without itself" (p. 28). Leibniz makes a suggestion: "God is not present to things by situation, but by essence." Spatial location is not the way God is present to things. The soul cannot be diffused over the whole body since that would be to make the soul extended and divisible, which it is not. Clarke does not know "how the soul of a seeing man, sees the images to which it is present," but he is certain that the soul "cannot perceive what it is not present to; because nothing can act, or be acted upon, where it is not" (p. 33). Similarly, God cannot operate where he is not. God is present to every thing essentially and substantially. The soul is not present to all parts of the body, only to the brain. Hence the soul can only operate upon the brain "or certain nerves and spirits," and they in turn, by God's arrangements, influence the whole body. Clarke did not deny that God is located in space, though his substantial presence is not clarified. Leibniz goes after this point again. To say God has a sensorium (Leibniz does not accept the appeal made by Clarke that this is an analogy only) is to make God the soul of the world. Leibniz allows that God perceives things in himself, but he insists that "space is the place of things, and not the place of God's ideas." Of course, for Leibniz, "The soul knows things, because God has put into it a principle representative of things without" (p. 41). The soul is immediately affected by images, but these images are within the soul and correspond to those of the body. Strictly, for Leibniz we do not see external objects. Clarke's response is to insist that space "is the place of all things, and of all ideas" (p. 50). He does not understand Leibniz's talk of images representing things. Clarke simply says, "The soul discerns things, by having the images of things conveyed to it through the organs of sense" (p. 51). It is present to the sensorium where those images come.

Leibniz replies by saying that space cannot be the place of ideas since "ideas are in the understanding." Ideas are not conveyed by the organs of sense to the soul: there is no way in which this can happen, as the new Cartesians have shown. Material does not affect immaterial. We perceive what passes outside us by means of what happens inside us. Clarke continues to speak of God being *actually* present everywhere. He also continues to say that space is the place of ideas, although he now (in his fifth reply) states that this is so because space "is the place of the substances themselves, in whose understandings ideas exist" (p. 109).

Leibniz was not alone in finding the notion of space being in the place of ideas an odd one. In his notes to his translation of William King's *De Origine Mali* (1702), *An Essay on the Origin of Evil* (1731), Edmund Law refers to the Leibniz-Clarke exchange on this point. "Few, I believe, besides Dr. Clarke, can apprehend how Space is . . .

the *Place of all Ideas*. I'm sure Space and Spirit, and the distinct Properties of each, appear to me as distant and incompatible, as the most remote and inconsistent things in nature" (p. 32, n.13). Space and place are also foreign to God's essence. Law says that the principle of no action at a distance has long ago been rejected. "Now to urge upon us the Old Maxim, that nothing can act where it is not, is still supposing a *Spirit* existing somewhere, or in some *Ubi*, or co-extended, or *co-expanded* with some part of *Space*, and *acting* in some other part of such imaginary Space (which supposition we have long ago discarded)" (p. 64).

Law does not name any persons who challenged or rejected this supposition. Perhaps a letter in the *Memoirs for the Ingenious* for 1693 reflects that rejection.[7] The writer is concerned with the problems that arise when the idea of extension or space is confounded or identified with that of matter. One difficulty with this identity is that then "Spirits and even God should be no-where," for to be somewhere (when space is the same as matter) would be to be matter. He remarks that "all mankind hitherto has look'd upon *not to be*, and *to be nowhere*, as synonimous Phrases" (p. 18). He agrees that spirits "are not circumscribed in a certain place," do not have "any determinate figure," and do not "fill up a certain space." But he still seems to want to hold on to the notion that spirits act *in* a place. Those he writes against, wanting to avoid any possibility of identifying spirit with matter, say that spirit is nowhere, not even "in the center of its operation."

Issac Watts (*Philosophical Essays on Various Subjects*, 1733, written, he says, "many years ago") also discusses what he characterizes as "the old maxim, *nihil agit in distans.*" He thinks Newton has exploded this notion by showing that planets at great distances from each other work by an attractive force. He says this attraction or gravitation is "but a powerful Appointment of the Creator" (p. 153). He then declares that the same holds for spirits: they can act on bodies only through the will of God. Hence, being in a place would not help spirits since they can act only by the will of God. Existing nowhere is, he says, not incompatible with being a spirit (p. 163). Moreover, if souls or spirits were in a place, "they must be extended, they must be Long, Broad, and Deep and then they must be of some Shape or Figure" (pp. 147-48). A spirit would then be a measurable distance from the north or south wall. He does not have any idea of "how a Thought can touch or lye near to a Piece of Flesh or a Bone" (p. 152).

Law did not go unchallenged in his easy rejection of the 'no action at a distance' principle for spirit. John Jackson's *The Existence and Unity of God* (1734)—a proposed defense of Clarke's Boyle lectures on the *Being and Attributes of God* (1705)—claimed that it is agreed that God is present everywhere. This means that his *substance* is present everywhere, since he cannot be present where his substance is not (p. 100). "As God cannot be *present* where his substance is not, so neither can he act where his Substance is not" (p. 101). In rejecting the maxim that nothing can act where it is not, Jackson says Law "plainly supposes God to know and act upon all Things, without a *local Presence* to any Thing." Jackson suspects that Law supposes that "if God was *present* where he acted, he must act by *Contact*, like *Bodies*, and so not be *immaterial*" (p. 102). Not even matter always acts by contact, Jackson says. Real presence does not entail or require contact. "The human Soul and Body do not touch each other, in their mutual impressions, but yet I hope they are *present* to each other" (p. 103). But local presence "is equally and absolutely necessary, where any agent can be conceived to act." We do not know the manner of God's acting, or of our action and perception, but "yet it is unquestionably true, that we do not *act* where we *are not*."

Law responds to Jackson in *An Enquiry into the Ideas of Space, Time, Infinity, and Eternity* (1734). Law grants that God is present to things, but only as a spirit, not in the way body is, i.e., spread out, extended (p. 116). He cites various words used in the past for immaterial (especially God's) presence: real virtue, force, vigor, energy, activity, substantial power. He is ready to accept the maxim, if liberalized as 'power':

From what has been said it may appear, that tho' we do not maintain our Author's Notion of *local Presence* (which is indeed the Ground of all the Objections against it) yet we hold such a Presence as belongs to all intellectual Beings, and which may be conceiv'd by our intellect; 'tis the actual Influence and Operation of a *Power* on its *Object*, which is all the Presentiality it is capable of, except it were render'd visible or tangible, i.e., made something else. (pp. 123-24)

In another book, published one year later, *A Dissertation on Matter and Spirit*, Jackson says that nothing can exist without extension or without being in space: "no Existence can be without a *Place* of Existence, or existing *somewhere*" (p. 3). Thus spirit exists and acts in space. Spirit is also capable of motion; it moves with the body. "*Soul* as well as *Body* hath evidently place of Existence; the Soul moves from one place to another as well as the Body. . . . Thinking Substance acts *in space* . . . it exists in *Space* and possesses Space by its Existence."[8] To deny this, Jackson claims, is to say the soul "exists and acts *where it is not*," which is absurd. Jackson was unable to offer any clear concept of the place of the soul: he stood by the principle that the soul, like everything else, must exist and (more important) act in and from a place. He was writing against Andrew Baxter's *An Enquiry into the Nature of the Human Soul* (1733). Baxter had given a firm foundation to the principle of no action at a distance. "Nothing can act where it is not. This is one of the plainest, most unexceptionable principles. To say a thing acts, and yet is not where it acts is to say nothing acts there."[9] Jackson quotes this remark from Baxter and then goes on to talk of the soul's presence in space. Every created thinking substance "has a sphere of Action in some Part of Space to which it is present, and in which it exists, and acts only where it is present. All substances act where they are, not where they are not" (p. 36). But the action of spirit does not require contact:

Spirit may act upon Spirit reciprocally, by being perfectly *present* to each other, without mutual *Contact* or *Solidity*; and even *Matter* may possibly act upon *Matter* by being *present* without *Contact* . . . since we have Reason to think it acts upon the *Soul*, to which it is united, by being *present* to it without Contact (tho' we know nothing of any such Thing in Fact). (p. 43)

This curious last parenthetical clause means, I assume, that we do not know how body acts on mind, but Jackson is sure it does act without contact. Jackson follows Newton and Clarke on God's substantial presence to all things, and he also compares this to our mode of knowing: "All other intelligent Agents know only by the Exercise of their intelligent Part on Objects receiv'd from External Things, to which Objects they are immediately present" (p. 56).

In 1737, William Porterfield published a long essay on the motions of the eyes.[10] In part one of this two-part essay, he laid down the principle that "nothing can act, or be acted upon where it is not," and went on from that principle to draw the conclusion: "and therefore our Mind can never perceive any thing but its own proper Modifications, the various States and Conditions of the *Sensorium* to which it is present."[11] Malebranche's walking-mind argument then reappears:

For when I look at the Sun or Moon, it is impossible that these Bodies so far distant from my Mind, can with any Propriety of Speech be said to act upon it. To imagine otherwise, is to Imagine Things can act where they are not present; which is as absurd, as to suppose that they can be where they are not.

It is, Porterfield insists, only the agitations in the sensorium excited by light (in the case of vision) "which can any way act upon the Mind, and therein excite those Modifications which we call Colours;

so that it is not the external Sun or Moon which is in the Heavens which our Mind perceives, but only their Image or Representation impressed upon the *Sensorium*."[12] Porterfield is not clear about the way the mind sees these images or "how it receives these ideas from such Agitations in the *Sensorium*," but he is certain that "it can never perceive the external Bodies themselves to which it is not present." This appeal to the principle of 'presence to mind' is reaffirmed toward the close of this essay: "strictly speaking" the mind "perceives nothing but what is present with it."[13] This claim is just as true of tangible ideas as with visible ones: "the Ideas or Perceptions that succeed one another, are all of them as much present with my mind as any visible idea can be."[14]

A few other examples of the pervasiveness of the principle of 'no action at a distance' are worth noting. The first is *An Essay on Spirit* (1750), by Robert Clayton, a controversial work in the debate over the Nicene and Athanasian Creeds. Clayton follows the common doctrine that matter is not capable of self-motion. Therefore, whenever we see anything moved, we can conclude "the first Author, or Cause of that Motion, to be what we call *Spirit*" (p. 10). Even the momentum of a falling body is ascribed to spirit: "Since, as *Nothing can act where it is not*, that Power whereby any Body continues in Motion, is as much the Effect of some concomitant Spirit, as the Power which put it first in Motion." Another interesting example of this principle is found in a brief essay, "Concerning the Perceptive Faculty," in the *Annual Register* for 1763. The author says, "As nothing can act where it is not, so the perceptive power of man cannot possibly perceive any thing without or beyond himself" (p. 182). He goes on to provide an example: "that man perceives colour we are sure of, and therefore it must be within him or he would act where he was not" (p. 183). The author cites Berkeley and Malebranche as having shown that color is not without the mind, but of course this was a doctrine about secondary qualities which had a wide acceptance in the eighteenth century.[15] Similarly, in *A Course of Lectures on the Principle Subjects in Pneumatology, Ethics, and Divinity* (1763), Philip Doddridge outlines his lectures and the reading assignments he had been using many years earlier in one of the non-Conformist colleges.[16] Doddridge reports on those who said that a spirit is "Present in Any Place, when it is capable of perceiving and immediately operating upon the body which fills that place, or on Spirits united to such bodies" (p. 77). While discussing the controversy over thinking matter, he says that those who claim the soul is extended do so in the belief that "nothing acts but *where it is*: therefore if the Soul were not extended, it could not act at all" (p. 210). Doddridge offers his own comment on this controversy: it is "inconceivable how the soul should move the nerves inserted in the brain, Any better by being near, than by being further off, unless we suppose it material" (p. 210). Doddridge, much like Arnauld, insisted that it "is not this proximity, which gives the mind a consciousness of bodily motion" (ibid.).

The debate over the place of mind continues right down to the closing years of the century. For example, in the correspondence between Richard Price and Joseph Priestley (published in 1778 as *A Free Discussion of the Doctrine of Materialism, and Philosophical Necessity*), Priestley referred to some modern metaphysicians "who said that spirit can have no relation to place, and is incapable of being present anywhere (p. 54). Priestley was defending a dynamic or organic version of materialism.[17] Price replied that only the Cartesians said this; everyone else accepts the maxim "that *time* and *place* are necessary to the existence of all things" (p. 55). Price confesses ignorance about the manner of existence of spirit, but holds that if it exists, it must do so in some place and at some time.

Price corresponded with another late eighteenth-century figure, Lord Monboddo, not as important or as sound an intellect as Priestley but one who reflects the extended debate over place and the action of mind or spirit. In a letter of 11 July 1780 to Price, Lord Monboddo writes that mind "acts and energizes in *some* part of Space. . . . And I allow that nothing can act except where it is. Mind therefore exists *in* space."[18] Monboddo does not think mind is extended; it is *in* but it does not *fill* space. In his reply of 2 August 1780, Price says that the soul, "as well as everything else, does exist in place, as well as time, but *how* I know not" (p. 121). He suspects that there are ways "of occupying place which do not imply *divisibility*," the question of whether mind is divisible as matter is being another disturbing question in these debates. Monboddo admits that he does not exactly know how mind exists, but he agrees that it exists in space, even in the same space as our body.

In a 1783 letter to Welborne Ellis, Monboddo suggests that mind does not exist in space the way body does (by filling it), but by acting there. It acts in space either by moving body or by perceiving. Monboddo then goes on to accept the walking-mind argument which Malebranche ridiculed. To Ellis, he writes that mind perceives not only things present where our bodies are, but distant things as well. Thus, "the mind must necessarily be there, where those things are, otherwise it could not perceive them" (p. 231). In these instances, we are out of ourselves "and acting somewhere else than at home."

The mind transports itself to a place where the body is not. The objects are present with the mind. "Now as we cannot suppose that the objects come to the mind, it is I think of necessity that the mind should go to the objects; for, some way or other, they must be present together" (ibid.). The same claims, with more discussion, are found in Monboddo's long and prolix work, *Antient Metaphysics* (vol. II, 1782).

Thomas Reid (*Essays on the Intellectual Powers of Man*, vol. I, 1786) discusses the appeal to union between knower and object (made by John Norris) and the appeal to the principle of no action at a distance for minds (made by Clarke, Newton, and Porterfield). Reid rejected union as inappropriate to cognition. He agreed that "nothing can act immediately where it is not" (p. 242), this principle being a consequence of the dictum, accepted by Newton, "that power without substance is inconceivable." But Reid does not think the principle that nothing can act or be acted upon where it is not applies to the mind and its perceptions. Perception is neither action nor reaction. "To be perceived, is what Logicians call an external denomination, which implies neither action nor quality in the object perceived" (p. 243). Moreover, "To perceive an object is one thing; to act upon it is another." Reid is confident in rejecting action and reaction in perception, although he confesses that "we are altogether ignorant how" perception occurs (p. 245). Like Arnauld, however, he firmly rejects the notion that in "perception, the object must be contiguous to the percipient" (p. 244).[19]

Reid and Arnauld were clearly right to reject contiguity of object to mind as relevant to perception. Some of the writers we have examined in this chapter did attempt to develop a nonphysical concept of space or place, one appropriate to the 'energizing' or action of mind. The absence of a developed set of concepts, and a vocabulary divorced from physics and physiology, raised problems in other areas as well. The puzzles about how mind can *know* body were matched by those of how mind can *move* body, including our own body.[20] Locke's suggestion, that God might be able to give to matter the power of thought, raised additional problems about the nature of mind and the locus of thought. New materialists arose to expand and defend the notion that thought is a predicate of the brain. Some of these materialists made use of the change in the concept of matter, from passive corpuscular matter to force and power.[21]

Questions about the nature of mind and the nature of perceptual acquaintance intersect around the concept of presence to mind. For perception theory, this concept, together with the principle about no cognition at a distance, forced writers to decide between what Hume called the single or double existence view. In trying to avoid the literalness of objects being united with or present to the mind, writers faced the option of mediating, immaterial *objects* (ideas, as with Malebranche) or some other kind of analysis with stress on cognitivity. This latter move is not so well marked among British writers as it is with Arnauld, but it is nicely illustrated in opposition to Malebranche in Locke's discussion of that Cartesian; there are also a number of examples in eighteenth-century writers on perception which stress meaning and understanding. The influence of optics and optical language is more apparent among these writers. That influence sometimes masks the cognitive analyses. Berkeley is a particularly good illustration here, for we will see in his account a very explicit cognitive reading of seeing and touching: he offers a phenomenological, experiential optics in which 'being in the mind' is analyzed in cognitive terms.

Notes

1. On the use of the term 'presentialness', see John Norris's *Cursory Reflections upon a Book call'd an Essay concerning Human Understanding* (1692), p. 20: "I account for the Mode of *Human Understanding* after a very different way [from Locke], namely by the Presentialness of the Divine *Ideas* or Ideal World to our Souls." Norris was of course a follower of Malebranche.

2. *The Mathematical Principles of Natural Philosophy*. Translated into English by Andrew Motte. 3 vols. New edition, 1819. The passage just cited is found in vol. III, pp. 311-12.

3. Ibid., p. 312.

4. Quoted by Arnold Thackray, *Atoms and Powers* (1970), p. 27.

5. *A Collection of Papers, Which passed between the late Learned Mr. Leibnitz and Dr. Clarke, in the Years 1715 and 1716* (1717). This has been reprinted, edited by H. G. Alexander, as *The Leibniz-Clarke Correspondence* (1956). My references are to this reprint.

6. God's omnipresence is discussed in *The Spectator* for 9 July 1714. God is said to inhabit essentially all things. "His Substance is within the Substance of every Being, either material, or immaterial, and as intimately present to it, as that Being is to itself." The discussion was continued in the issue for 23 July. Bayle also notes that all modern theologians say that "the substance of God is extended in infinite spaces." Bayle insists that this is to make God material, for to be extended is to have parts, be divisible, and so on. "In a word, if matter is matter only because it is extended, it follows that everything extended is matter." (Article on Simonides, Remark F in his *Dictionnaire*.)

7. See letter III, dated 21 Jan. Cf. Locke, writing about the motion of spirits: "If it be said by anyone that it cannot change place because it hath none, for spirits are not in *loco* but *ubi*, I suppose that way of talking will not now be of much weight to many in an age that is not much disposed to admire or suffer themselves to be deceived by such unintelligible ways of speaking" (*Essay*, 2.23.21). In his *Philosophical Essays* (1733), Isaac Watts notes Locke's ridicule of this distinction (p. 147). Locke did, however, accept the general principle: "that spirits as well as bodies cannot operate but where they are" (2.23.19). In

his *Dictionnaire* Bayle tells us that three kinds of local presence were distinguished by theologians: *ubi circumsriptivum* for bodies, *ubi definitivum* for created spirits, and *ubi repletivum* for God.

8. Cf. Locke, *Essay*, 2.23.20: "Nobody can imagine that his soul can think or move a body at *Oxford* whilst he is at *London*, and cannot but know that, being united to his body, it constantly changes place all the whole journey between *Oxford* and *London*, as the coach or horse does that carries him, and I think may be said to be truly all that while in motion; or, if that will not be allowed to afford us a clear *idea* enough of its motion, its being separated from the body in death I think will; for to consider it as going out of the body, or leaving it and yet to have no *idea* of its motion, seems to me impossible."

9. Citations from Baxter are to the second edition of 1737.

10. "An Essay concerning the Motion of Our Eyes," in *Medical Essays and Observations of the Philosophical Society of Edinburgh*, 2nd edition, corrected, volumes III and IV. Much of this material, including the passages cited here, is used in Porterfield's *A Treatise on the Eye*, 1759, vol. II, pp. 306, 356-57.

11. "An Essay Concerning the Motion of Our Eyes," vol. III, p. 220.

12. Ibid., p. 221.

13. Ibid., p. 233.

14. Ibid., p. 234.

15. *The Spectator* can again be taken as an indicator of those philosophical doctrines that were known by the general reader. In the issue for 24 June 1712, the conclusion of one of the many essays on the imagination is as follows: "I have here supposed that my Reader is acquainted with that great Modern Discovery, which is at present universally acknowledged by all the inquirers into Natural Philosophy: Namely, that Light and Colours, as apprehended by the Imagination, are only Ideas in the Mind, and not Qualities that have any Existence in Matter. As this is a Truth that has been proved incontestably by many Modern Philosophers, and is indeed one of the finest Speculations in that Science, If the *English* Reader would see the Notion explained at large," he may find it in Locke's *Essay*, 2.8. The author of the article in the *Annual Register* for 1763, "Concerning the Perceptive Faculty," went even further to say "that figure, extension, and motion, are not perceptible objects, but that sensations alone are such, the former being only imagined by an operation of the mind, to exist external to it" (p. 184).

16. These lectures, with their references, are an excellent guide through the eighteenth-century literature on topics then under debate by philosophers and theologians. Unlike the traditional universities, these non-Conformist institutes and colleges, especially the one to which Doddridge was attached, instructed from contemporary books, pamphlets, and tracts.

17. For a discussion of this aspect of Priestley, see chapter VI of my *Thinking Matter*.

18. In *Lord Monboddo and Some of His Contemporaries* (1900), by William Knight.

19. William Drummond (*Academical Questions*, 1805) notes Reid's discussion of this principle, cites Clarke's use of it in the exchange with Leibniz, but uses it himself as a way of defending some sort of idealism. "If we assert, that the soul either acts, or is acted upon, we must still acknowledge, that nothing can act but where it is" (p. 30). Like Reid, Drummond denies action in perception, certainly action of objects on the mind. "Now if nothing can act, except where it is, how can the mind be acted upon by external objects? It would, besides, be absurd to say, that the immaterial intellect is in contact with any thing" (p. 31).

20. For a detailed discussion of eighteenth-century accounts of action, including answering the question "how is it that I can move my arm?" see chapter VII of my *Thinking Matter*.

21. Chapter V of *Thinking Matter* surveys the different views on the nature of matter.

Chapter V

Locke and Malebranche: Two Concepts of Idea

The doctrine that what is known must be present to the mind is found in Locke's *Essay*. In discussing the question of how bodies produce ideas in us, especially ideas of the original or primary qualities, Locke says this can only be done by impulse, "the only way which we can conceive bodies operate in" (2.8.11). He then gives a more detailed account of the production of ideas.

If then external objects be not united to our minds when they produce *ideas* in it and yet we perceive *these original qualities* in such of them as singly fall under our senses, it is evident that some motion must be thence continued by our nerves or animal spirits, there to *produce in our minds the particular* ideas *we have of them.* (2.8.12)

This passage works with the same alternatives cited by Malebranche: either *objects* themselves are united to the mind, or *ideas* of objects are united to the mind. In one of his replies to Bishop Stillingfleet, Locke confronts him with the absurdity of following the first alternative: his cathedral exists in his mind when he thinks of it. Locke expresses confidence that the bishop's thoughts do after all contain ideas.[1] At the end of the *Essay*, there is an even more Malebranchian remark: "For, since the things the mind contemplates are none of them, besides itself, present to the understanding, it is necessary that something else, as a sign or representation of the thing it considers, should be present to it: and these are *ideas*" (4.21.4). Locke disagrees with Malebranche on the causation of ideas: not God, but corpuscular action is their cause. Nor does he take ideas to be real beings. There *are* many passages where Locke uses the language of 'objects' while talking about ideas, e.g., "whatsoever is the object of the understanding when a man thinks" (1.1.8); the mind "hath no other immediate object but its own *ideas*"; it is these ideas alone that the mind "does or can contemplate" (4.1.1). More of these passages can be found. It may seem then that, although the objects of the mind when it thinks are not God-given ideas, it is nevertheless ideas and not things that are present to the mind. The question then becomes, how important is it that Locke's ideas are not real beings?

Before we pursue this question, we should note that Malebranche's concept of idea is not the only doctrine echoed in Locke's *Essay*. The 1.1.8 definition of 'idea' was linked with "whatever is meant by *phantasm, notion, species*," a clear echo of some portion of the scholastic doctrine (for 'species' certainly; 'notion' may be a reference to John Sergeant's adaptation of the Aristotelian-Thomistic account) and Hobbes's talk of phantasms. In addition, Locke's "Epistle to the Reader" includes Descartes's adaptation of the scholastic doctrine. Locke there explains that instead of the terms 'clear' and 'distinct' for ideas (terms from the Cartesian tradition), he proposes using 'determinate' and 'determined'. He then says that "by those denominations, I mean some object in the mind, and consequently *determined*, i.e., such as it is there seen and perceived to be." That we are hearing Cartesian echoes in the talk of "some object in the mind," and of the object being "there seen and perceived" is confirmed by Locke's elaboration: "This, I think, may fitly be called a *determinate* or *determined* idea, when, such as it is at any time objectively in the mind and so *determined* there, it is annexed and without variation *determined* to a name or articulate sound." Whereas Descartes spoke of the 'objective reality of ideas', meaning the reality of objects as they exist in the mind, Locke talks of *ideas* being in the mind objectively.

Locke did not become involved, as Descartes did, with the ontological aspect of objective reality, but he did give an unequivocal account of what he meant by the notion of 'being in the mind': "For if these words (*to be in the understanding*) have any propriety, they signify to be understood" (1.2.5). Here we have an almost verbatim repetition of Arnauld's remark: "I say that an object is present to our mind, when our mind perceives or conceives it."[2] The echoes from Arnauld are more pronounced on another important issue that divided Arnauld and Malebranche, namely, the nature of ideas.

Arnauld insisted that ideas were not real beings and that having ideas and perceiving were virtually the same. In several places in the *Essay* Locke repeats this linking of having ideas and perceiving.

"Whatever *idea* is in the mind is either an actual perception or else, having been an actual perception, is so in the mind that by the memory it can be made an actual perception again" (1.4.21).

In 2.1.3, Locke speaks of our senses conveying into the mind "several distinct *perceptions* of things." He refines his meaning of 'convey' by saying the senses "from external objects convey into the mind what produces there those *perceptions*."

External objects are said to "*furnish the mind with the* ideas *of sensible qualities*, which are all those different perceptions they [external objects] produce in us" (2.1.5).

"To ask *at what time a man has first any* ideas is to ask when he begins to perceive: having *ideas* and perceptions being the same thing" (2.1.9).

In answer to the question "*when [does] a man [begin] to have any ideas,*" Locke says, "when he first has any *sensations*." 'Sensation' is here used to designate the physiological process: it is defined as "an impression or motion made in some part of the body," and he says that that impression produces "some perception in the understanding" (2.1.23).

In discussing memory, Locke declares that "our *ideas* . . . [are] nothing but actual perceptions in the mind." Memory is said to be "a power in many cases to revive perceptions which it [the mind] has once had" (2.10.2).

"For our *ideas*, being nothing but bare appearances or perceptions in our minds" (2.32.1). In 2.32.3, he repeats this remark: "and so I say that the *ideas* in our minds, being only so many perceptions or appearances there . . ."

Locke's Critique

The contrast in these passages with Malebranche's strong characterization of ideas as distinct, real beings is marked. With the variety of references to other doctrines on ideas and perception in the *Essay*, with Locke using the different languages of these diverse doctrines, is there any reason for saying that he was following Arnauld? I think there is. The passages from the *Essay* that I have just cited are reinforced by Locke's Comments in his *An Examination of P. Malebranche's Opinion of Seeing All Things in God*. Section 3 of that tract cites Malebranche's appeal to the principle that "whatever the mind perceives 'must be actually present and intimately united to it'." In a later section (30). Locke recognizes that for Malebranche, "it is *ideas*, not *things*, that are present to the mind," because "the soul cannot perceive things at a distance, or remote from it." Ideas are present to the mind "only because God, in whom they are, is present to the mind." Locke does not think the notion of being intimately united to our soul or mind is very clear. He wants to know how can there be a union of two spirits, or of two beings, "that have neither of them any extension or surface." The notion of union is, he suggests, taken from bodies, "when the parts of one get within the surface of the other, and touch their inward parts" (§3). Locke insists that without an explanation of union with soul, Malebranche's account of seeing in God is no better than simply stating that ideas are produced in the mind. Locke notes that Malebranche said our bodies are united to our souls, but not in the way "which is necessary that the soul may perceive them" (§5). Locke wants to know what makes one union (with God) appropriate for perception but not the other (with bodies). Malebranche's reason for saying that bodies are not united to the soul in order to be perceived is that there is no proportion between them. To this, Locke responds, "if it shows anything, [it] shows only that a soul and a body cannot be united because one has surfaces to be united by, and the other none." What the claim of no proportion fails to show is why the union of soul and body is not sufficient to allow ideas to be excited in the soul by means of the body, instead of by God (§5). Locke thinks there is as little proportion between the soul and God as there is between soul and body. Later, in section 30, Locke notes that presence alone is not, according to Malebranche, sufficient for perception: God must *disclose* those ideas to us. It is the *disclosing* that Locke wants to know more about. The only point that Locke can find Malebranche making about *disclosure* is that "when God shows them, we see them; which in short seems to me to say only . . . that when we have these ideas, we have them, and we owe the having of them to our Maker." Locke thinks that it is just as intelligible to say "God has made our souls so, and so united them to our bodies, that, upon certain motions made in our bodies by external objects, the soul should have such and such perceptions or ideas" (§8). Note the phrase here, 'perceptions or ideas'. The physical account offered by Locke tells us just as much about the production of ideas as does Malebranche's account:

We have the ideas of figures and colours by the operation of exterior objects on our senses, when the sun shows them us; but how the sun shows them us, or how the light of the sun produces them in us; what, and how the alteration is made in our souls; I know not: nor does it appear by any thing our author says, that he knows any more what God does when he shows them us, or what it is that is done upon our minds, since the presence of them to our minds, he confesses, does it not. (§30)

Locke employs the corpuscular account, in terms of motion of particles of matter striking our sense organs, as the best explanatory hypothesis of perception (§9). He gives considerable details about the workings of each sense; his example of light is especially detailed (§9, 10). But Locke does not claim to know how we see the object, once the image has been made on the retina. He thinks, though, that it is easier to conceive a visible image in "variously modified matter" than in the invariable essence of God. He repeats his physical account of impressions on the retina, motions to the brain, and ideas in the mind. He suggests that it is more intelligible to say we see things in the bottom of our eyes than it is to say we see them in God (§11).

Just as Locke thinks the notion of the mind's union with God is a relation borrowed from physical objects, so he charges Malebranche with making the soul literally extended when the latter talks of our soul not being able to *contain* infinite ideas. Locke must have known that Malebranche did not believe the soul to be literally extended, but he tries to show the ambiguity and nonexplanatory nature of the concept of union by taking that word literally. He treats the notion of all things being in God in a similar fashion: he does not understand how material things can be in God "after a spiritual manner." He confesses that he thinks Malebranche is close to making God material (a charge made by Arnauld as well) (§23). When, in his sixth chapter, Malebranche says God is the place of spirits in the way that space is the place of bodies, Locke professes that there is not one word of this remark that he understands. Since Malebranche considers body to be the same as extension, body is the same as space.[3] Thus Malebranche has in effect said bodies are the places of bodies. When this notion is applied to spirit, either space is being used metaphorically "and so signifies literally nothing, or else being literal, makes us conceive that spirits move up and down, and have their distances and intervals in God, as bodies have in space" (§25). Again Locke asks whether the ideas that are in God are parts of God or modifications of God, or "comprehended in him as things in a place." Malebranche had also spoken of God *penetrating* the mind. Locke asks how it is possible for an unextended thing to penetrate (§43). This is a way of speaking taken from body and tells us nothing when applied to spirits. Locke was, in these passages, relentlessly charging that the notion of seeing all things in God was either a metaphor (in which case it was unclear and ambiguous) or a literalist reading of God's presence and of our union with him (in which case the resultant materialism would reduce Malebranche's doctrine to absurdity).

When Locke turns to some of the details of Malebranche's theory, e.g., to the distinction between 'sentiment' and 'idée', Locke has difficulty with that distinction. What is of interest is that on several occasions he identifies his own doctrine as making ideas the same as perceptions: Locke sounds like Arnauld. For example, when Malebranche tries to confute the "opinion of those who think our minds have a power to produce the ideas of things on which they would think, and that they are excited to produce them by the impressions which objects make on the body," Locke remarks:

One who thinks ideas are nothing but perceptions of the mind annexed to certain motions of the body by the will of God, who hath ordered such perceptions always to accompany such motions, though we know not how they are produced; does in effect conceive those ideas or perceptions to be only passions of the mind, when produced in it, whether we will or no, by external objects. (§15)

In another passage (§3), Locke says that the following three expressions say the same thing or have the same meaning: 'to have an idea', 'to have my soul modified', and 'to have a sensation'. In section 47, Locke links 'thinking on' with "having an idea of the colour or hardness."

The strongest affirmation of ideas as perceptions comes in those passages where Locke discusses Malebranche's treatment of ideas as *real things*. Locke remarks that although Malebranche does not say ideas are *substances*, this must be what the phrase 'real spiritual beings' means (§17). 'Substance' of course was a term Malebranche would have reserved for God. Locke sees that, within the ontology accepted by Malebranche, what exists must be a substance or a mode of substance. Thus he infers that ideas as spiritual beings must fit into one of these two categories. Neither of these categories for explaining ideas helps Locke understand ideas. "So that supposing ideas real spiritual things ever so much, if they are neither substances nor modes, let them be what they will, I am no more instructed in their nature, than when I am told they are perceptions, such as I find them" (§18). In another passage (§42), while referring to the physiology of animal spirits, Locke writes indifferently 'idea' or 'perception', 'discovering ideas to the soul', and 'producing perceptions in the soul'. Still later (§45), Locke remarks, "But if by ideas be here meant the perceptions or representation of things in the mind," and contrasts this with ideas "as the real object of our knowledge." In section 47, Locke uses interchangeably 'thinking on a figure' and 'having the idea of a figure'. In section 5, he confesses that beyond knowing what simple ideas are by experiencing them, we "know nothing at all, but only that they are perceptions in the mind."

These assertions that ideas are perceptions, not entities, are repeated in two draft replies Locke wrote to John Norris, the English follower of Malebranche.[4] Locke asks Norris to explain to him "what the alteration in the mind is [when we perceive], besides saying, as we vulgar do, it is having a perception" (§2). Locke also repeats to Norris the objections he has against Malebranche's treatment of ideas as real entities (§17). He professes ignorance as to what ideas are "any farther than as they are perceptions we experiment in ourselves" (§18). When Locke defines ideas as "whatsoever is the object of the understanding when a man thinks," he means explicitly to avoid all attempts at an ontological account of ideas. In another draft of a reply to Norris, he makes this point emphatically: "If you once mention ideas you must be presently called to an account *what kind of things you make these same ideas to be* though perhaps you have no design to consider them any further than as the *immediate objects* of perception."[5] The point of this last remark is that Locke did not consider ideas to have an ontological status; he wanted to concentrate upon their role in perception and knowledge. Having Malebranche's theory as an example of a theory that gave to ideas an ontological status, Locke had a twofold reaction: he rejected Norris's attempts to fit ideas into the standard ontological categories of substance or mode, and he stressed the cognitive, awareness features of ideas. The language of 'having ideas' is identified with being aware, with perceiving.[6]

Gerdil's Defense

When Locke's *Oeuvres diverses* appeared in France (in 1710), Father Barnabite Gerdil came to Malebranche's defense. Gerdil had one year earlier mounted a full-scale attack on Locke's suggestion that matter might be made to think. Both this suggestion and Locke's way of ideas Gerdil considered dangerous to religion. It is clear from what Gerdil says that in attacking Locke he is attacking a man whose views are generally accepted and a man of wide reputation. Gerdil thinks Locke's principles wrong, his reasoning contradictory. He attacks Locke in the name of the church and of religion. Malebranche is the defender of religion: "The philosophy of Malebranche leads straight to Christianity."[7]

The language of penetration and of presence to mind appears in

Gerdil's defense. Most philosophers teach, he says, that in order to know an object, the object must make a species penetrate right up to the mind, "which, in making it into an intelligible image affecting the mind immediately, makes the mind perceive the reality of the object" (p. iv). Augustine is appealed to when Gerdil talks of our being related to God through intelligible and immutable principles: Gerdil considers this notion as the basis for Malebranche's doctrine. He also remarks that Augustine believed that in order for us to know an immutable object, "such as the essence and properties of things, it is necessary that the object, insofar as it is intelligible and immutable, be immediately present to the mind." The object in this case is an idea in God (p. xix). Gerdil also attacks Arnauld's true and false ideas, in particular Arnauld's denial of a distinction between the perception of an object and the idea or the immediate object that represents the material object (p. xxiii). He refers to Bayle's discussion of the Arnauld-Malebranche dispute.[8]

Gerdil also cites St. Thomas's notion that "when any created intellect sees the essence of God, the essence of God itself becomes the intelligible form of the intellect."[9] In order to know God, God must be immediately present to us (p. xxvii). Gerdil goes on to argue, with some support from St. Thomas, that because all things are contained in God, in having the essence of God immediately present to our minds, we also have other things represented to us by that essence (p. xxix).[10] For Gerdil, it is a resemblance of the object that is present to the mind, but his example is of geometrical objects (p. xxx). He speaks of such images as "the intelligible resemblance," and he says that the resemblance "must contain the act, or be in the reality, and the perception of the essence of the thing which one knows" (p. xxx). The resemblance must contain all that it represents, but the concept of 'contains' is not given much analysis. Since no finite mind can have an intelligible resemblance which contains all that it knows of objects, that resemblance is ultimately found only in God (p. xxxii).

With that background, Gerdil then formulates Malebranche's doctrine by saying that that which is immediately present to the mind when it perceives an object external to it "is not a created species which carries the resemblance of it, but the archetype or eternal and intelligible idea, by means of which God knows it from all eternity" (p. 2). If we know objects by means of ideas (we neither know nor see [voir] external objects immediately), "it is necessary that the idea, which represents immediately some object to the mind, be something real in that mind" (p. 5). Either that idea is a reality distinct from the mind, or it will be the perception of the mind, where that perception represents objects distinct from the mind. The latter is the view maintained by Arnauld, and, Gerdil observes, Locke "is of the same opinion." Gerdil is clear about the two concepts of ideas, and he is clear also about which one of these concepts Locke accepted.

When Locke objects to applying the literal notion of union to minds, either union of mind to body or union of mind to God, Gerdil says surely we can extend this talk to noncorporeal things. He does not explain such an extended use of this concept, but later he gives a part-metaphorical, part-action account of it. Gerdil insists that Locke's account of the union of mind and body can only be the correspondence between thought and movements that have been established by God (pp. 15-19). There is no other possibility consistent with Locke's principles, for extended bodies acting by impulse cannot affect the indivisible mind (p. 20). The only conclusion is that God can act on our minds.

Gerdil suggests that Locke's remarks about images on the eyeball imply that Malebranche did not know optics, which is absurd. More important, Gerdil insists that images on the retina are not ideas (p. 25). Even if the movements that carry right up to the brain were, *per impossibile*, to go to the mind and cause ideas, those ideas could not represent the object because they do not resemble it; representation requires resemblance (p. 26). There is of course no causal connection between movement of particles with primary qualities and the sensations of secondary qualities, since "every efficient cause must contain the reality of the effect which it produces." For Gerdil, neither the retinal image nor the material object is what is immediately present to us: only the intelligible object is present to us (p. 28). In an argument reminiscent of Berkeley on distance perception, Gerdil credits Voltaire (he does not give a reference) with saying that, when I see a tower from a distance and then go up to the tower and touch it, I am experiencing two different objects:

What I saw is certainly not what I see and what I touch, and what is the measurable and touchable object other than the visible object; thus it is *not* this external building, which has always been the same, but an intelligible building which I perceive immediately and which is different. . . . (p. 28).

Gerdil insists that when we see or touch some object, we must be careful to distinguish in that seeing or touching "that which is idea or what represents to the mind the object of sight and touch, and that which makes it known and distinguishes its nature and properties, from what is only sensation, which represents nothing to the mind" (p. 44).

These intelligible objects, these ideas, are for Malebranche very real beings since they have real properties. They are spiritual beings; they are more perfect than the material objects that they represent (p. 48). A spiritual idea could not be made by a material impression, because the former has more reality than the latter. Gerdil is reluctant to say ideas are *substances*, in the traditional sense. "It is true that ideas are not separate substances, such as Aristotle and the Scholastics attribute to Plato; they are the substance of God, in being representative of created Beings" (p. 61). Locke's claim that ideas are perceptions of the mind has been shown by Malebranche to be false: ideas are the *objects* of perceptions (p. 51). Those intelligible beings are present to us through God's presence. God is "completely present where I am, and completely present everywhere else" (p. 62). Gerdil does not profess to understand God's presence, nor does he understand God's containing ideas of all things, but he offers some scholastic and Cartesian terminology to help explain these spatial terms. For example, "material things are in God because their archetype ideas, which contain all reality and perfection, are in God" (p. 79). He cites as a comparison with the way God contains all things by containing the ideas of all things, a "gold louis" which contains several crowns, not formally, but in an equivalent manner and more perfectly (p. 79).

Returning to the spatial talk, Gerdil remarks that Locke's question about God being the place of spirits misses the point; this is a metaphor without any literal sense (p. 83). God's union with us is his action on us. His general union with all things, bodies as well as minds, is his sustaining the created world. Gerdil also points out that if Locke asks Malebranche, "does union by itself cause me to see ideas?" then bodies would also perceive (because they too are united to God), and the same argument could apply to Locke: for the sun's rays strike rocks as well as eyes, yet only eyes see (p. 86). The word "presence' cannot mean the same when applied to God and to objects: God is not present as a body is present in a place. The different phrases that Malebranche uses—'present ideas to the mind', 'discover ideas to us', 'unite himself to us in an intelligible way'—signify only that action of God on us (p. 99). Gerdil goes on to deal with the notion of all things being contained in God. The reality of finite beings cannot be in God *formally*, only *eminently* (p. 100). The ideas of things in God are the reality of things in God, without any of their defects: they are there more perfectly, eminently. Gerdil tries to argue that this explication gives these spatial words a literal sense, after having said they must be taken metaphorically. In a later passage, he tells readers that in order to understand the notion of 'penetration' as used by Malebranche, they need only consult a dictionary. He thinks Locke makes the mistake of taking the first meaning of a word for its only meaning (p. 171). 'To penetrate the mind' means nothing other than 'act on the mind' (p. 172).

There are many other details in Gerdil's long analysis of Locke's critique of Malebranche, but only one other remark of his needs to be noted. After explicating for Locke what Malebranche means by 'voir'—Gerdil simply gives a straightforward account from Malebranche without catching the special, inverted sense of 'voir'—he comments that Locke's distinction between primary and secondary qualities is the same as the distinction drawn by Malebranche between ideas and sensations. He then observes: "Mr. Locke recognizes here two sorts of perception, for perception and idea according to him are the same thing" (p. 137). Gerdil thus clearly identified the difference over the nature of ideas between Malebranche on the one hand and Arnauld and Locke on the other.

Other Recognition of the Two Concepts

Most of the eighteenth- and early nineteenth-century writers who looked at the doctrine of ideas recognized the two different concepts employed by Malebranche and Arnauld. Many of these writers also linked Locke with the Arnauld concept. Although Ellis (*Some Brief Considerations upon Mr. Locke's Hypothesis that the Knowledge of God Is Attainable by Ideas of Reflexion*, 1743) misunderstands Locke's account, he does get Malebranche's concept of idea correct. Ellis reads Locke as saying (citing *Essay*, 4.4.3 as support), "The mind knows not Things immediately." Ellis's commentary on this passage is as follows: "For as Things themselves cannot enter the Cabinet of the Mind, the Representations or ideas of them stand in their stead, which Mr. *Locke* rightly calls Prints, Inscriptions, Pictures, Imagery, Images, Characters" (p. 14). The reference to Malebranche is more accurate.

Without going so far as some have done (who maintain that Ideas are real things, as they have real Properties, vary one from another, represent opposite Things, and are of a spiritual Nature, very different from the Bodies represented by them) . . . (p. 23).

Thomas Reid was not certain about Locke's view. He lists Descartes, Arnauld, Locke, and John Norris as all holding that the mind "perceives nothing but a world of ideas in itself."[11] In discussing Locke's use of 'idea', Reid refers to "those representative beings called *ideas*" (p. 171), to "those internal objects of thought" (p. 175), and to those "shadowy . . . beings intermediate between thought" and the world (pp. 180-81). Reid does not claim that Locke always used ideas in this strong 'object' sense: "in many places [Locke] means nothing more by it ['idea'] but the notion or conception we have of any object of thought, that is, the act of mind in conceiving it" (pp. 178-79). In other words, Reid saw Locke's use of the term 'idea' encompassing both concepts: ideas as acts of thinking and ideas as entities, real beings.

Thomas Brown (*Lectures on the Philosophy of the Mind*, 1820) said that in crediting Locke with the view of ideas as real beings, Reid misread Locke. Brown remarks that even in older traditions, the term 'idea', like the term 'perception' now, "was expressive, not of one part of a process, but of two parts of it. It included . . . the *organic* as well as the *mental* – in the same way as *perception* now implies a certain change produced in our organs of sense, and a consequent change in the state of the mind" (p. 5). Besides thinking that all those philosophers who spoke of ideas took them as *third things*, as entities, Reid errs, Brown thinks, by taking in a literal way that which was intended in a metaphorical sense. For example, we speak of impressions *on* the mind, ideas as *bright* and *obscure*, the senses as *inlets* (p. 6). Brown warns us not to use the language of metaphor, unless we carefully explain our meaning. He names Locke as one whose language is especially figurative. This fact accounts in part, he thinks, for Reid's misreading. The question is, did Locke ever take ideas as *things* in the mind, separate from perception, intermediate between the organic and the mental? (p. 8) The alternative is that Locke meant idea and perception to be the same, as Arnauld did. Brown insists that this alternative view, the view Reid identified with the ordinary person, has been the view of most philosophers since the fall of the peripatetic philosophy. He excepts only Berkeley and Malebranche (p. 23).

Another historian of philosophy, J. M. de Gérando (*Histoire de la philosophie moderne*, 1858) thinks it was useful for Locke to refute Malebranche, for it led Locke to replace what de Gérando calls Malebranche's "clever story on the origin of ideas" with an attempt at tracing the true genealogy of ideas.[12] De Gérando believes that "the great discussion which had been raised between Arnauld and Malebranche had alerted Locke to the mistake, so ancient and so general, of considering *ideas* as something intermediary between the mind and objects, having a sort of existence distinct from the mind itself, serving as an item in its contemplation, as a picture for the view which is directed upon it" (pp. 11-12).

Still another writer looking back over the way of ideas from early in the nineteenth century identified Reid's mistakes. Frederick Beasley (*A Search of Truth in the Science of the Human Mind*, 1822) defends Locke against Reid's charge of accepting the ideal theory. He denies that Locke ever said that an impression is made on the mind as well as on the brain (p. 132). Locke does not, Beasley says, attempt to explain how ideas arise, save to say it is after the sense organs and brain have been activated. Beasley thinks Locke's *Examination of Malebranche* is important for our understanding of Locke's views on perception. He cites Reid as saying the images that (on the ideal theory) are the immediate objects of the mind are literally physical images in the brain. He insists that, although this may be the theory of the Schoolmen, it is not that of Locke. He argues that, in saying "an idea is the immediate object of the mind in thinking," he means "nothing more than that it is so in the same sense in which a thought or perception is the immediate object of the mind in thinking" (p. 153). Beasley cites those passages where Locke uses ideas and thoughts, or ideas and perceptions, interchangeably.

Beasley and de Gérando are correct in finding Locke's critique of Malebranche and his knowledge of Arnauld of importance for the sense of 'idea' employed by Locke. Locke was carefully reading the exchange between these two Cartesians while completing his *Essay*. As we have seen earlier, Arnauld centered his attack on Malebranche's 'representative beings', those idea-entities against which we have seen Locke reacting. Arnauld insisted that Malebranche had confused *cognitive* with *spatial* presence: to be in the understanding means to be understood. Working within Descartes's concepts of formal and objective reality, Arnauld says that the immediate object of my perception when I see the sun is the objective reality of the sun. It is the objective reality of the sun which is present to the mind. The possible or actual sun in the world is the *mediate* object. Arnauld firmly denies the need for any representative *beings*, though he is happy to talk about representation, representation without representative entities, proxy objects. How are we to understand this notion of representation?

If, as Arnauld says, to be objectively in the mind is to be understood, then in speaking about representation, he is saying that *my understanding* of the object is my access to the object. My understanding is representative and indirect only in the sense that I cannot be aware of the object without understanding it, without knowing that I have that awareness. The having of an idea for Arnauld (he insisted, as we saw, against Malebranche that this was Descartes's meaning also) is to have a thought that contains objectively that which is formally in the object. That is, 'to have an idea' means 'to understand or conceive what exists formally'. More specifically, 'to see the properties of things in their ideas' is rendered by saying 'to see in the idea of extension, e.g., *that* it must be divisible'. *Seeing that* is the sense of *seeing in* or *by means of* ideas. Arnauld also linked his ideas and understanding with the fact that awareness is self-reflective. Thought knows itself. Thus, to say that ideas are the immediate object of my thought is just to say that when I think, I am aware of what I am thinking. It is the information content of ideas, of awareness, that is the representative aspect of awareness. Locke's treatment of ideas as signs was another way of stressing the fact that ideas as the content of awareness inform us about the world.

In a recent discussion of the representative theory of perception in relation to Locke, J. L. Mackie distinguishes between "a 'crudely representative' theory and some more sophisticated and defensible kind" (*Problems from Locke*, 1976, p. 41). He cites Ryle's description of the first kind "as the use of the term 'ideas' to denote certain supposed entities which are 'in the mind'."[13] Mackie also characterizes a version of realism that "distinguishes appearances from reality," but appearances in this theory "are not a special kind of entity: to speak of appearances is just to speak generally of such matters as how-it-looks or how-it-feels" (p. 65). Mackie suggests that once we cease taking appearances as real objects, we may be able to treat causal relations among our appearances as a basis for asserting causal relations between appearances and objects in the world. I do not want to follow any further Mackie's interesting treatment of the representative theory. I wanted only to call attention to his discussion because it is a very recent recognition of the difference between a representative theory that takes ideas to be themselves real objects and a representative theory that takes the talk of ideas as a way of talking about appearances or, as I would prefer, about perceptual acquaintance. The world is not cognitive, though it is cognizable. To cognize the world is not to have objects literally in our minds, nor is it to have special objects that stand proxy for objects in the world: to cognize the world is to be aware of the world. Locke's analysis of awareness was made in terms of act and content. On such an analysis, it is easy to slip into talking of the content as if it is an *object*; but Locke's discussion of Malebranche, with some explicit passages from the *Essay*, gives us a clear warning against reading his account of ideas in that way.

The terms in which the subsequent debate over perceptual acquaintance has been conducted—direct realism or representationalism—have not helped us avoid becoming lost inside the metaphors. Even if we treat direct realism as saying the object of awareness is numerically identical to the object in the world, we must ask, "what is the status of awareness?" On any theory of perception, perceiving the table in front of me is a conscious, cognitive process. How can the table in the room be numerically identical with the cognitive content of my awareness? The answer may be that this is possible only on a particular ontology that allows for tables to exist in two different media. The scholastic version rests upon such an ontology. This ontology is not found in Locke's account, but there is a part of that scholastic analysis which *is* retained by Locke, the part that allows for a cognitive translation of external objects. The question we should ask at this point is, "in recognizing that of course cognition must take place in terms appropriate to awareness, i.e., conscious mental contents, is Locke (or anyone else) forced into an indirect realism?" If the answer is "yes," direct realism is impossible without an ontology such as the scholastics had.

We might then distinguish kinds of indirectness. One kind involves another ontology, an ontology where 'object in the mind' is taken as 'immaterial substance' (special things) and where 'exists in' also has an ontic meaning. Another kind of indirectness rejects this ontology, preferring to read 'ideas' not as things but simply as 'conscious mental contents', and it translates 'exist in' as 'understood'. On this second kind of indirectness, perceiving an object is having or receiving ideas. On this point, Locke and Malebranche agree. The difference is in the nature of ideas. For Malebranche, an idea is God-given and thing-like. For Locke, ideas are the result of a physical process and of a psychological process, but they are not thing-like.

There may still be problems associated with our knowledge of the external world, but on the Locke-Arnauld concept of ideas those problems do not involve ideas as entities standing between us and external objects. Once we are clear about this, once we follow the lead of most eighteenth-century historians of the way of ideas, we should be able to avoid ascribing to Locke the standard representative theory.[14]

In chapters VIII and XI I shall discuss the nature of the realsim that the Locke-Arnauld account of ideas yields. What I wanted to show at this point in our examination of the term 'idea' was that there are two distinct concepts, one of which clearly does lead to indirectness. Whether that concept gives a *perceptual* indirectness is doubtful because, as we have seen, Malebranche's ideas provide an understanding, not a perception, of objects. This difference between perception and understanding was not always so marked by writers in Britain. Questions about our knowledge of external objects were linked with that principle about presence to mind. That principle was given different interpretations, ranging from the literalist one accepted by Monboddo and used by others, to the cognitive reading of Arnauld and Locke. Where the literalist interpretation governs one's reactions, and when the subject-mode categories are controlling one's ontology, it is easy, as with Malebranche, to end with idea-entities. The other route, the one followed by Arnauld and Locke, enables one to escape the spatial metaphor and to concentrate upon awareness, upon one's perceptions of the world.

Notes

1. Locke's *Second Reply*, in *Works*, vol. IV, p. 390. For a brief discussion of these remarks, see my *Locke and the Compass of Human Understanding*, p. 128.

2. Definition 4 in his *Des vraies et des fausses idées*, p. 198: "Je dis qu'un objet est présent à notre esprit, quand notre esprit l'apperçoit et le connoit."

3. Locke is equivocating on the word 'extension' here, it would seem. At least, for Locke, space is extended as well as body, though not in the sense of solid particles. But to make extension the same as space without argument is not quite fair to Malebranche. For a discussion of Locke's notion of the extension (he uses the term 'expansion') of space, along with other writers who ascribed extension to both space and body, see my *Thinking Matter*, chapter IV.

4. *Remarks upon Some of Mr. Norris' Books, Works*, vol. X. For the second set of remarks, see next note.

5. These have been printed by Richard Acworth as "Locke's First Reply to John Norris," in *The Locke, Newsletter* 2 (1971):7-11.

6. There was one other example, well known to Locke, of a theory that treated ideas as real beings. Most of the innatists against whom Locke wrote held such a view. Norris was only more explicit about ideas as spiritual beings, since he related his view with that of Malebranche. But other innatists (e.g., William Sherlock, Thomas Burnet) took a Platonic view of ideas as existing in the mind before any perception, to serve as criteria for recognition.

7. Giacinto Sigismondo Gerdil, *Defense du Sentiment du P. Malebranche sur la nature & l'origine des idées, contre l'examen de M. Locke* (1748), Preface.

8. *Nouvelles de la République des Lettres*, April 1684, art. 2; May 1685, art. 3.

9. *Summa Theologica*, I, Q. 22, art. 5.

10. St. Thomas raises the question "Whether Those Who See the Essence of God See All in God? (*Summa Theologica*, art. 8). He is concerned to combat the thesis that finite minds see all things in God, in the sense that our knowledge is as great as God's. Not even angels know all things. What we can know by knowing the essence of God is "the species and genera of things and their essences."

11. *Essays on the Intellectual Powers of Man* (1785), vol. I, p. 169.

12. J. M. de Gérando, *Histoire de la philosophie moderne, à partir de la renaissance des lettres jusqu'a la fin du dix-huitième siècle* (1858), 4 vols. The passage cited is in volume 3, p. 3.

13. Mackie is referring to Gilbert Ryle's "John Locke on Human Understanding," originally published in *Tercentenary Addresses on John Locke* (1933), ed. J. L. Stocks, and now reprinted in *Locke and Berkeley, A Collection of Critical Essays* (Garden City, N.Y.: Anchor Books, 1968), ed. C. B. Martin and D. M. Armstrong.

14. For a good discussion showing that Locke's text does not support the interpretation that Locke's ideas are entities or 'dummy objects', see "Locke's Mental Atomism and the Classification of Ideas," by M. A. Stewart, *The Locke Newsletter* 10 (1979):53-82. Another recent writer, while disagreeing with my reading of Locke on ideas, calls attention to a passage from William of Ockham that expresses what I take to be the Arnauld-Locke view. "But what in the soul, is this thing which is a sign? It must be said that with regard to this there are various opinions. For some say that it is nothing but a certain fiction produced by the soul. Others say that it is a certain quality existing subjectively in the soul, distinct from the act of understanding. Others say that it is an act of understanding. And in favour of these is to be said: what can be explained on fewer principles is explained needlessly by more. Something, however, which is explained through positing something distinct from the act of understanding can be explained without positing such a distinct thing. For to stand for something and to signify something can belong just as well to the act of understanding as to this fictive entity; therefore one ought not to posit anything else beyond the act of understanding." (Quoted by R. F. McRae, "On Being Present to the Mind: A Reply," *Dialogue* 14 (1975):664-65. The passage is from Ockham's *Summa Totius Logicae*, I.12.6r.) McRae was replying to my earlier "On Being Present to the Mind: A Sketch for the History of an Idea." *Dialogue* 14 (1975):373-88. Another discussion of this article of mine is "representationalism, Judgment, and Perception of Distance: Further to Yolton and McRae," Thomas Lennon, *Dialogue* 19 (1980):151-63.

Chapter VI

Ideas in Logic
and
Psychology

The terminology of ideas was part of a general and developing interest in the workings of the mind, of human understanding. Locke's *Essay* on that topic was just one in a long line of treatises devoted to perceiving, understanding, and reasoning. Such treatises fell into two categories. The first comprised works of psychology, or works that contained sections on psychology. In Britain, most of these treatises have the word 'soul' in the title, but other works addressed to principles of religion or to the search for truth included some discussion of the cognitive faculties. These treatises were modeled after, in some cases they were extensions of, the standard logics of the day whose divisions were those of the faculties. The newer logics (the second category of treatises), both on the continent and in Britain, concentrated more upon the nature and operation of the faculties than upon arguments and valid inference forms. Most of these logics show the influence of Locke, or of a combination of Locke and the Port Royal logic. Locke's *Essay* is in effect a combination of both these sorts of books: logic and psychology. In both, ideas play a central role. The same two concepts of ideas as found in Malebranche and Locke are present in these works. There are also some variations on ideas as modes of mind. In a few cases, ideas are even thought to be modes of the brain.

Something of the importance of the role of ideas in these various writings up to 1705 is conveyed in a careful discussion of ideas in an anonymous tract published the same year, *A Philosophick Essay concerning Ideas*. This author sets out, as he says, to "State the Notion of Ideas" (p. 3). He views this as a difficult task because "there is hardly any Topick we shall meet with that the Learned have differ'd more about than this of Ideas" (p. 4). In a quick summary of the different views about ideas, this author goes on to say: "Some make them to be *Material*, others *Spiritual*; some will have them to be *Effluvia*, from the Bodies they Represent, others Totally Distinct *Essences*; some hold them to be *Modes*, others *Substances*." Malebranche was one who considered ideas to be totally distinct essences, even substances distinct from our mind, resident in God. Some Cartesians insisted that ideas were modes of thought, others (even Descartes himself sometimes) talked of images on the brain. The effluvia were a reference to the Epicureans. The author of this tract warns of the danger of using the language of matter to describe mind. Thus, many writers on ideas talk of them as images and signatures, marks and impressions, characters, notes, and seeds of knowledge. This vocabulary was mainly used by the defenders of innate ideas in the previous century, but the warning about the danger of borrowing from the language of body when talking about thought and ideas was repeated later by other writers.[1]

The author of this tract defines 'idea' as "the Representation of something in the mind" (p. 6). He remarks that this definition fits either of the two main hypotheses: that ideas are modifications of the mind, or that they are distinct beings. He identifies Malebranche as holding to the second hypothesis; the first is said to be "the more Common and General Hypothesis." There is considerable evidence from the two centuries to support his claim that the view of ideas as modes of mind was in fact the more common. This author's further specification of this hypothesis suggests that it is the position taken by Arnauld against Malebranche that he has in mind. His subsequent definitions tell us that to think truly of any object is to perceive, understand, or know that object (Def. 3), and that a "Representation of something in the Mind, and to frame such a Representation of an object, is to Think" (Def. 6). That is, "Thought and Idea are the same thing" (p. 8).[2] The echoes from Locke and Arnauld are especially strong.

This hypothesis about ideas and thought being the same, which this author identifies as the common and general one, is also explicitly found in one of the more important English predecessors of Locke, Richard Burthogge. Burthogge also emphasizes another aspect of this hypothesis, the meaning carried by ideas. In his 1678 work, *Oganum Vetus & Novum; or, A Discourse of Reason and Truth*, Burthogge identifies the immediate object of apprehension as "Sence or Meaning," that "Conception or Notion that is formed in the Minde, or a proposal to it of an Object, a Word, or Proposition" (pp. 11-12). Burthogge points out that

things are nothing [to us] but as they stand in our *Analogie*; that is, are nothing to us but as they are known by us; and they are not known by us but as they are in the Sense, Imagination, or Minde; in a word, as they are *in our Faculties*; and they are in our *Faculties* not in their *Realities as* they be without them; no nor so much as *by Pictures* and proper Representation, but only by certain *Appearances*, and Phaenomena, which *their* impressions on the Faculties do either cause or occasion in them. (p. 13)

The appearances of things in us are of three sorts: entities of sense (e.g., color, sound, etc.), of the imagination (images), or "of *Reason* and *Understanding*, Mental Entities, the Meaning or Notions" (p. 14). Notions are carefully distinguished from sensations and feelings. Using the language of formal and objective reality, Burthogge says that the only formal being that notions have is as conceptions, *noemata* (p. 15). In his 1694 *An Essay upon Reason* (dedicated to Locke), he characterizes these meanings as *"Modus Concipiendi*, a certain particular *manner* of conceiving" (p. 56).

In the same year, a Cartesian work by Le Grand was translated into English as *An Entire Body of Philosophy, according to the Principles of the Famous Renate des Cartes*. The Arnauld reading of Descartes is firm in this work. Ideas are defined as *"Conceptions*, or rather the Things themselves conceived and understood by the *Mind*; by which Intellection things are said to be Objectively in the Intellect" (p. 22). We cannot, Le Grand says, express anything in words without having some ideas. I cannot know what I am talking about if I do not have some conception of it "besides the bare sound of the words" (p. 23). An idea for Le Grand is not an image "represented in our Bodily Imagination, and delineated in some part of the Brain, but all that which is in our Mind, when we assert with Truth, that we do conceive a thing, after any manner whatever" (ibid.).

The anonymous author of 1705 provides us with one of the clearest statements of this Arnauld view of ideas. Writing with the defenders of innatism in mind, this author echoes Locke: *"If To Imprint a Thing on the Mind* has any Sense in it, it must be only to *make it Perceiv'd"* (pp. 12-13).[3] He also points out that the question "What becomes of . . . *Ideas when they go out of the mind?"* is "nowise proper for those who make Thought and Idea to be the same" (p. 13). To have an idea is for the mind to operate "after *such* and *such* a Manner, just as the Roundness of a Body, and its Motion are nothing but the Body itself figur'd and translated after such and such a sort."[4] This author insists that "our Ideas do not come from without, but are wholly owning to the Mind, and are indeed nothing else but *the natural Operations of the Mind upon the several Objects presented to it*" (p. 20).

That John Norris is following the other hypothesis about the nature of ideas—that they are distinct essences or substances—is evident from the questions he puts to Locke in his *Cursory Reflections* (1690).

I would know what kind of things he makes these Ideas to be as to their *Essence* or *Nature*. Are they in the first place Real Beings or not? Without doubt Real Beings, as having Real Properties, and really different one from another, and representing things really different. Well if Real Beings, then I demand, are they Substances, or are they Modifications of Substances? (pp. 22-23)

Norris thinks ideas cannot be modifications of a substance because there is no likeness between a substance and a mode, and hence a mode cannot represent a substance, likeness being for him a necessary condition for representation. Ideas cannot be material substances, particles from objects, because of a variety of difficulties, chief among them for Norris being the problem of how so many corporeal substances could find room in the brain, or how the brain, being fluid, could retain them (p. 25). The soul cannot receive material impressions. Material substances cannot represent immaterial and intellectual objects. The conclusion for Norris is clear: all ideas must be immaterial substances (p. 26). They are, following Malebranche, "the Omniform Essence of God" (p. 31).

One critic of this second hypothesis of ideas as distinct entities was Henry Layton (*Observations upon a Treatise, Intitl'd Psychologia: Or, An Account of the Nature of the Rational Soul* [by John Broughton], 1703). Although Broughton remarked that some writers take ideas as "those Impressions which by the Presence of sensible Objects, or the Powers of Memory, are made on the Imagination," he preferred to follow the more general definition used by Descartes and Locke: "the immediate Object of our Thoughts, while we do think." But something Broughton said led Layton to think he considered ideas to be substantial, extraneous, "and different from all other Organs and Powers of the Person" (p. 5). Layton followed the scholastic theory according to which the species from the object are transmitted to the common sense and to the phantasy, where the form of the object is retained. Ideas for him are the form of the object in the understanding. As such, they "have no more Reality in them, than what by this Description is allow'd them, nor have any other Subsistence in the world, save in the Minds of Men" (p. 57). The term 'idea', like the terms 'thought' and 'skill', are words invented by "Human Art, to signify such Activities or Motions"; they signify modes or qualifications of the organic whole which Layton saw as the person (p. 59).

Some eighteenth-century writers, agreeing that ideas are modes of mind, took them in the more restricted sense of images. Chambers's definition of 'idea' in his *Cyclopaedia; or, An Universal Dictionary of Arts and Sciences* (1728) uses the Cartesian and Lockean language: "A Term by which we mean that immediate Object of the Mind about which we are employ'd when we perceive or think: Thus, we look at the Sun, we do not see that Luminary itself, but its Image or Appearance convey'd to the Soul by the Organ of Sight; and this Image we call *Idea*." Peter Browne (*The Procedure, Extent, and Limits of Human Understanding*, 1728) limits ideas to the sensible ideas of objects. He follows Malebranche and Berkeley in holding that there are no ideas of thinking, willing, and so on. Ideas are likenesses of things (p. 65). Sense ideas are, for Browne, immediate. They suppose the presence of the objects to the sense organs (p. 103). But even though ideas are likenesses of objects, Browne does not think this fact canceled the directness of our awareness of objects. When an object is present to our sense organs, "there is an *Immediate* and direct Representation of the Object, and it is perceived without the mediation or *Intervention* of any other Object or Idea whatsoever." There is an interesting echo of Arnauld in Browne's talk of direct perception through ideas. With his firm equation of idea and perception, it may have been easier for Arnauld to retain directness, than for Browne, for whom ideas were images. Arnauld agreed that all perception, all ideas, are representative of that which is not idea, but he had seen the representative nature of ideas as lying in their cognitive or meaning role, not in any likeness of their image quality.

One of the more important essays on ideas and awareness in eighteenth-century Britain was the work attributed to Zachary Mayne, *Two Dissertations concerning Sense and the Imagination* (1728). In that work, Mayne carefully distinguished sense and imagination from understanding, a distinction with Cartesian origins. Sensitive perception is "a bare Representation of some corporeal Phenomenon or external Appearance, as *Colour, Sound, Taste, Odeur*, etc." (p. 9). The understanding works with notions and meaning. Sense exhibits to us the matter or appearance of things, the understanding has to get at the meaning or significance (pp. 38, 60). Strictly, we do not see body, body as a material substance "does not fall under the Cognizance of *Sense*, but only of the *Understanding*" (p. 13). Pushing this Cartesian distinction still further, Mayne remarks that people fancy that they see what they understand or that they "see the *Intelligible* (as I may call it) of an Object" (p. 14). The term 'idea' signifies an image or copy; it is more appropriate when the object is absent; but when we use the term 'idea' we "Mean and Intend the Object itself which it represents, as if we immediately perceived it by any of our *Senses*" (p. 59). Ideas in the imagination enable us to contemplate or think abut the object as we might have done when perceiving the object originally. In imagination "we perceive, virtually and in effect, what is absent as if it were present" (p. 124). Ideas are of use when the object is not present to sense. "By an *Idea* (according to the Common and most usual Significance of the Word) I mean the *Image, Picture*, or *Representation in the Mind of a sensible Appearance or of an Object which hath before been perceived by Sense*" (p. 104).

Even with ideas in the imagination, we need notions before we can understand what the idea represents. We cannot understand anything without having a notion of it: the "Notion of a Thing is really, That which" we understand of that thing. With this strong distinction between ideas and notions, Mayne saw Locke's equation of idea with phantasm, notion, or species as a misuse of the term 'notion'; it turned notions into ideas, i.e., into "visible Appearances within the mind" (p. 122). The way of ideas fails to distinguish sensing from understanding. Mayne observed that it is now taken for granted that the way to explain knowledge is in terms of the perception of ideas (p. 93). This view says, according to Mayne, that "in having the Idea of a Thing, we actually understand it". Clearly having Locke's definition of knowledge in mind, as the perception of the agreement or disagreement of ideas, Mayne seeks to show what is wrong with this view by claiming that (1) perception is not an act of understanding, (2) an idea is not a notion, and (3) by giving an analysis of ideal perception, i.e., nonsensitive or intellectual perception. When we think or judge, we never attend to our perceptions but to the things themselves, "we consider the object as it is in itself" (p. 101). To perceive, whether it be sense perception or the perception of relations between ideas, is never to understand. What Mayne has in mind is understanding in terms of general concepts such as existence, unity, essence, property, cause, effect, whole, part.

It is important, especially in the light of the 1705 anonymous author's identification of two main hypotheses about ideas (but also in the light of what I have cited from Locke), to see Mayne taking that passage in Locke (1.2.5) as evidence that Locke did sometimes take ideas as equivalent to notions, since to have a notion for Mayne is to have an intellectual understanding. To have an idea means to understand, but Mayne prefers to replace 'idea' with 'notion'. He notes that most people now use 'idea' instead of 'notion', even when they mean "no more than the *Appropriation* of their *Notion* to the *Object* of it" (p. 137). He says further, in *An Essay on Consciousness* (appended to his *Two Dissertations*),[5] that some people "hold that to *understand* any Thing, is only to have an *Idea* of it, and nothing else more" (p. 170). Mayne rejects this close connection of having an idea and understanding, but his reference confirms that this hypothesis about ideas was held. His rejection of this concept of idea occurs in the midst of his discussion of those writers who said that instinct in animals is "true genuine *Reason* and *Understanding*" (p. 169). He says that "they . . . are most stiff and peremptory in his Opinion, who hold that to *understand* any thing, is only to have an *Idea* of it, and nothing else more" (pp. 169-70). He thinks that by showing that animals are not conscious and hence not rational, he will have demonstrated "that to have an *Idea* cannot be the same thing with an Act of *Understanding*" (p. 170).[6] However, when Mayne discusses our knowledge of external objects, it is perceptions as the appearances of those objects which he stresses. He does not explicitly use the language of 'present to the mind' when talking about the objects, but what he does say is tantamount to stating, as Porterfield and Hume did later, that all that is present to us are our perceptions. His general claim is that "whatever the Mind is employed about in the Exercise of any of its Faculties, it is *conscious* of it, as its Object. . . . And whether an Object be *External*, as in *Sensitive Perception*, or *Internal*, as in perceiving the *Idea* of any sensible Object, the Mind is *conscious* of such its Appearance: and likewise of Time and Place, and other Circumstances which, as an intelligent Being, it takes notice of; for all these do enter into its *Perception*, and may be considered as Parts of it" (p. 146). It is impossible to "consider or regard any thing, as having such an Appearance to me in my Act of perceiving it (which is the true and proper Notion of an Object) any otherwise than by being *Conscious* of my own *Perceptions*, and of the Appearance to which it refers" (pp. 146-47). Moreover, Mayne claims that there is "no possibility of separating the Object or Thing *perceived*, from the Act of *Perceiving*" (p. 168).

Mayne's three essays are an unusually sophisticated analysis of sense, imagination, and consciousness. He does not seem particularly indebted to other writers. He cites Hobbes once or twice in disagreement, but it was mainly Locke and Locke's influence that stimulated Mayne's first two essays. The "late frequent and continual use of the Word *Idea*, in almost all Discourses and Conversations, and its having in a manner supplanted *Notion, Conception, Apprehension*, and the like; and which, I believe, is owing chiefly, if not entirely, to what Mr. *Locke* hath written about *Ideas*," was the object of his attack (pp. 136-37). Mayne was concerned to distinguish our understanding or comprehension of the world from our sensing and imagining. Curiously, he believed that "Mr. *Locke's Doctrine of* Ideas" had as "a direct and immediate Consequence" a "very dangerous and pernicious Opinion, which prevails almost everywhere, *viz*. 'That Brutes have the same Powers or Capacities of Understanding, with Mankind'" (Preface to the Reader). What was needed, Mayne believed, to combat this dangerous opinion was "a fair and impartial Enquiry into the Nature of *Human Understanding*," an inquiry that would sort out the different operations of the mind, discover the function and nature of each. Such an inquiry is "at present very much wanted." The first step toward that inquiry—the step Mayne thought he was supplying—is "the removal of those Prejudices arising from *Sense*, and the *Imagination*, which hinder Men from discovering the Truth, or discerning it, tho' fairly offered to them." Such a clarification may, he believes, "be of some use to any one who shall hereafter undertake to explain and set forth, in a clear and perspicuous Light, the nature and genuine Operations of the *Understanding*, as they are in Themselves, without mixing or confounding them with any Others" (p. 2).[7]

Locke's *Essay* was, of course, just such an inquiry. Mayne does not appreciate the details on mental operations that are in that work. Attention to the various operations of the mind did not originate with Locke, though he perhaps discerned more of them and gave more details than other writers had. Locke's influence in the eighteenth century *was* massive. His doctrines and his language are found everywhere. Especially important were the new logics that began to appear in Britain, at first French logics in translation, then by 1725 British logics proper. The terminology of ideas is prominent in these logics. The Port Royal logic of 1642 of Arnauld and Nicole, which appeared in an English translation of 1685 (other editions were published in the eighteenth century), had set the tone and direction for logics in the eighteenth century, especially British logics. Cartesianism was again the base upon which much English-speaking philosophy was built. But there were also some indigenous British foundations for new logics, even though these bases may have drawn from (this is certainly true for Locke) Cartesian and scholastic traditions. The citing of Locke as a logician sounds strange to our ears, especially since he was so outspoken against traditional logics.[8] But it was precisely his strong attack against the syllogism and his demand for a logic of use which typified the new logics. The line from the Port Royal to the logic of Issac Watts or William Duncan goes straight through Locke's *Essay* and his *Conduct*.[9] The subtitle of the Port Royal logic—*The Art of Thinking*—set the mold for British logics in the eighteenth century.[10]

Both old and new logics took their divisions from the faculties or acts of the mind, but the analysis of those acts became in most of the new logics a major part of their account. Usually, the division was into three, as it is in the logic of Richard Burthogge: (1) apprehension of simple terms, (2) the composition of those terms as in affirmation and negation, and (3) discourse or illation.[11] This threefold division of acts of the mind appears not only in works on logic and theory of knowledge. Typical of many works on religion in the latter part of the seventeenth century (and as well, another interesting predecessor of Locke) is John Wilkins's *Of the Principles and Duties of Natural Religion* (1675). Wilkins says it is generally agreed that the acts of the mind are reducible to three: (1) "Perception of such single objects as are proposed to them, which is called *simple Apprehension*," (2) "Putting together such single objects, in order to our comparing of the agreement or disagreement betwixt them, by which we make Propositions, which is called *Judging*," and (3) "The discerning of that connexion or dependence which there is betwixt several Propositions, whereby we are enabled to infer one Proposition from another, which is called *Ratiocination, or Discourse*."[12] The use of the same threefold distinction in an older logic can be found in one written in English as early as 1654. Zachary Coke (*The Art of Logick; or, The Entire Body of Logick*) speaks of degrees rather than of acts of the understanding: (1) "the apprehension of a single Term or Theme, as *Peter, Paul*, a living Creature," (2) the "conception of two Terms by way of composition, as when we think, *A man is a living Creature*," and (3) "when in order we think of more then two Terms passing the thought from one to the other, till you come to a third. This is discourse" (p. 6). Robert Sanderson's much better known and more widely used logic, *Logicae Artis Compendium* (1615), identifies the three operations of the mind as simple perceiving (which deals with terms), unifying and dividing (which deals with propositions), and discoursing (which deals with argumentation and method). Henry Aldrich's *Artis Logicae Compendium* (1691) lists the three operations as simple apprehension, judgment, and discourse. In a few works, such as the Port Royal logic, Peter Ramus's logic, and some of the eighteenth-century British logics, there are four divisions: conceiving, judging, reasoning, and ordering or method.

We have seen how Burthogge put sense or meaning as the immediate object of apprehension. It became in order, then, to give some account of ideas or notions as the meanings apprehended. Logic in the sense of reasoning comes under the third act, discourse, or illation. Burthogge distinguished logic, as the method of reasoning, into artificial and natural. Logical truth was defined by him as "a Truth of things as standing in our analogy" (p. 48). We discover such truth, in the Cartesian way, by clear and distinct perceptions. Another early English writer who anticipated much of Locke's vocabulary of ideas was Richard Cumberland, in his *De Legibus Naturae* (1672). Cumberland also starts with simple apprehension.

Seeing therefore it is well known by the Experience of all Men, that those *Ideas* or Thoughts, which Logicians call *simple* Apprehensions, are *two* ways excited in the Mind of Man; (1) By the *immediate Presence* and Operations of the Object upon the Mind; after which manner the Mind is conscious of its *own Actions*, and also of the Motions of the Imagination, or of the *Ideas* [of] its Objects . . . (2) By the *Means* of our external *Senses*, Nerves, and Membranes, in which manner we perceive *other Men*, and the rest of the Parts of this *visible World*. . . .[13]

The terms of propositions for Cumberland are "the *simple Apprehension* of Ideas, and their *Composition*" (p. 49); in Latin original, p. 14). Sometimes simple apprehensions are said to be ideas (here, the Latin text uses 'cogitationes', p. 83). They are spoken of as images of things; their truth and perfection consists in the correspondence to the object they represent or to which they refer (p. 103; in Latin, p. 83). True propositions "are the *Joining, by Affirmation, of Apprehensions impress'd upon the Mind by the same Objects*, or the *Separating, by Negation, of Notions representing different Objects*" (p. 104; in Latin, pp. 83-84).[14] He goes on to distinguish conditional propositions, those whose truth "consists only in an *agreement* among the *Terms*, of which they are composed," and those that are trifling, conditional propositions about things that cannot exist. These latter are only equivocally called 'true'.

The Port Royal definitions of each of the four operations of the mind are as follows (using the English translation of 1685):[15]

(1) We call *Apprehension* ['concevoir'] the simple Contemplation of Things

that present themselves to the Mind, as when we consider the *Sun*, the *Earth*, a Tree, Rotundity, a Square, Cogitation, Entity, pronouncing nothing expressly concerning 'em; and the form under which we consider 'em is call'd an *Idea*.

(2) We call *Judgment*, that Action of the Mind, by which assembling together several *Ideas*, we either deny or affirm this to be That. Thus considering the *Idea* of the *Earth*, and the *Idea* of *Round*, we affirm or deny the *Earth to be round*.

(3) *Discourse* ['raisonner'] we call that Operation of the Mind, by which out of several Judgments we frame another. . . .

(4) We call *Disposition* that Action of the Mind, by which we range various *Ideas*, *Judgments*, and *Ratiocinations* upon one and the same Subject; in that Order which is most proper for its Explanation; and this by another Name we call Method (p. 42)

The first part of the Port Royal logic had insisted that an account of ideas — their nature and origin, their difference from the objects they represent, their simplicity and composition, their universality and particularity — is necessary for logic (a logic concerned with aiding genuine knowledge) because "we cannot have any knowledge of what is without us, but by the assistance of *Ideas* which are within us" (p. 44). In their definition of 'conceiving', reflecting a remark Descartes had made to Arnauld in reply to Arnauld's objections to the *Meditations*, they characterize ideas as 'forms of thought'. Ideas are distinguished from images: "When we speak then of *Ideas*, we do not call by that name those Images that present themselves to the Fancy, but whatever offers it self to our *thought*; at what time we may truly affirm, that we apprehend a certain *Thing*, after whatever manner we apprehend it" (p. 48).

The Cartesian, Port Royal influence on the art of thinking in Great Britain, on the eighteenth-century epistemic logics, was strengthened by many features of Locke's *Essay* and his *Conduct*. The Lockean formulation and vocabulary doubled back on to the continent by the medium of Jean LeClerc's writings. LeClerc, the editor of a number of journals published in Holland, one of which printed in 1688 a long portion of Locke's *Essay*, wrote a logic in Latin that appeared both in Amsterdam and in London in 1692.[16] Like LeClerc's, another continental logic, that of Jean Pierre de Crousaz (1712) was a combination of Port Royal and Lockean concepts.[17] Crousaz's book was translated into English in 1724 as *A New Treatise of the Art of Thinking*. A number of aspects of this logic are important to note for their heavy use of the way of ideas.

The first part, on perception, characterizes simple perceptions as "the Representation of objects, without determining anything about them, either affirmatively or negatively" (p. 2). Crousaz speaks of perceptions or representations, also of comparing perceptions together to observe "their Connexion, or Opposition." Ideas are distinguished from sensations, the latter being perceptions that perceive themselves, e.g., perceptions of thirst, pain, sorrow, desire. Ideas are perceptions of objects different from themselves. "A sensation represents nothing but a sensation," ideas represent objects (p. 11). Thinking in a certain way, after a particular manner, represents to me a tree, a triangle, and so on. Thinking this way makes me know the object that we name. "These three Things, *Faculty, Object*, and *Manner of perceiving*, are the sources of the Varieties of our Ideas" (p. 14). Perceptions of the understanding (what Locke refers to as reflections) are also said to be ideas (p. 24). Words as the signs of things do not excite sensations; only the sounds or written characters of words can do that. Words excite ideas. Perceptions of objects involve judgment as well. When we see a tree, three things are compounded: (1) the bodily organs are affected by the external object; (2) the corporeal impressions left or aroused by the external object are usually followed by a perception; and (3) we judge that there is an object external to us (pp. 38-39). He makes a point of saying that to perceive and to receive impressions are two different operations.[18]

In these passages, Crousaz sometimes hovers between taking ideas as perceptions and talking as if they may be something else as well. In a later section, he declares that "philosophers are at a loss to know what an idea is" (vol. I, p. 298). He then cites various hypotheses about ideas. Some people, he says, "suppose an Idea to be a certain internal Object, different from Thought, and to the Contemplation of which the Thought does immediately apply it self." He suggests that this notion of idea arises because its holders "judge of the Understanding, as they judge of the Senses, and fancy that because, when we see, there is always an Object of our Sight, which is different from Perception, whereby it is represented and known to us, in the same manner, the Understanding has its Eyes and its Objects" (pp. 298-99). In contrast (and this does indicate his own preference) Crousaz says that *thoughts* proceed from one another, that thought is self-conscious; "it is its own immediate Object, and by that Self-consciousness it represents to it self at the same time Things different from it self" (vol. I, p. 299). Even if there were images as internal objects, they would have to be thought about, and hence be their own immediate objects. Even if ideas were images, it would be the thought itself which gives us knowledge of the external object. It is more natural and simpler to say, however, that "the Thought is self-conscious, and that by such a Consciousness of its Way of thinking, it learns to know what a Tree is, and so with other Objects" (p. 299). Images, in short, would need to be augmented by thoughts, so why not eliminate images? An added advantage to taking ideas as thoughts, or as a way of thinking, is that the innate controversy about idea is resolved, for "we are not born with a great many Thoughts."[19] It is clear that for a variety of reasons, Crousaz sees no need to take ideas as entities: "every idea is an Act, which perceives itself" (vol. II, p. 2).

The first of the indigenous eighteenth-century British logics is that of Isaac Watts, *Logick; or, The Right Use of Reason in the Enquiry after Truth* (1725). The subtitle is the same as that of Descartes's *Discourse*. Watts was an admirer and sometime follower of Locke, but his logic moves away from Arnauld's definition of ideas, as identical to perceptions, toward a more scholastic reading of Descartes. A preliminary definition of idea makes it the form under which things appear to the mind, "or the Result of our Conception or Apprehension" of things (p. 7). The act of the mind whereby it becomes conscious of anything is called perception. A more precise definition of 'idea' is as "a *Representation of a Thing in the Mind*," a representation of something we have seen, felt, heard, and so on. Reflecting Descartes's discussion of the objective reality of ideas, Watts insists that "'Tis not the outward Object, or *Thing which is perceived*, (viz.) the Horse, the Man, etc. Nor is it the very *Perception or Sense*, and *Feeling* (viz.) of Hunger, or Cold, etc., which is call'd the *Idea*; but the *Thing as it exists in the Mind by Way of Conception or Representations*, that is properly called the *Idea*" (p. 13). The horse, man, or tree are outward objects of perception, archetypes or patterns of our ideas. Sensations of hunger, cold, etc., are inward archetypes of our ideas. It is "the *Notions* or *Pictures of these* Things, as they are considered, or conceiv'd in the Mind" that are the ideas dealt with by logic (p. 13).

Perhaps a more important British logic is that of William Duncan, *The Elements of Logick* (1748).[20] The link between logic and knowledge is quite explicit in Duncan's *Elements*.

We find ourselves in this World surrounded with a Variety of Objects; we have Powers and Faculties fitted to deal with them, and are happy or miserable in proportion as we know how to frame a right Judgment of Things, and shape our Actions agreeably to the Circumstances in which we are placed. (p. 1)

He continues in this Lockean vein: by studying ourselves, "we become acquainted with the Extent and Capacity of the Human Mind, and learning to distinguish what Objects it is suited to, and in what

manner it must proceed, in order to compass its Ends" (p. 2). Reason
for Duncan is the boundary "by which Man is distinguished from the
other Creatures that surround him," but reason is not equal in all
men. "It is therefore by Culture, and a due Application of the Powers
of our Minds" that we can perfect human reason (p. 3). By strength-
ening our knowledge and understanding, we can survey the "vast
Fabrick of the World . . . and search into the Causes of Things."
Thus it is important to examine the powers and faculties of our understanding, in order to show "the Ways by which it comes to attain
its various Notions of Things" (p. 3). Such an examination is the design of logic. Duncan even calls logic "the History of the human Mind,
in as much as it traces the Progress of our Knowledge, from our first
and simple Perceptions" (p. 4).

Duncan follows the usual distinctions of the mental operations,
saying of perception that "we find ourselves surrounded with a Variety of Objects, which acting differently upon our Senses, convey distinct impressions into the Mind, and thereby rouse the Attention and
Notice of the Understanding" (p. 5). We reflect and become conscious
of the operations of our own mind. The attention of the understanding to the object that acts upon it is called by logicians 'perception',
and "the *Notices* themselves, as they exist in the Mind, and are there
treasured up to be the Materials of Thinking and Knowledge, are distinguished by the name of *Ideas*." A bit later, he speaks of ideas as
renewed impressions which arise only after the objects that first produced the impressions are removed (p. 16). However, simple ideas are
sometimes identified with the impressions of sense; they are conveyed
into the mind by external objects.

One of the more important aspects of Duncan's logic is its very
close following of Locke. Locke is mentioned only once or twice,
but Duncan's book is in many ways an abridgment of Locke's *Essay*.
His language, his examples, and the order of his exposition copy
Locke. There are numerous verbatim similarities. While reading
Duncan, one can begin to appreciate why Locke was viewed as a
logician by the eighteenth-century writers. The operations of the mind
on which these new logics were based—simple apprehension or perception, judgment, reasoning—are, in that order, the framework of
Locke's *Essay*, as well as of the logics of Watts and Duncan.[21]

Edward Bentham (*Reflexions upon Logick*, 2nd ed., 1755; 1st ed.
was published in 1739) even compares "the logical Theory contained
in *Mr. Locke's Essay*" with "that of the Schools." Locke departed
from logic, in Bentham's eyes, by going into too much detail on the
operations of the mind (p. 7). Bentham is trying to find a middle

way between old and new logics. Thus his *Reflexions* maintain that "enquiries into the nature of our Souls, and our Sensations, our Passions and Prejudices, with other springs of wrong judgment, make a part of the natural History of man, rather than a part of Logick" (pp. 6-7). Logic for Bentham is rather "a collection of such rules and Observations, as may enable us to make the best of our intellectual faculties, both in our own enquiries after truth, and in the communication of it to others" (p. 1). But in his *Introduction to Logick* (not published until 1773 but written and printed, he claims, much earlier), Bentham begins with a chapter on the soul, its powers and operations. Although it is brief, this chapter follows the pattern of Duncan and Watts. Simple apprehension is defined as the bare contemplation of anything, "whether absent or present, without determining any thing concerning it" (p. 2). Idea is defined as "the form, under which a thing is represented within the mind." He recognizes that 'notion' is sometimes used instead of 'idea', and, in a footnote, he identifies the two main views about ideas that we have found running throughout the century.

The word *idea* is sometimes taken in a large sense, only for the thing that is thought upon, as it is thought upon; and in this sense there are as many ideas as there are intelligible objects; since, whatever we understand, is some way or other in the understanding: and in this sense we may be said to have an idea of God himself. Sometimes it is taken, according to its strict propriety, for that, whereby we perceive any Being, as by its intelligible representative; in which sense we have no ideas, but of such things as are material, whereof they are the *Images*. (pp. 2-3)

The same duality of the concept of idea is noted by Thomas Reid a few years later. In his *Essays on the Intellectual Powers of Man* (1785), Reid devotes his second long essay (pp. 81-343) to an account and criticism of the various theories of ideas (and of seeing and sensing, as well as perceiving) in the seventeenth and eighteenth centuries. He says that "in the popular meaning, to have an idea of any thing, signifies nothing more than to think of it" (vol. I, p. 173). He elaborates on this notion of idea:

To think of a thing, and to have a thought of it; to believe a thing, and to have a belief of it; to see a thing, and to have a sight of it; to conceive a thing, and to have a conception, notion, or idea of it, are phrases perfectly synonymous. In these phrases, the thought means nothing but the act of thinking; the belief, the act of believing; and the conception, notion, or idea, the act of conceiving. To have a clear and distinct idea, is, in this sense, nothing else but to conceive the thing clearly and distinctly. When the word *idea* is taken in this popular sense, there can be no doubt of our having ideas in our minds. To think without ideas would be to think without thought, which is a manifest contradiction. (p. 174).

Reid identifies one very prevalent principle that led to this conclusion, the principle we traced in chapter III: "that the operations of the mind, like the tools of an artificer, can only be employed upon objects that are present, in the mind, or in the brain, where the mind is supposed to reside" (p. 174). We now know how extensive the use of this principle was, but we also can now say that the view Reid characterized as the popular one was in fact held by many writers in the fields of philosophy, religion, logic, and psychology. Reid also identified as the ordinary, nonphilosophical view, the belief that "it is the external object which we immediately perceive, and not a representative image of it only" (p. 165). Reid seems to have thought that this belief follows from the view of ideas as acts of thought. To see an object is, in Reid's language, "to have a sight of it." And to have a sight of an object is for Reid immediately to perceive that object. Thus representative realism is replaced by direct realism.

This survey of a wide variety of books and pamphlets, including the eighteenth-century British logics, confirms the presence of two concepts of idea. The term 'image' appears rather frequently in these writings. Although no precise definition of that term is offered, it is clearly a term that designates some kind of entity, mental or physical impression. In those discussions where ideas are distinguished from notions, e.g., in Mayne, it is the latter that bears the weight of meaning and that leads to understanding. If notions are characterized as mental contents, they are not 'objects' in the sense of being a substance or resembling things. Reid gives the strongest and clearest formulation of this concept of mental content. Not only does his conflation of having a conception, notion, or idea of some thing pick up the conflation we have found in Arnauld and Locke, by characterizing the idea in this sense as an act of conceiving; Reid also guards against reifying the concept, notion, or idea. The prominence that his characterization gives to *conceiving* also highlights a feature of Hume's epistemic logic that we will examine in chapter VIII.

To say that Reid's following of the second concept of idea, as an act of conceiving, enables him to defend some form of direct realism is not, of course, to ignore the fact that some ideas are false in their purportedly informing us about the world. To reject the form of representative realism whereby ideas resemble things does not mean that all perceptual experiences are veridical. Nor does Reid's direct realism avoid some form of representationalism: we learn about the world through our ideas, through our acts of conceiving. Those acts are numerically different from the objects to which they refer. The issue of representative or direct realism gradually gets transformed as we move through the eighteenth century from Berkeley to Hume to Reid. Instead of debating whether ideas stand between objects and perceivers, preventing direct access to objects, the question becomes whether our ideas, notions, concepts, or perceptions are *specifically* or only *numerically* different from objects. In this transformation, a large role was played by perceptual optics.

Notes

1. Cf. Berkeley, *The Principles of Human Knowledge*: "But nothing seems more to have contributed towards engaging men in controversies and mistakes, with regard to the nature and operations of the mind, than the being used to speak of those things, in terms borrowed from sensible ideas" (§ 144, p. 107 in the *Works*, ed. Luce and Jessop, vol. 2).

2. Berkeley employs similar language: "for to have an idea is all one as to perceive" (ibid., § 7, p. 44).

3. Cf. Berkeley, *Dialogues*: "Look you, Hylas, when I speak of objects as existing in the mind or imprinted on the senses; I would not be understood in the gross literal sense, as when bodies are said to exist in a place, or a seal to make an impression upon wax. My meaning is only that the mind comprehends or perceives them" (in *Works*, vol. 2, p. 250).

4. Father Claude Buffier uses the same comparison. He defines ideas as modifications of the mind when it thinks. Like Arnauld, Buffier maintains that these modifications are ideas in relation to the object represented, and perceptions in relation to the mind which thinks on the object. He then declares, "it is evident that our ideas, taken in this latter sense, are no more distinct from our understanding than movement is from the body moved" (*Traité de premières vérités*, chap. VIII, p. 187, *Oeuvres*, 1843). Or again, the mind, Buffier says, "which receives an idea differs from the idea received only as a ball which receives motion differs from the motion which is received by it." In *Questions sur l'Encyclopédie* (1771) Voltaire holds that an idea is not a sensation or a volition, it is "I perceiving, I sensing, I willing." He goes on to say: "We know that there is no more a real being called *idea* than there is a real being called *motion*; but there are bodies moved."

5. Printed as a separate essay but paged with *Two Dissertations*. This essay is especially important for its careful, sustained attempt to articulate a notion of self and self-consciousness.

6. It is of some interest, in the light of Hume's discussion of instinct in animals and his remark that human reason is "a wonderful and unintelligible instinct in our souls" (*Treatise*, p. 179), to note Mayne's remark about the natural instinct of animals: "their natural instinct (which I conceive to be nothing else but the Power and Force of their *Imaginations*, working upon, and actuating their Souls, according to the particular Frames and Constitutions of their several Beings . . ." (p. 172).

7. Was Hume in 1739 responding to Mayne's call for such an inquiry? Hume's discerning the specific roles of sense, imagination, and reason is very similar to Mayne's. One example used by Mayne reappears in Hume's *Abstract*: when "one Body, in Motion, moves another which is at Rest, by striking it: The Appearance of this to Sight, is a Body in Motion, striking another at Rest, whereupon follows a Motion in the Body which is struck" (p. 11). It is, for Mayne, the *understanding* that concludes that the first body caused or produced the motion of the second. The action of striking, "which here means a violent Shock or

Impulse, and implies such a force or strength of Motion as will Push or bear forwards what stands in its way, and is capable of being Moved by it, is not perceived by *Sense*: all that it perceives being, that 'one Body, which is at rest, or stands still, is touched by another Body which is in Motion, and that, when Touched, it is Moved.'" Mayne goes on to analyze exactly what sense discovers in such an example (p. 12).

8. In his *Letters concerning the English Nation* (1733), Voltaire said of Locke: "Perhaps no Man ever had a more judicious or more methodical Genius, or was a more acute Logician than Mr. *Locke*" (p. 73). Gerdil (*Défense du Sentiment du P. Malebranche sur la nature & l'origine des idées, contre l'examen de M. Locke*, 1748), spoke of Locke as an exact logician, even though he went on to charge that Locke's reasoning was contradictory.

9. The role played by Locke's *Essay* in the changing logic and philosophy curriculum at Oxford has been detailed in my contribution to a volume on the history of the University of Oxford in the Eighteenth Century, to be published in 1984 by the Oxford University Press.

10. For an account of these logics, see W. S. Howell, *Eighteenth-Century British Logic and Rhetoric* (1971). Also useful is W. H. Kenny, "John Locke and the Oxford Training in Logic and Metaphysics" (1959, University Microfilms), although Kenny's work deals with the pre-eighteenth-century logics then in use.

11. *Organum Vetus & Novum; or, A Discourse of Reason and Truth* (1678), p. 9.

12. Late in the century, Edward Bentham (*An Introduction to Logick*, 1773) said that he borrowed from this work of Wilkins.

13. *A Treatise of the Laws of Nature. Made English from the Latin by John Maxwell* (1727), pp. 42-43. The Latin text is virtually the same, see pp. 5-6. The fact that Maxwell translates 'cogitationes' as 'ideas' may be significant, as showing what Mayne said was the general use of the term 'idea'. Maxwell's introductory definition of the scope of logic is also interesting, in reflecting the new attitudes: "all Arts, or *Methods of Reasoning*, such as the *Algebraical, Geometrical, Metaphysical*, & c." (p. ii, note).

14. That this way of characterizing reasoning or judgment was common, and that it came out of the Cartesian tradition, is suggested by a review of a book in Bayle's journal for November 1685. The book, by M. Vieussens, shows Malebranchian influence. Judgment is defined as follows: "it is nothing other than the soul, which considers several ideas which it has received, unites or separates them, depending upon whether they agree or disagree with one another." (See Pierre Bayle, *Oeuvres diverses*, vol. I, pp. 410-11).

15. *Logic; or, The Art of Thinking* . . . Translated into English by Several Hands (1685).

16. Jean LeClerc, *Logica; sive, Ars ratiocinandi* (1692).

17. The French title is symptomatic of the new logics: "Système de Réflexions qui peuvent contribuer à la netteté et à l'étendue de nos connaissances."

18. See p. 50: "It is a Truth universally acknowledged, that the Impressions of Objects upon the Senses pass to the Brain, and produce there what we call the Perceptions of the Imagination. The Custom which we have of connecting continually Ideas with Signs, is moreover the Cause that the Understanding hardly ever forms any Thought, but that the Imagination furnishes at the same time Names and Signs."

19. The frequent association of ideas with thoughts runs throughout the century. The author of an anonymous work, *A Theological Survey of the Human Understanding* (1776), says that "Ideas and Thoughts" are synonymous terms (p. 51).

20. Duncan's logic was first published in 1748 in *The Preceptor*, a compendium of learning designed for students and general readers, and many editions of the work appeared throughout the century. His logic also makes up the bulk of the article on logic in the first edition of the *Encyclopaedia Britannica* in 1768-71.

21. Locke's influence on eighteenth-century logics appears in many places. An anonymous work already mentioned in note 20 includes a long section on the nature of knowledge,

acts of the mind, and the role of ideas in knowing. Lockean language pervades this part of the work. The author's following of Locke, and of the other logics, is not complete, however. In fact, there is an interesting attempt to classify the faculties and acts of the mind differently than was usually done in the logics. At the end of the work, in the section entitled "A Psychological Stricture," the author offers a division of the mind into four components. (1) "The *Percipient*, or that by which we correct, abstract, and compare our *Ideas*"; (2) "The Percepta; or the *Ideas* thus corrected, abstracted, and compared"; (3) "the *Sentient*; or that *Body* of Nerves, which surrounding the *Percipient*, gives it Notice from without; and affords it the *Ideas* just mentioned"; (4) "the *Nestens Intellectualis*; or *that* by which the Three former are joined together, so as mutually to impel Each Other" (p. 248). In the next century, there were a number of works that recognized the importance of Locke's writings as contributions to logic. In 1840 there was published, anonymously, *Lectures on Locke; or, The Principles of Logic Designed for the Use of Students in the University*. This is in large part an outline of Locke's *Essay*. The author divides logic into practical and speculative, the latter being mental philosophy. Before Locke, the author says, this kind of logic was never carried very far. In his *Historical Sketch of Logic* (1851), Robert Blakey declares that Locke's *Essay* "has given birth to a more diversified sense of logical systems and speculations, as well as modes of tuition, than any other work since the days of Aristotle" (p. 27). For another late eighteenth-century logic that follows Locke closely, see William Barron, *Lectures on Belles Lettres and Logic* (1806). Barron gave these lectures at the University of St. Andrews in the latter half of the eighteenth century.

Chapter VII

Perceptual Optics

In disagreeing with those who claimed that thought might be a property of matter, Humphrey Ditton was careful to distinguish between perception and the physical causes of perception. Motion produces reaction in the sense organs, but that reaction is not perception. "How is this Reciprocal Agitation of an *Eye* or an *Ear*, my apprehension of the Thing seen or heard?" Ditton finds neither *"Similitude nor Relation, between mere Vibrations or Undulations of some fine Threads or Fibrillae in the Machine, and that Acquaintance which I have with an Object, in what I call an Act of Perception."*[1] Along with works detailing the physiology of perception, and with works devoted to optics, there were people in eighteenth-century Britain who were attempting to characterize what Ditton identified as perceptual acquaintance. These philosophical approaches to perception often employed optical language and made use of optical examples, e.g., objects seen in mirrors, the eye compared to a lens, the understanding compared to a *camera obscura*. Many of these works were concerned (some might say obsessed) with the question "do I see an external world?" The skeptical answer to this question, as well as the debate over a single and double existence, has been due in large part to a reliance upon optical examples. It is only when the optical model is replaced by a cognitive one that writers are able to point the way around skepticism with regard to external objects. When perceptual acquaintance is considered in visual and optical terms, the tendency is to relate or match the image seen with the object—or reach the conclusion that everything seen is an image.

The Perspective Box as a Model for Perception

Locke is a good example of a writer who often uses visual, even optical language to describe perception. When he compares the mind, early in book 2, to "white paper void of all characters" on which the fancy paints ideas, we are reminded of the optician's talk of rays of light making "a Picture of the Object upon any white Body on which they fall."[2] The *camera obscura* metaphor is more explicit in Locke's 2.11.17 passage, where he compares sensation to "the windows by which light is let into this *dark room*" of the understanding. "For, methinks, the *understanding* is not much unlike a closet wholly shut from light, with only some little opening left, to let in external visible resemblances, or *ideas* of things without." Comparing the *eye* to a *camera obscura* was standard in writings on optics. Robert Hooke remarks in his *Lectures on Light* (1680) that Della Porta, Kepler, and Galileo, among others, used this way of explaining the workings of the eye. Hooke refers to Descartes's use of this model:

He explains then . . . the Organ of Vision the Eye, by the Similitude of it to a dark Room, into which no other light is admitted but what enters by one round Hole, in which a convenient Convex refracting *Lens* is placed so as to collect all the Rays from Objects without, and to unite them in their distinct and proper places upon a Wall or Sheet of Paper at a convenient Distance within; whereby the Picture of all those Objects that are without the Room, is made as it were and placed upon the Wall or Sheet within: This Sheet says he in the Eye, is the *Tunica Retina*, on which the Picture of all Objects without the Eye are as it were painted and described.[3]

In the same lectures, Hooke describes a "Perspective Box, in which all the Appearances that are made in the Eye are in some manner represented" (p. 127). This box contains a hole "large enough to put one's Face into it," as well as the necessary small hole with a lens for letting in light. With such a box, one can look in and "see the Species or Picture of outward Objects upon the bottom." (p. 128)

For Hooke, not only were the eyes our special access to the world, but they were also a "Microcosm, or a little World," a duplicate of the outer world. The eye, he says, has "a distinct Point within it self, for every distinct Point without it self in the Universe; and when a

Hemisphere of the Heavens is open to its view, it has a Hemisphere within it self, wherein there are as many Respective Points for Reception of the Radiations, as there are differing Points for emission of Radiations" (p. 121). Since Hooke accepted a plenum, the eye informs us in an instant of what is happening in the world. In another passage, he compares the action of the eye in collecting rays to a lens for collecting light from the sun in order to start a fire:

Now the Action of the Eye being much the same upon the Rays of light, from any Luminous Object with this of the Burning Glass; it follows that the Eye does by its Power bring all visible Objects into the bottom of it, and make an Impression on the *Retina*, the same as if the very Action of the Object were immediately there. (p. 123)

The substance of the retina "is affected or moved by the very same Action, as if it touched the Object." These impressions are then communicated to the brain. The eye in fact "becomes as it were a Hand, by which the Brain feels, and touches the Objects, by creating a Motion in the *Retina*, the same, and at the same Instant, with the Motion of the lucid Object it self" (p. 124).

With his notion of the eye providing the brain with hands to touch objects, Hooke's optics give us something close to direct realism. At least, we have "a perfect Picture, or Representation of all outward Objects" preserved point by point on the retina. Hooke was unable, however, to explain our awareness of these little images. We find in his further account a material or corporeal notion of ideas. Memory, he says, is an organ in the brain. It is a "repository of Ideas formed partly by the Senses, but chiefly by the Soul it self" (p. 140). Impressions from the senses—those impressions being actual motions—are carried to the memory, where they become powers "sufficient to effect such Formations of Ideas as the Soul does guide and direct them in" (p. 140). The soul's action is necessary for the formation of ideas. This action is attention: "the Soul in the Action of Attention does really form some material Part of the Repository into such a Shape, and gives it some such a Motion as is from the Senses conveyed thither" (p. 140). He seems to mean this talk quite literally, although he proceeds to help us understand it by making "a mechanical and sensible Figure and Picture thereof" (pp. 141-42). The talk then becomes that of *supposing*, of supposing that ideas have size and bulk, supposing that they occupy a place (p. 142). The soul is incorporeal, but it is "every where as it were actually present, in every point of the Sphere of its Radiation, though yet it may be supposed to be more immediately and powerfully present in the Centre of its Being"

(p. 146). He does not understand how the incorporeal soul can act on corporeal ideas, but he drops a hint that the sphere of influence of the Soul may extend "out of the Body, and that to some considerable Distance" (p. 147).[4]

Nor did Locke profess to understand the transition from brain impression to awareness. As he said to Malebranche: "Impressions made on the retina by rays of light, I think I understand; and motions from thence continued to the brain may be conceived, and that these produce ideas in our minds, I am persuaded, but in a manner to me incomprehensible."[5] Locke's ideas were not brain impressions. That Locke was well acquainted with the physiology of perception, especially with optical accounts of the eye, is indicated by his detailing the facts about the eye to Malebranche. He was writing to show how an optical species theory—different from the Peripatetic species theory against which Malebranche wrote—explains vision. He spoke of the "visible appearances of bodies, being brought into the eye by the rays of light"; of how "the bottom of the eye is far from being a point"; of the way in which the rays of light "cause their distinct sensations, by striking on distinct parts of the retina"; of how the "figures they paint there must be of some considerable bigness, since it takes up on the retina an area whose diameter is at least thirty seconds of a circle, whereof the circumference is in the retina, and the centre somewhere in the crystalline"; and of how "few can perceive an object less than thirty minutes of a circle, whereof the eye is the centre."[6] Thus, when Locke compared the *understanding* of humans to a *camera obscura*, he did so in full knowledge of this model for the eye. In using that model for the understanding, was he unduly influenced by the optical details? When he talked of ideas *resembling* primary qualities, of ideas *conforming* to things, of ideas and not objects being present to the mind, was Locke transferring Hooke's microcosmic notion to the understanding? Was there some temptation to think of our awareness being like the face at the perspective box scanning the images on the wall of the box?[7]

There was one other striking use of the perspective box in the early eighteenth century. In the Preface to his *An Essay towards a Demonstration of the Soul's Immateriality* (1718), Henry Grove replied to Arthur Collier's recent *Clavis Universalis* (1713). Grove wanted to state the evidence that he thought we have for rejecting Collier's subtitle: "Being a Demonstration of the Non-Existence, or Impossibility of an External World." Collier seems to have argued for a single existence view; what he denied is the "extra-existence of a material world, that such a world exists independent of humans. Grove accepts a double-existence view, of perceptions and object. He agrees with Collier that "the World, which is the immediate Object of Perception, is not external."[8] We gain our knowledge of the visible world through ideas: "we see nothing but our own Ideas" (p. 10; cf. p. 17). The fit of ideas to the world is, however, very close. Grove compares them to a "thin Varnish spread over the Face of Nature, which do[es] not hinder us from passing a Judgment of it; because they express outward Objects, much as the Varnish takes the Form of the Work upon which it is laid" (pp. 11-12). Grove offers a number of arguments against Collier's position, but the one that makes use of the perspective box illustration is introduced by his saying that if there were in fact no external world answering to our ideas of it, God would "have so contrived our Ideas, that they should appear to be at home in the Mind," and not appear, as even Collier agrees, to be external (p. 16). He then provides the following illustration:

Suppose then a hollow Globe endued with Perception, and painted on the Inside with Birds, Beasts and Fishes, and to have the Knowledge of all that is delineated within it; the whole Delineation being within the Globe, and the Perception the Globe hath of it but one Act, is it not certain that the Appearance which this Representation would most naturally make to the Globe must be of something comprehended within it self? And the same it would probably be with the Mind, if there were not some external World, to signify and represent which our Ideas, by the Rules of divine Perspective appear External. (pp. 16-17)

The perceiver and the perspective box have been collapsed into one, the box now becomes percipient. Perspective and distance perception (which I presume are what Grove means by saying our ideas appear as external) save us from the skeptical and even idealist conclusions with which Grove's optical example is threatened.[9]

Image and Object

When perception is considered in visual and optical terms, the question tends to be that of relating or matching the image seen with the object. Either the image seen is taken to be the very thing itself, or we are said to see both image and object: "As in a *Looking-glass*, in which he that looks does indeed immediately behold the *Species* in the Glass, but does also at the same time actually behold *Peter* or *Paul* whose Image it is."[10] Henry Lee, in his careful critique of Locke (*Anti-Scepticism*, 1702) says that the proper sense of 'idea' is "a visible Representation or Resemblance of the Object, and, in some measure at least, *like* the thing of which it is the *Idea*. Thus a man's Face in the Glass is properly the *Idea* of that Face" (p. 2). Locke too used the looking-glass analogy.

To think often and never to retain it so much as one moment is a very useless sort of thinking; and the soul in such a state of thinking does very little if at all excell that of a looking-glass, which constantly receives variety of images or *ideas* but retains none: they disappear and vanish and there remain no footsteps of them; the looking-glass is never the better for such *ideas*, nor the soul for such thoughts. (*Essay*, 2.1.15)

In a later passage, speaking of simple ideas, Locke remarked that the understanding "can no more refuse to have, nor alter them when they are imprinted, nor blot them out and make new ones itself, than a mirror can refuse, alter, or obliterate the images, or *ideas* which the objects set before it do therein produce" (2.1.25). In his account of perception, in trying to sort out the respective roles of the senses and the activity of the mind, Cudworth resorted to the mirror analogy in an extended passage. He compares three things: "*First*, a Mirror, Looking-glass, or Crystal Globe; *Secondly*, a Living Eye, that is, a Seeing or Perceptive Mirror or Looking-glass; *Thirdly*, a Mind or Intellect Superadded to this Living Eye or Seeing Mirror."[11]

Sometimes the optical comparison is with eyeglasses. John Witty (*The First Principles of Modern Deism Confuted*, 1707) speaks of our eyes as natural glasses. Those glasses do not give us direct access to objects: "For not the Things themselves, but their *Ideas in us* are the immediate Objects of Human Understanding in its search after Truth" (p. 4). Later in this work, Witty elaborates:

we have no impressions of the *Primary* attributes of External Objects, immediately from the Objects themselves, but by the *mediation* and interposition of the Organs of our own *Sensations*; so that we are beholden to their Representations for the *Ideas* which we are furnish'd with of Things: And were External Objects to act upon our Souls *immediately*, we can't say but that they would represent themselves otherwise to us. (p. 129)

In a standard work on nervous disorders, George Cheyne cites an optical account while discussing perception.

Seeing, or the Perception of the Bulk, Distance, Situation, or Colour of Objects, is nothing but the Action of Light . . . reflected or refracted from the Surfaces of Bodies or outward Objects . . . which being variously refracted in the Humours of the *Eyes*, [is] at last united on the *Retina*, so as there to form an *Image* analogous to that of the outward Objects, which by striking the Nerves of the *Retina* (in the same Manner that the object it self would have done) is by them transmitted to the *sentient Principle*.[12]

Optical writers were concerned to understand how it is that the images or appearances of things are sometimes located by us on the object, at other times not. Vasco Ronchi has described the various accounts by opticians of the location of visual images.[13] More recently, he has set Hobbes's treatise *De Homine* in that context.[14] Both Ronchi and the editor-translator of this treatise help us understand Hobbes's sometimes complex optical accounts. Interestingly, Maurin compares Hobbes's account of sensible qualities as the observer's translation of the movement of rays of light to the passages (cited in chapter I) in which Descartes spoke of motion in the world and in the nerves as natural signs. Maurin says that for Hobbes too, the variety of rays from objects constitute "a code which, analyzed instant by instant by the observer, gives him the possibility of re-creating at each instant a universe of phantasms which constitutes a good imitation of the real universe."[15]

In chapter 2 of his treatise, Hobbes speaks of a distinct and figured vision occurring when light (lumen) or color forms a figure of which the parts originate from the parts of the object; the parts of the figure stand in a one-to-one correspondence to those of the object. Light thus figured is called *an image*. By an institution of nature, all animate beings judge that that vision is the vision *of* the object. People have not always understood that the sun and stars, for example, are larger than they appear to be. That writers on vision have so far been unable to explain why objects appear now larger, now smaller, now farther away, now closer, does not surprise Hobbes because no one so far, he claims, has had the idea of considering light (lux) and color, not as emanations from the object but as phenomena of our inner world.[16] Later chapters of this treatise identify the apparent place of the object as the place of the images in direct vision (p. 59). Maurin reads Hobbes as saying all that we are aware of are our images, our phantasms (pp. 55-56, n. 12). He interprets such a view as *idealism*, and he wonders how such an idealism can be superimposed upon Hobbes's materialism. Whether we can so quickly take the distinction between 'lumen' and 'lux', between physical events and psychological awareness, as idealism, is open to some doubt. The same question is discussed by subsequent writers in Britain, especially Berkeley and Hume. But it is important to appreciate that Hobbes has not changed his views in this late treatise. He never did deny *appearances*. Exactly what their status was may not always be clear; but his use of 'thought' or 'conception' in earlier writings, as well as 'idea', reinforces the fact that he was not saying *all* is matter and motion.

For instance, in the *Elements of Philosophy* Hobbes considers the effects and appearances of things to sense as "faculties or powers of bodies, which make us distinguish them from one another."[17] Later in this work, he says that "the first beginnings, therefore, of knowledge, are the phantasms of sense and imagination; and that there be such phantasms we know well enough by nature" (p. 66). Sometimes he uses the term 'idea' in close conjunction with, sometimes even as a synonym for 'phantasm'. "A man that looks upon the sun, has a certain shining idea of the magnitude of about a foot over, and this he calls the sun, though he knows the sun to be truly a great deal bigger; and, in like manner, the phantasm of the same thing appears sometimes round . . . and sometimes square" (p. 75).[18] The question then is "whether that phantasm be matter, or some body natural, or only some accident of body" (p. 75). As a way of answering this question, he assumes that the whole world, save humans, was annihilated. A man would still have the ideas of the world, of bodies, etc., "that is the memory and imagination of magnitude, motions, sounds, colours, etc.," as well as their order (p. 92). Hobbes continues: "All which things, though they be nothing but ideas and phantasms, happening internally to him that imagineth; yet they will appear as if they were external, and not at all depending upon any power of the mind" (p. 92). Even when the world does still exist, we work only with our phantasms. "For when we calculate the magnitude and motions of heaven or earth, we do not ascend into heaven that we may divide it into parts, or measure the motions thereof, but we do it sitting in our closets or in the dark" (p. 92). He then proceeds to consider the species of external things, "not as really existing, but appearing only to exist, or [appearing] to have a being without us" (p. 92). It is the way the world appears that he analyzes.

Later, in part IV on "Physics, or the Phenomena of Nature," in the chapter "Sense and Animal Motion," 'perception' is linked with 'ideas'. "In the first place, therefore, the causes of our perception, that is, the causes of those ideas and phantasms which are perpetually generated within us whilst we make use of our senses, are to be enquired into . . ." (p. 389). The act of sense differs from sense "no otherwise . . . then *fieri*, that is, being a doing, differs from *factum esse*, that is, being done" (p. 392). Sense is also said to be "the judgment we make of objects by their phantasms; namely, by comparing and distinguishing those phantasms" (p. 393). In some passages, Hobbes writes 'thought or phantasm' (e.g., p. 398). *Leviathan* speaks of human thoughts, characterizing them as "a *representation* or *appearance*, of some quality, or other accident of a body without us."[19] Mental discourse is a "train of thought" (p. 11). The word 'conception' is also used. Hobbes's *Human Nature: or, The Fundamental Elements of Policy* even speaks of "certain images of conceptions of the things without us."[20] The having of images is what "we call our *conception, imagination, idea, notice* or *knowledge* of them" (p. 3). The faculty by which we have such knowledge is the cognitive power. He goes on in the same work to speak of conceptions "proceeding from the action of the thing itself." By sight, "we have a conception or image composed of *colour* and *figure*." He cites seeing the sun and other visible objects reflected in water and glasses. These experiences show us that color and images generally "may be there where the thing seen is not" (pp. 4-5). The image seen by reflection in a glass "is *not* any thing *in* or *behind* the glass." The image and color "is but an apparition to us" of the motion of object and nerves. Thus again, two senses of light are distinguished: motion in and from the object, and the appearance or image.

We should perhaps guard against crediting too strong a psychological content to these various words used by Hobbes. What seems certain, however, is that he did employ different terms, all of which were his attempt to distinguish the way the world appears to us from the world itself. *Leviathan* made this point firmly: "And though at some certain distance, the real and very object seems invested with the fancy it begets in us; yet still the object is one thing, the image or fancy is another."[21] Similarly, in *Seven Philosophical Problems*, one of the speakers, B, cites as examples of fancy both "the appearance of your face in a looking-glass" and an afterimage, "a spot before the eyes that hath stared upon the sun or fire."[22] The other speaker, A, then asks why that which "appears before your eyes" when you look toward the sun or moon is also not fancy? B replies, "So it is. Though the sun itself be a real body, yet that bright circle of about a foot diameter cannot be the sun, unless there be two suns."[23]

To the question raised by Hume later, of whether there is a single or double existence, Hobbes clearly answered 'double'. Moreover, Hobbes seems to have taken the visual image as his standard, although such terms as 'thought' and 'conception' indicate his generalizing of the double-existence view. It was optics that provided Hobbes, certainly in his last work, *De Homine*, with some convincing evidence for his distinction between image and object.[24]

Berkeley's Double-Existence View

The most striking example of a perception theory based upon vision is that of Bishop Berkeley. His *New Theory of Vision* (1709) addressed itself to the way in which we determine the distance of objects. He begins that work with a quick summary of different theories advanced by opticians to explain how we determine the apparent location of objects (§ 4-8). Instead of claiming, as the geometrical opticians did, that distance is judged by the "bigness of the angle made by the meeting of the two optic axes" (§ 12), Berkeley argues that the perception of distance is based upon (1) the sensations we feel in our eyes when we try to bring a near object into focus (§ 16) and (2) the degree of confusion in our vision of the object (§ 21). Both these ways of determining or judging distance (or the location of objects) are a function of the coexistence of these experiences: coexistence of the sensations with the discovery of the location of objects, coexistence of degrees of confusion with varying distances of objects (§ 25). He attempts to explain a problem raised by Dr. Barrow about the 'locus objecti' and the 'locus apparens', citing Molyneux's use of these two phrases. To explain this problem, Berkeley appeals to the second of the ways of judging distance, the degrees of confusion in vision. But as he proceeds, his account of these two places becomes more radical. The 'locus apparens' is always *near to* the perceiver (present to the mind) and the 'objectum' constantly changes. To speak more accurately on this last point, the 'objectum' becomes a series of 'apparens'.

We can witness this double change by examining Berkeley's remarks about the man born blind who later is made to see. For such a person, "The objects intromitted by sight would seem to him (as in truth they are) no other than a new set of thoughts or sensations, each whereof is as near to him as the perception of pain or pleasure, or the most inward passions of his soul" (§ 43). Continuing to use language that places sensations, passions, and thoughts near to the mind, he asks rhetorically "whether the visible extension of any object doth not appear as near to him as the colour of that object." Because "those who have had any thoughts of that matter" agree that colors (which Berkeley calls 'the immediate objects of sight') are not without the mind, and because Berkeley here argues that extension, figure, and motion are inseparable from color, the suggestion is that what is seen does not exist outside the mind at any distance. Berkeley then offers an analysis of what is meant, in ordinary discourse, by saying that the moon that I am looking at is "fifty or sixty semidiameters of the earth distant from me" (§ 44).

Suppose, for example, that looking at the moon I should say it were fifty or sixty semidiameters of the earth distant from me. Let us see what moon this is spoken of: It is plain it cannot be the visible moon, or anything like the visible moon, or that which I see, which is only a round, luminous plain of about thirty visible points in diameter. For in case I am carried from the place where I stand directly towards the moon, it is manifest the object varies, still as I go on; and by the time that I am advanced fifty or sixty semidiameters of the earth, I shall be so far from being near a small, round, luminous flat that I shall perceive nothing like it; this object having long since disappeared, and if I would recover it, it must be by going back to the earth from whence I set out. Again, suppose I perceive by sight the faint and obscure idea of something which I doubt whether it be a man, or a tree, or a tower, but judge it to be at the distance of about a mile. It is plain I cannot mean that what I see is a mile off, or that it is the image or likeness of anything which is a mile off, since that every step I take towards it the appearance alters and from being obscure, small, and faint, grows clear, large, and vigorous. And when I come to the mile's end, that which I saw first is quite lost, neither do I find any thing in the likeness of it.

What leads me to think I am seeing a distant object such as a tree is that I have found that my seeing has usually been accompanied or followed by touching, after a certain movement of my body. But Berkeley claims even further that I do not touch what I see. Both seeing and touching reveal sensations *near to me*; they reveal both *sensations* and sensations *near to me*. Thus, "in truth and strictness of speech I neither see distance it self, nor anything that I take to be at a distance" (§45). I have only ideas, my perceptions, my phantasms. Hooke's microcosm duplicate world turns out to *be* my world. We seem to have a single existence, my perceptions. That dictum about no cognition at a distance, that what is known must be present to the mind, seems to be at work here: "the things we see being in truth at no distance from us" (§52), all visible objects "are only in the mind" (§77).

Berkeley's explication, in his *Principles* and *Dialogues*, of this notion of objects existing in the mind was summarized by his dictum 'esse est percipi'. This principle was meant to identify two features of his general account: that there is no aspect of objects that is insensible (his negative claim against the materialists) and that objects as known are *in* the mind. This second feature is consistent with the various traditions from Aristotle to the Schoolmen and to Descartes according to which the object is present to the mind. Berkeley was fond of pointing out that the materialist's object—the insensible, corpuscular particles of matter—cannot be present to the mind. Nor does the corpuscular account of perception explain how ideas or perceptions arise. He agreed with many other writers that corporeal events cannot cause awareness. If the physical objects that we take to exist in external space distant from us can neither cause ideas in us nor be present to our mind, what *is* present there? Berkeley's answer is 'visible objects' and 'ideas', where these two terms mean and designate the same thing. 'Tangible objects' or 'ideas' follow the same analysis. He was quite clear about his analysis of 'present to' and 'exist in': they mean 'perceived', 'known', or 'comprehended' (i.e., understood). Early in the *Principles*, where he is explaining what he means by 'mind', 'spirit', 'soul', or 'my self', he says these words denote "a thing entirely distinct from them [his ideas], wherein they exist, or, which is the same thing, whereby they are perceived."[25] In the third of his *Dialogues*, Philonous says, "I know what I mean, when I affirm that there is a spiritual substance or support of ideas, that is, that a spirit knows and perceives ideas" (p. 234). To reinforce the point that 'exist in' has no literal sense, Philonous tells Hylas that "when I speak of objects as existing in the mind or imprinted on the senses; I would not be understood in the gross literal sense, as when bodies are said to exist in a place, or a seal to make an impression upon wax. My meaning is only that the mind comprehends or perceives them; and that it is affected from without, or by some being distinct from itself." (p. 250) More important still, Berkeley's ideas are not modes of mind: they exist in the mind "not by way of mode or property, but as a thing perceived in that which perceives it" (p. 237). The *Principles* says that qualities (a term frequently used interchangeably with 'idea') "are in the mind only as they are perceived by it, that is, not by way of *mode* or *attribute*, but only by way of *idea*" (*Principles*, §49). In these important but overlooked passages, Berkeley clearly echoes Descartes's notion of the objective reality of ideas. Berkeley's denial of ideas as modes of mind is a forceful reminder that he is working within the Cartesian tradition, trying to find a way to say that ideas *are* the things themselves existing in, i.e., cognized by, the mind.[26]

In his study of Berkeley (*Berkeley, the Philosophy of Immaterialism*, 1974), I. C. Tipton recognizes this close linking of 'exist in' with 'perceived by' (p. 87). He even allows that Luce's stressing of this linkage (Luce reads 'in the mind' as an abbreviation for 'in direct cognitive relation to the mind'; see p. 93 in Tipton's book) is "in a way right." Tipton's reluctance to accept this as Berkeley's full meaning is not clearly explained. What he says is that "if it is true Berkeley regards existence in the mind as amounting to perception by the mind, it is also true that he thinks of perception by the mind as coming down to existence of an idea in the mind" (pp. 93-94). Whereas Berkeley's translation of 'exist in' by 'perceived or known by' does give us an intelligible explication, I do not see what we are told by the second part of Tipton's remark, that 'perception by the mind' means 'existence in the mind'. The troublesome phrase is 'exist in', not 'perceived by'. We need to know, especially in the light of the history of the appeals to 'present with the mind', exactly what Berkeley means by 'exists in the mind'. The passages I have cited seem to tell us unequivocally what that phrase means. It means 'to be perceived by'. And *what* is perceived by the mind is *not* a mode of mind. If it is not a mode of mind, it must be the object as it exists for, or is present to, the mind, i.e., as perceived, known, or understood by the mind.

It is this last notion that leads Tipton to hang back from accepting Berkeley's explication of 'exists in', for Tipton is sure that, not being a mode, ideas for Berkeley must be things, entities. Berkeley, Tipton says, "does want us to think of the appearance as itself a thing" (p. 187). This claim is correct, provided we keep in the mind the Cartesian objective reality; but Tipton takes the appearances to be a different sort of thing: "he really does hold that each sense datum is an entity" (p. 185). In other words, Tipton's inference from the disclaimer that ideas are modes of mind is that they are *things*, substances, or entities; they are not things in the usual physical-object sense, but new kinds of things: sense-data. Berkeley's ideas become things. My inference from the same passage about ideas not being modes of mind is also that ideas are things, but not new kinds of things; they are the *very things themselves*, the ordinary objects of our and of Berkeley's environment.

Tipton makes some good comments earlier about how reifying sensations or appearances leads us away from direct realism and toward representative realism (see pp. 23-24, 35, 66). We have seen how ideas as entities function for Malebranche as a proxy for objects that cannot be present to the mind. Ideas for Malebranche were *real beings*, even though there was no clear category in his metaphysics for characterizing these beings. They were substance-like, if not substances. Berkeley's ideas are clearly not such spiritual things. Tipton comes closer to what I am suggesting is Berkeley's view when he says of the appearances that "they are themselves the basic things in the sensible world" (p. 191). As Hume was later to say of the ordinary view, "the very image which is present to the senses, is with us the real body."[27] Berkeley's way of expressing this view is succinctly put at the end of his *Dialogues*: the vulgar opinion is that "*those things they immediately perceive are the real things*" (p. 262). His own position combined this vulgar view with the view of the philosophers:

"that *the things immediately perceived, are ideas which exist only in the mind*" (ibid.).

To understand Berkeley, we must appreciate what the combination of the vulgar and philosophical views yields. The most obvious product of that combination, because it is stressed so often by Berkeley, is the 'esse est percipi' principle: the mind dependence of sensible things. Of even greater importance is Berkeley's repeated disclaimer that such a principle violated the ordinary view. Berkeley never wavered from the claim that with the definition of 'existence' as 'percipi' and 'percipere', "the horse is in the stable, the Books are in the study as before."[28] Putting an objection to himself — "Well say you according to this new Doctrine all is but meer idea, there is nothing wch is not an ens rationis" — he replies: "I answer things are as real and exist in rerum natura as much as ever, the distinction betwixt entia Realia and entia rationis may be made as properly now as ever" (PC, 535). The corresponding passage in the *Principles* is in section 34:

First then, it will be objected that by the foregoing principles, all that is real and substantial in Nature is banished out of the world: and instead thereof a chimerical scheme of ideas takes place. All things that exist, exist only in the mind, that is, they are purely notional. What therefore becomes of the sun, moon, and stars? What must we think of houses, rivers, mountains, trees, stones; nay, even of our own bodies? Are all these but so many chimeras and illusions on the fancy? To all which, and whatever else of the same sort may be objected, I answer, that by the principles premised, we are not deprived of any one thing in Nature. Whatever we see, feel, hear, or any wise conceive or understand, remains as secure as ever, and is as real as ever.

Both here and in the *Dialogues*, what Berkeley is concerned to deny is the philosopher's matter, that insensible, colorless something that was said to cause our sensations. The familiar world, the world we normally take for granted, is the world Berkeley saw himself supporting and explicating. The "things I see with mine eyes and touch with my hands do exist, really exist, I make not the least question" (*Principles*, §35). Similarly, Philonous affirms that

the real things are those very things I see and feel, and perceive by my senses. These I know, and finding they answer all the necessities and purposes of life, have no reason to be solicitous about any other unknown beings. A piece of sensible bread, for instance, would stay my stomach better than ten thousand times as much of that insensible, unintelligible, real bread you speak of. It is likewise my opinion, that colours and other sensible qualities are on the objects. I cannot for my life help thinking that snow is white, and fire hot. (*Dialogues*, pp. 229-30)

In another frequently quoted passage Philonous says: "I am not for changing things into ideas, but rather ideas into things; since those immediate objects of perception, which according to you, are only appearances of things, I take to be the real things themselves" (p. 244). Entry 807 in PC makes a similar point about the term 'idea': "Say you, at this rate all's nothing but idea meer phantasm. I answer every thing as real as ever. I hope to call a thing idea makes it not the less real. Truly I should perhaps have stuck to ye word thing and not mention'd the Word Idea were it not for a Reason and I think a good one too wch I shall give in ye Second Book."

Berkeley could hardly be more explicit in defense of the vulgar view. What does the view of the philosopher—that things immediately perceived are ideas in the mind—add to the vulgar view? There are two components in the philosophical view, ideas and things. What can we say about Berkeley's use of the term 'idea'? In his Notebooks, we find that term used in two ways, both of which seem close to the Arnauld-Locke sense. One of these usages treats ideas as thoughts or perceptions, the other makes ideas the content of perceptions. In neither case are ideas special sorts of objects. In the first group are the following entries in PC:

280—Our simple ideas are so many simple thoughts or perceptions, and that a perception cannot exist without a thing to perceive it or any longer than it is perceiv'd, that a thought cannot be in an unthinking thing, that one uniform simple thought can be like to nothing but another uniform simple thought. Complex thoughts or ideas are only an assemblage of simple ideas and can be the image of nothing or like unto nothing but another assemblage of simple ideas, etc.

299—But say you the thought or perception I call extension is not itself in an unthinking thing or matter But it is like something wch is in matter. Well, says I, do you apprehend and conceive w^t you say extension is like unto or do you not. If the latter, now know you they are alike, how can you compare any things besides y^r own ideas. If the former it must be an idea i.e. perception thought, or sensation wch to be in an unperceiving thing is a Contradiction.[29]

378.8—All our ideas are either sensations or thoughts.

578—Consciousness, perception, existence of ideas seem to be all one.

706—No Perception according to Locke is active. Therefore no perception (i.e. no idea) can be the image of or like unto that wch is altogether active and not at all passive i.e. the Will.

In the second group are the following:

572—I Defy any man to Imagine or conceive perception without an idea or an Idea without perception.

582—The having Idea is not the same thing with Perception. A Man may have Ideas when he only Imagines. But then this Imagination presupposes the Perception.

609—The Distinguishing betwixt an Idea and perception of the Idea has been one great cause of Imagining material substances.

656—Twas the opinion that Ideas could exist unperceiv'd or before perception that made Men think perception was somewhat different from the Idea perceived.

In the *New Theory of Vision*, 'idea' occurs with 'sensation' and with 'perception'. For example, in section 16 Berkeley asks "what ideas or sensations there be that attend vision"; in section 28 he tells us that he has "set down those sensations or ideas that seem to be constant and general occasions of introducing into the mind the different ideas of distance"; in section 53 he says that "the same perceptions or ideas which suggest distance do also suggest magnitude"; in section 73 he speaks of "faintness, as well as all other ideas or perceptions"; and in section 135 he declares that "the ideas of sight are all new perceptions." There is also a passage in which he links *thoughts* with *sensations*: "The objects intromitted by sight would seem to him (as in truth they are) no other than a new set of thoughts or sensations" (§41).[30]

In the *Principles* and the *Dialogues*, the two words that are linked most frequently are 'ideas' and 'sensations' (e.g., *Principles*, 5, 25, 90; *Dialogues*, pp. 203, 215, 249). There are two longer lists of synonyms or near synonyms: sensations, notions, ideas, impressions (*Principles*, 5); sensations, ideas, actions, or passions (*Dialogues*, p. 233). Principle 87 speaks of "Colour, figure, motion, extension and the like" as "only so many sensations in the mind." These sensations are said to be "perfectly known, there being nothing in them which is not perceived." There are numerous passages in which 'idea' is said to "signify the several combinations of sensible qualities," those combinations being called 'things' (e.g., *Principles*, 38, 56, 82, 95; *Dialogues*, p. 175). There is also the passage I quoted in a previous chapter, "to have an idea is all one as to perceive" (*Principles*, 7).

In the light of these passages about the nature of ideas, and those other passages showing Berkeley defending the vulgar view, we might summarize his position as follows.

1. Ideas are perceptions, sensations, or thoughts.
2. Perceptions or ideas *are* the things themselves.
3. What is known or perceived is present to (near to) the mind.
4. To exist in the mind means to be perceived or known by the mind.
5. To be perceived by the mind is the way things are in the mind.
6. Perceptions or ideas do not (cannot?) exist apart from mind.
7. Things do not (cannot?) exist apart from mind.

Other writers accepted propositions 1, 3, 4, and 5. But propositions 2 and 7, which are distinctive of Berkeley's analysis, proved puzzling to his contemporaries; they were the basis for the mocking and satire leveled at him. It was easier for people to accept proposition 3, identifying what is present to the mind as our perceptions, while insisting (as Porterfield did) that there is a world of objects independent of our perceptions, to which we ascribe our perceptions. It was apparently even easier to accept a veil of perception doctrine, as Henry Grove urged, taking ideas or perceptions as a screen (albeit in Grove's case, a very thin screen) between perceivers and the world. Skepticism seemed to many an easier, more intelligible position than Berkeley's propositions 2 and 7.

There are, however, reasons for suggesting that proposition 7 should not be included in our summary, at least not without some commentary. That commentary may relieve 7 of its objectionable features, for it may show us why Berkeley did not think the philosophical view in any way contradicted or was incompatible with the vulgar view. Berkeley was read, when anyone took notice of him, as accepting proposition 7 in its most objectionable form: according to the standard interpretation, he turned the real world into an illusion, things into ideas. In his influential work, *An Enquiry into the Nature of the Human Soul* (1733), Andrew Baxter devoted over two hundred pages to "An Essay on the Phenomenon of Dreaming," which is followed by his discussion of "Dean Berkeley's scheme against the existence of matter, and a material world examined, and shown inconclusive" (vol. II, p. 239). The very objections Berkeley anticipated and denied, from his earliest notebook jottings to his *Principles*, were taken as his sincere conclusions. William Porterfield also charged Berkeley with compounding ideas with things, thereby with a skepticism that substituted a phantom world for the external world (*A Treatise on the Eye*, 1759, p. 329). The same author, in an earlier work objects to taking away all "Difference between Space and Time, and to make both consist in a Consciousness of a Succession of different Ideas or Perceptions in the Mind" ("An Essay concerning the Motion of the Eyes," in *Medical Essays . . .* , vol. 3, p. 234). Neither space nor time depends upon our ideas. To claim that they do leads, Porterfield insisted, to "a Scepticism that at once banishes this external World and Space itself out of the Field of Existence," substitutes a visionary world, "a World of Ideas and Phantoms existing no where but in his own Mind." Porterfield considers such a view to be a "wild and unbounded *Scepticism*."

Collier is never mentioned in the tracts of the eighteenth century, but one wonders if those who criticize Berkeley in this way did not confuse him with Collier. For Collier did make much of dreams and illusions. He agreed that we see objects *as* external, but the way they seem does not support their real externality (*Clavis Universalis*, p. 15). His way of explicating 'exist in'—as objects of vision were said to exist in the mind or visive faculty—was to talk of mirrors, or of persons who are "light-headed, ecstatic, etc., where not only colours, but entire bodies are perceived or seen" (p. 8). In a looking glass, "I see moon, and stars, even a whole expanded world" (p. 26). He points out that the objects in the glass are not the same as the objects supposed to be external to the glass. He draws the parallel with normal seeing: its objects are no different from those seen in a glass.

There were two considerations that tended to lead people toward the extreme single-existence view, that only perceptions exist. The first of these were claims such as Berkeley's about distance perceptions. The second was the generally accepted doctrine that a vast array of supposed qualities (the secondary ones) were only perceptions. The more radical persons quickly moved to the claim that *all* perceived qualities are only perceptions. These two considerations are of course closely related. If perceptions are 'near to us', Berkeley's concern with the apparent place of our perceptions must be answered. Even those who were trying to espouse some sort of materialism (making sensations properties of organized matter, e.g., the brain) had to meet this probem, for, as Thomas Morgan remarked, "the apparent Place of the Sensation, where the Object, from whence it arises, and by which the Motion is modified and impressed, is external, and at a distance from the sensative Organ; for in this Case, the apparent Place of the Sensation is at the external Object, and not in the Organ which receives the impression."[31] All the ideas and impressions of external, sensible objects are, Morgan says, "referred to the Place of the Object themselves." From this arises "the vulgar Error of ascribing those Sensations to the external Objects, by which they are impressed, as if they were real Attributes and Properties of those Objects themselves, and not Affections of the sensative Nerves within us."[32]

Morgan makes perceived qualities (our sensations) properties of the brain and nervous system. The accepted philosophical view was that some of those perceived qualities (the secondary ones) were properties of the mind. For Morgan and the accepted view, there was a distinction between perceptions and objects, between appearance and reality. Berkeley identified this distinction as the source of skepticism. Richard Popkin[33] has reminded us of the importance Berkeley gave to refuting skepticism. The double existence of corpuscular matter and perceived qualities takes us, Berkeley insisted, to skepticism; for the attempt to retain the primary qualities as qualities of body, qualities which our ideas resemble, fails. Popkin suggests that all the arguments used by Berkeley to show that primary and secondary qualities are both mind-dependent were found in Bayle's *Dictionnaire*. Popkin argues that Berkeley defends a common sense realism by adopting the skeptical position on qualities—their 'esse' is 'percipi'—while insisting that those qualities *are* the things themselves. I think Popkin is right, but his article does not explain how Berkeley's ideas are turned into things. We can now understand how that is done. Instead of ideas being modes of mind (as secondary qualities became for Locke and as both secondary and primary qualities were for the strong skeptic represented by Bayle), they are the very things themselves. Berkeley's twofold assertion that he had not turned things into ideas (just the reverse) and that ideas are not modes of mind (thus things are not modes of mind) enabled him to articulate a realism within the terminology of the way of ideas. If we take him seriously on these two claims, he could not have accepted a single-existence ontology. What he did was to reformulate Descartes's notion of the existence of objects in the mind. Along with this reformulation, he insisted that we cannot conceive of objects in any other terms than in those of ideas. The being of objects in the mind—that is, their being conceived or known—cannot be mind-independent. 'Esse est percipi' addresses itself to, and holds for objects as known. His single-existence ontology includes a duality: ideas and things, but the ideas are the things as known.

The double-existence view rejected by Berkeley claimed, as he interpreted it, that objects were (to use Hume's vocabulary) *specifically* different from perceptions. This corpuscular account of objects is, Berkeley insisted, incoherent, just because it requires a specific difference. We can think of or conceive of the world only in experiential terms. Thus, if Berkeley did not turn things into ideas, if throughout his writings he followed the Cartesian and scholastic practice of saying that objects exist in the mind, and if, as Descartes, Locke and Arnauld held, 'exist in the mind' means 'known by or perceived by', we must see his efforts as a defense, just as he said, of the vulgar direct realist view. But the vulgar view was seen by Berkeley (and by Hume later) as ignoring the cognitive nature of that realism. In using existential language ('exists in'), Berkeley retained the ontological features in the analysis of perception. What Hume did was to replace that ontology by the epistemic feature of belief. But Hume worked with the very same notion as Berkeley did, and as the vulgar do, that what we see are the things themselves. Both Berkeley and Hume worked to find a way of protecting this view, while recognizing that what is present to the mind are perceptions.

The Transition to Hume

One of the more interesting writers who accepted the view that *all* perceived qualities are really only perceptions was William Porterfield. Porterfield is of particular importance for the way in which, on the question of single or double existence, he bridges the way from Berkeley to Hume. In his 1737 "Essay concerning the Motion of the Eyes," he speaks of each eye impressing the "Mind with an idea of the same Object," asserting that "the Impression must be more strong and lively when both Eyes concur" and that the mind receives a living idea of the object.[34] Both this essay and his 1759 *Treatise on the Eye* identify five ways of conceiving of colors: (1) as properties of light, (2) as qualities of body, (3) as passions of our sight or retina, (4) as sensations or perceptions of the mind, i.e., the idea excited there by the agitation of our sense organs, and (5) as judgments of the mind.[35] As qualities of body, colors are dispositions of the surfaces of objects reflecting rays of light. Only 4 deserves the name 'color': "to speak truly, Colours are Sensations produced in our Mind" (*Treatise*, p. 353). In his "Essay," he generalizes this conclusion about color. No quality is a property of objects—no perceived quality, that is. He goes on to draw some distinctions between the perceptions or sensations of our mind. They are of three sorts: some are very strong and lively, others weak and faint, the third are of moderate nature ("Essay," vol. III, p. 222). The first "touch our Mind very sensibly, and as it were, surprise it and rouse it up with Force and Vigour." He cites agreeable and painful sensations. These we do not attribute to the object. The second sort of sensations are "weak and languishing"; the mind does not think of attributing these to itself. Examples include light that is not too strong, colors, tastes, smells. Examples of the third sort of sensations are moderate heat and cold. He recognizes that "a weak and languishing Sensation may become both a middle or a strong one" (ibid., p. 224).

Even though he is firm in his claim that what we experience in perception are our own sensations, Porterfield recognizes that the "mind never considers any of them [save those he has just excepted] as belonging to itself, but as belonging to something external . . . Now, since there is no essential or necessary Connection betwixt these Perceptions and the Judgments we form concerning them, it follows that those judgments must either depend upon Custom and Experience, or on an original, connate and immutable Law" ("Essay," pp. 226-27). He thinks it is a contradiction to say that *all* of them depend upon custom and experience, since it is "impossible for us to have any Experience, till some how or other we have formed a Judgment." It is this first judgment that depends upon "an original, connate and immutable Law." The connate law is formulated as follows: "the mind traces back its own Sensations from the *Sensorium* to the *Retina*, and from thence along the perpendicular Lines above mentioned [those talked of by the opticians] to the Object itself; and thence concludes what it perceives to be in the external Object, and not in the Mind" (ibid., pp. 228-29). His appeal to such an innate law is in effect an objection to Berkeley's account in the *New Theory of Vision*. He does, however, agree with Berkeley that there are no necessary connections between our judgments and our experience of color. He paraphrases Berkeley in a way that reminds us of Hume:

> There is no essential or necessary Connection between the Ideas of Sight and Touch; the Ideas suggested by Sight, of the Distance, Situation and Magnitude of external Things, must depend entirely on Custom and Experience; for that one Idea may suggest another to the Mind, it is sufficient that they have been observed to go together, without any Demonstration of the Necessity of their Coexistence. (ibid., p. 232).

Appealing to the principle of no action at a distance, and echoing Malebranche's use of the walking-mind argument, Porterfield concludes (as I have noted earlier) that the "Mind can never perceive any thing but its own proper Modifications, and the various States and Conditions of the *Sensorium* to which it is present" (ibid., p. 220). Here and later, he insists that he does not know how "the Soul of a seeing Man sees these Images, or how it receives those Ideas from such agitations in the *Sensorium*," but he is certain that the soul "can never perceive the external Bodies themselves to which it is not present" (p. 221).

Notes

1. See the Appendix to his *A Discourse concerning the Resurrection of Jesus Christ* (1712), p. 497. Speaking of nerves as 'threads' or 'fine strings' was commonplace. For details on the different physiological theories at this time, see chapter VIII of my *Thinking Matter*.

2. Newton, *Opticks*, Axiom VII.

3. Robert Hooke, *Lectures on Light* (1680), in *Posthumous Works*, ed. Waller, p. 98. The following references to Hooke are all to these lectures.

4. B. R. Singer recently reprinted selections from these writings of Hooke, with some

useful discussion of those on memory. See his "Robert Hooke on Memory, Association, and Time Perception," *Notes and Records of the Royal Society* 31 (1976):115-31.

5. *Examination of Malebranche, Works,* vol. IX, p. 217, § 10.

6. Ibid., § 9.

7. In his recent discussion of Locke and the representative theory, J. L. Mackie makes use of a device very much like Hooke's Perspective Box. "What if someone ever since birth had had a large box attached in front of his eyes, on the inside of which, for him to see, fairly faithful pictures of outside, surrounding things were somehow produced?" (*Problems from Locke*, 1976, p. 44)

8. Grove says that "I have pleaded for the same Thing in a Discourse which only waits till the favorable Reception of this shall encourage it to appear abroad" (pp. 8-9). So far I have been unable to discover any such work.

9. Cf. Cudworth, *A Treatise concerning Eternal and Immutable Morality* (1731), p. 134: "The Mind being a kind of Notional of Representative World, as it were a Diaphanous and Crystalline Sphaere, in which the Ideas and Images of all things existing in the real Universe may be reflected or represented."

10. John Norris, *An Essay towards the Theory of the Ideal or Intelligible World* (1701), vol. I, p. 166. Norris is here giving a commentary on Christopher Scheibler's discussion of the question "Whether Created things are the Object of the Divine Understanding of their own Beings, or only as they are Eminently, Ideally or Vertually contain'd in God." Norris insists that in perceiving, "I do not feel any thing that is out of my self, but I feel my very self otherwise Modified, and existing after Another manner than I did before" (p. 199).

11. Cudworth, *Treatise,* p. 150. The passage runs from page 150 to page 156, with considerable detail. The mirror analogy was not restricted to Britain. We have seen that Arnauld used it. Compare also La Mettrie, *L'Homme machine,* p. 162, in *Oeuvres philosophiques,* vol. 3 (Berlin, 1796): "The sun, the air, water, organization, form of bodies: all are arranged in the eye as in a mirror which presents faithfully to the imagination the objects which are painted there, according to laws which this infinite variety of bodies which serve vision require."

12. *The English Malady* (1733), pp. 71-72.

13. *L'Optique, science de la vision* (1966). This is a French translation of his *L'Ottica, scienza delle visione* (1955).

14. *Traité de l'homme.* Traduction et commentaire par Paul-Marie Maurin. The Preface is by Vasco Ronchi (1974).

15. Ibid., p. 29. See also his note 2, p. 51.

16. The editor points out that the two different Latin words, 'lumen' and 'lux', distinguish light as a physical phenomenon from light as a visual appearance. Ronchi stresses the importance of this distinction in the history of vision, a distinction which he laments has not always been followed. See chapter IV in his *L'Optique.* Cf. Locke's *Essay,* 3.4.10, where he distinguishes the cause of light from the *idea* of light "as it is such a particular perception in us." It is interesting, especially in view of Malebranche's inversion of 'voir', to note that St. Thomas used the same distinction between 'lumen' and 'lux' for light as a way of contrasting created light with God's intelligible light (*Sum. Theo.*, I, Q. 22, Art. 5).

17. In his *Works,* ed. Molesworth, vol. I, p. 5.

18. 'Idea' occurs with 'Phantasm' in the following passages: "As a body leaves a phantasm of its magnitude in the mind, so also a moved body leaves a phantasm of its motion, namely, an idea of that body passing out of one space into another by continual succession" (p. 94). "Now, by space I understand, here as formerly, an idea or phantasm of a body" (p. 108).

19. *Works,* vol. III, p. 1.

20. *Works,* vol. IV, p. 2.

21. Ibid., vol. III, pp. 2-3.

22. Ibid., vol. VII, pp. 27.

23. Ibid., pp. 27-28.

24. Ronchi called attention, both in his book and in the Preface to the edition of Hobbes's *De Homine*, to the differences between the optical treatises that use geometry to explain vision (most of them fall into this category) and those that attempt to examine our experience of seeing (for example, Kepler's and Hobbes's treatises). Ronchi is, as I indicated in the Introduction to this study, convinced that we are only aware of appearances, phantasms, from which we may construct, infer, or assume a world of objects. Ronchi's writings are important in helping us see at least one of the dimensions of perception theories in the seventeenth and eighteenth centuries.

25. *Works*, ed. Luce and Jessop, vol. 2, p. 234. Both the *Principles* and the *Dialogues* are in this volume.

26. The same analysis of 'exist in' is given for 'ideas in God's mind'. For example, in denying that he is following Malebranche, Philonous maintains that he does not say "I see things by perceiving that which represents them in the intelligible substance of God. This I do not understand; but I say, the things by me perceived are known by the understanding, and produced by the will, of an infinite spirit" (p. 215). It is the *"Omnipresent eternal Mind*, which knows and comprehends all things" (p. 231); the "real tree existing without" our minds "is truly known and comprehended by (that is, *exists in*) the infinite mind of God" (p. 235). To emphasize that the 'that is' phrase is meant to explicate by offering a synonym, Philonous a bit later says: "All objects are eternally known by God, or which is the same thing, have an eternal existence in his mind" (p. 252).

27. *Treatise*, p. 205.

28. *Philosophical Commentaries*, in vol. I of the Luce-Jessop edition of the *Works*. I will refer to these as PC.

29. There is in this last clause an interesting echo of Locke's suggestion that thought might be added to matter, and of the controversy that this created. In light of Berkeley's keen intention to subvert materialism, the transition from denying that thoughts can be properties of body, to denying that ideas are such properties, and thence to his assertion about ideas or thoughts being near to us, is perhaps more understandable.

30. It may also be relevant to remember those notes in PC where Berkeley says the mind or the understanding is a congeries of perceptions. See entries 580, 587, and 614. One of these (587) uses the phrase 'perceptions or ideas'.

31. *Physico-Theology; or, A Philosophico-Moral Disquisition concerning Human Nature, Free Agency, Moral Government, and Divine Providence* (1741), pp. 82-83.

32. Ibid., p. 83.

33. Richard Popkin, "Berkeley and Pyrrhonism," *Review of Metaphysics* 5 (December 1951):223-46. Reprinted in *A Treatise Concerning the Principles of Human Knowledge*, with Critical Essays, ed. Colin M. Turbayne, 1970.

34. Vol. III, p. 184.

35. *Treatise*, p. 334.

Chapter VIII

Hume on Single and Double Existence

In the 1730s, when Hume began reading in preparation for writing a treatise on the human understanding, there were a number of traditions in philosophy that had been widely explored, concepts and principles that were generally used in dealing with perception and knowledge. One tradition invoked the dictum that what is known must be present to the mind: i.e., there is no cognition at a distance. Several optical treatises addressed the question of where and how the visual image is located on or near the object. Some philosophers, such as Hobbes and Berkeley, had adapted the knowledge of the structure and workings of the eye to cognitive theories about our perception of objects. Another tradition was the dual concept of ideas, whereby ideas either became separately existing objects or were used interchangeably or in close connection with perceptions. Almost all writers believed that it was ideas or perceptions, not objects, that were present to the mind.

The move from what is present with the mind to knowledge of objects distant from the mind was sometimes made by claiming that a resemblance existed between ideas and objects, without giving much attention to the analysis of 'resemblance'. The metaphor of optical images hovered in the background. At other times, the claim was that ideas carried an internal mark of external causation: when, as Locke said, I am actually receiving sensory ideas, I cannot doubt that there are objects causing those ideas. External reference for some writers (e.g., Grove) was a matter of features built into our perceptual world by God. Skepticism was kept at bay even though ideas screen the world from us. Porterfield thought he could avoid skepticism, even though all that is present to us are our perceptions, because he retained the optical information about locating images external to us, making this external reference part of our natural, instinctive, equipment. What none of these routes to external reference yielded was a direct acquaintance with the objects of the supposed physical world. Collier's denial of an external world, while extreme, expressed the frustration engendered by what was taken to be the inevitable if natural indirectness of our perceptual knowledge.

Numerical and Specific Difference between Ideas and Objects

Both Berkeley and Hume took seriously the notion that our ideas or perceptions are objects; it was for them the ordinary, natural view of all of us. One consequence of this vulgar view seemed to be that objects took on some of the characteristics of perceptions: mind-dependency, interruptedness, relativity to perspective, discreteness of each quality. Hume saw that if sense could be made of this ordinary view, we would have to find an explanation for how we come to take perceptions, which are discontinuous and mind-dependent, to be objects, which we believe to be continuous and mind-independent. His account of how we come to believe in the existence of body is a long and involved psychological description of the workings of the mind. His summary of that account, which he calls "a short sketch or abridgment of my system," is given in the middle of his section in the *Treatise* entitled "Scepticism with regard to the senses."

When we have been accustom'd to observe a constancy in certain impressions, and have found, that the perception of the sun or ocean, for instance, returns upon us after an absence or annihilation with like parts and in like order, as at its first appearance, we are not apt to regard these interrupted perceptions as different, (which they really are) but on the contrary consider them as individually the same, upon account of their resemblance. But as this interruption of their existence is contrary to their perfect identity, and makes us regard the first impression as annihilated, and the second as newly created, we find ourselves somewhat at a loss, and are involv'd in a kind of contradiction. In order to free ourselves from this difficulty, we disguise, as much as possible, the interruption, or rather remove it entirely, by supposing that these interrupted perceptions are connected by a real existence, of which we are insensible. (p. 199)

Hume was not entirely satisfied with his account of this way of

viewing perceptions ("This supposition, or idea of continu'd existence"). His dissatisfaction reflects a suspicion that no systematic
account is possible. But in his discussion of that view, and of the
double existence of perceptions and objects, we find the most detailed
analysis in the century of both the single- and the double-existence
views.

Berkeley provided in the early part of the century a clear statement
of the two points of view. In Principle 56, he says that

men knowing they perceived several ideas, whereof they themselves were not the
authors, as not being excited from within, nor depending on the operation of
their wills, this made them maintain those ideas or objects of perception had an
existence independent of, and without the mind, without ever dreaming that a
contradiction was involved in those words. But philosophers having plainly seen,
that the immediate objects of perception do not exist without the mind, they in
some degree corrected the mistake of the vulgar, but at the same time run into
another which seems no less absurd, to wit, that there are certain objects really
existing without the mind, or having a subsistence distinct from being perceived,
of which our ideas are only images or resemblances, imprinted by those objects
on the mind.

Hume agrees with Berkeley that the notion of an external world utterly different from what we experience is inconceivable: "the notion
of external existence, when taken for something specifically different
from our perceptions" is absurd (*Treatise*, p. 188). The key phrase
here is 'specifically different'. The denial of *specific* difference does
not rule out the existence of *numerical* difference. A later passage
shows how the application of the principle about what is present to
the mind yields his conclusion of no specific difference between perceptions and external existence. "We may observe," Hume says, "that
'tis universally allow'd by philosophers, and is besides pretty obvious
of itself, that nothing is ever really present with the mind but its perceptions or impressions and ideas, and that external objects become
known to us only by those perceptions they occasion" (p. 67). In
order to conceive something specifically different from ideas and impressions, something other than ideas and impressions (i.e., objects)
would have to be present to the mind from which we could then derive an idea. We never "can conceive any kind of existence, but those
perceptions, which have appear'd in that narrow compass" of our
mind (pp. 67-68). In fact, Hume remarks, we do not think of external objects as specifically different; we only ascribe different relations
to them, e.g., continuity through time, independence of mind. Hume
does not, then, turn ideas into things (as Berkeley said he did), as his
remark about perceptions being *occasioned by* external objects

indicates, but he insists (as Berkeley did before him) that we do not and cannot think of things being essentially different from our perceptions. Hume retains an idea-object distinction.

That Hume accepts a double-existence view is clear from his remarks early in I.IV.II: "'tis in vain to ask, *Whether there be body or not*? That is a point, which we must take for granted in all our reasonings." (p. 187) His interest lies in identifying the causes that "*induce us to believe in the existence of body*." Hume is also concerned to discover what idea of body is compatible with the limitations on what we can conceive. That idea cannot be *specifically* different from our perceptions. This psychological fact (as he took it to be) about our faculty of conceiving eliminated several traditional concepts of body: the ancient appeal to substance and the modern version of substance, the corpuscular theory of matter.

Hume's discussion of both these concepts of body illustrates his appeal to conceivability. His rejection of these concepts of body is similar to Berkeley's rejection of corpuscular matter. The fundamental principle of modern philosophy is the "opinion concerning colours, sounds, tastes, smells, heat and cold; which it asserts to be nothing but impressions in the mind, deriv'd from the operation of external objects, and without any resemblance to the qualities of the objects" (p. 226). The only reason offered for this principle that Hume thinks is sound is the one based on variability of impressions. From this phenomenon it is certain, Hume argues, that "when different [incompatible] impressions of the same sense arise from any object, every one of these impressions has not a resembling quality existent in the object" (p. 227). He invokes the notion that the same object cannot at the same time have different and incompatible qualities (e.g., round and square) of the same sense. Thus "many of our impressions have no external model or archetype." These impressions are "internal existences" coming from causes they do not resemble. What this conclusion does, in treating impressions as internal existences, is to deny that they are "continu'd independent existences." Modern philosophy then moves to the next conclusion, that the primary qualities are the only real ones of which we have adequate notions. Hume cites figure, motion, gravity, and cohesion. All changes in the material world, according to this philosophy, are due to figure and motion.

Hume then offers one decisive objection to this system of secondary and primary qualities, to the attempt to distinguish internal and external existences. His objection follows Berkeley's arguments. Hume says that instead of this system explaining external objects, it utterly annihilates those objects from our conception and, as Philonous urged against Hylas, reduces us to skepticism (p. 228). For if the secondary qualities are "merely perceptions," we are unable to conceive of "a real, continu'd and independent existence." The conclusion of his argument is that modern philosophy "leaves us no just nor satisfactory idea of solidity, nor consequently of matter" (p. 229; cf. Berkeley's *Principles*, § 10-11). The steps to this conclusion are the following:

1. Motion can be conceived only with reference to some object.

2. A moving body (or our idea of a moving body) resolves into the idea of extension and solidity. That is, the reality of motion depends upon these other qualities.

3. Extension cannot be conceived except as compounded of parts that have color and solidity.

4. Unless the parts of extension are colored or solid, they are only nonentities. Without color, which the modern philosopher holds to be not real, extension can be conceived only with reference to solidity.

5. Solidity is "perfectly incomprehensible alone," without reference to other bodies, for the "idea of solidity is that of two objects, which being impell'd by the utmost force, cannot penetrate each other" (p. 228).

6. The only idea of bodies we can have, on this modern view, is of a moving, extended, solid object. But we are now back at the beginning, with step 1 above. The conclusion, then, is that we have no idea of solidity without reference to several extended, impenetrable bodies, and we can have no idea of such extended bodies without color. Thus, on the modern view, we cannot form an idea of body.

When he analyzes the more general appeal to substance, rather than that of extended, solid, and impenetrable particles, Hume traces the path that the mind takes from perceived qualities to a substance and to substantial forms. There are strong echoes of Locke and Berkeley in Hume's discussion of this notion.

'Tis confest by the most judicious philosophers, that our ideas of bodies are nothing but collections form'd by the mind of the ideas of the several distinct sensible qualities, of which objects are compos'd, and which we find to have a constant union with each other. But however these qualities may in themselves be entirely distinct, 'tis certain we commonly regard the compound, which they form, as ONE thing, and as continuing the SAME under very considerable alterations. (p. 219)

It is the "smooth and uninterrupted progress of the thought" from one successive quality to another that leads us to ascribe an identity to that series of coexisting qualities. The referent of that identity cannot be found in the series itself. Thus "the imagination is apt to feign something unknown and invisible, which it supposes to continue the same under all these variations; and this unintelligible something it calls a *substance, or original and first matter*" (p. 220).

Hume recognized that he must find a way of distinguishing between this fiction of the imagination—"that unintelligible chimera of a substance" (p. 222)—and the less objectionable fictions of his own analysis of our perceptual acquaintance, but for the moment we need only notice that his appeal is to unintelligibility: "the whole system" of substance, substantial form, and accidents "is entirely incomprehensible" (p. 222). False philosophy is distinguished from true philosophy; the latter "approaches nearer to the sentiments of the vulgar" (pp. 222-23). As with Berkeley, so with Hume: it is the beliefs of the vulgar, "the simple dictates of Nature" (Berkeley, *Dialogues*, p. 168), or our natural beliefs that serve as the touchstone of his analysis. What is the view of the vulgar? Hume lists three different kinds of qualities: (1) figure, bulk, motion, and solidity; (2) colors, tastes, smells, sounds, heat and cold; and (3) pains and pleasures. He tells us that "both philosophers and the vulgar suppose the first of these to have a distinct continu'd existence." The vulgar take the second kind in the same way. Both take the third kind to be "merely perceptions" (p. 192). Philosophy tells us that "every thing, which appears to the mind, is nothing but a perception, and dependent on the mind." The vulgar, on the other hand, "confound perceptions and objects, and attribute a distinct continu'd existence to the very things they feel or see" (p. 193). Hume points out that if our perceptions are taken to *be* objects, then of course we cannot infer objects from perceptions, nor can we form any causal argument involving both.

Presence to Mind

Hume says that it will "readily be allow'd, that . . . nothing is ever really present to the mind, besides its own perceptions" (p. 197). He does not say this time that it is philosophy that teaches this truth. He makes it clear a few pages later that he is here trying to account for "the opinions and beliefs of the vulgar with regard to the existence of body." The generality of mankind perceive only one being, he says, and "can never assent to the opinion of a double existence and representation. Those very sensations . . . are with them the true objects, nor can they readily conceive that this pen or paper, which is immediately perceiv'd, represents another, which is different from, but resembling it" (p. 202). Thus, in order to explicate the vulgar view, he tells us that he will use 'object' and 'perception' indifferently, meaning by either what "any common man means by a hat, or shoe, or stone, or any other impression, convey'd to him by his senses." The general principle is repeated: "all the unthinking and unphilosophical part of mankind (that is, all of us, at one time or another) . . . suppose their perceptions to be their only objects and never think of a double existence internal and external, representing and represented" (p. 205). He repeats this claim: " 'Tis certain, that almost all mankind, and even philosophers themselves, for the greatest part of their lives, take their perceptions to be their only objects, and suppose the very being, which is intimately present to the mind, is the real body or material existence" (p. 206).

Hume's explication of this Cartesian notion of the intimate presence of objects to the mind includes both an ontological and an epistemological component. In trying to make sense of the notion that perceptions are our only objects but nevertheless the real body or material existence is present to the mind, he distinguishes two questions. The first question is: "How we can satisfy ourselves in supposing a perception to be absent from the mind without being annihilated" (p. 207). His answer: the mind is nothing but a heap of different perceptions, united by certain relations; every perception is distinguishable and hence can be separated from this collection; hence any perception can exist apart from mind. In this way, Hume's explication provides a way of thinking about perceptions that gives them the object-like property of independence from mind. Although we may believe that the conceivability of mind-independent perceptions is questionable, it does rest on a principle that Hume argued for earlier: what is distinguishable is separable. A more puzzling feature of Hume's answer to this first question is that it appears to assume that a single perception can satisfy our notion of a body or material existence. However, I suppose that if a single perception can be conceived to exist apart from mind, a group of perceptions can also be so conceived. The point is, "this very perception or object is suppos'd to have a continu'd uninterrupted being, and neither to be annihilated by our absence, nor to be brought into existence by our presence" (p. 207). Thus perceptions can be conceived as being the very object itself. The being of objects in the mind, on this reading, is not interpreted, as with Descartes, Arnauld, Locke, and Berkeley, as 'being known'. There is a single reality—perceptions—which can be thought of as changing relations, joining or separating from the heap or collection of perceptions that is the mind. When joined, awareness of these perception-objects occurs.

Such might be called Hume's ontological analysis of objects being present to the mind, on this vulgar view of perceptions being objects. Whether Hume accepted this analysis, whether this part of the vulgar view coincides with true philosophy, may not be clear from what Hume says. He does maintain that there is no absurdity in this supposal of "separating any particular perception from the mind" (p. 207).

There is, I think, more reason to think Hume's answer to the second question does reflect his own opinion. That second question is: "After what manner we conceive an object to become present to the mind, without some new creation of a perception or image."[1] This last phrase seems to refer to his answer to the first question: new perceptions are not involved, only old ones rejoining the heap. But as he continues with his answer, we discover that a different analysis of 'present to the mind' is being suggested. The question also contains another clause: "what we mean by this *seeing*, and *feeling*, and *perceiving*," the seeing, feeling, and perceiving of objects. Here is his answer: "External objects are seen, and felt, and become present to the mind; that is, they acquire such a relation to a connected heap of perceptions, as to influence them very considerably in augmenting their number by present reflexions and passions, and in storing the memory with ideas" (p. 207). This is Hume's epistemic component in his explication of 'present to the mind'. He talks of the external object influencing the heap by augmenting the number of perceptions through reflections and passions. It is as if his account here is that objects can be present to the mind in the effects they bring about, not effects in the form of new sense perceptions, but effects in stimulating reflection on the contents of the mind. It is present reflections and passions that augment the number of perceptions in the heap.

That this epistemic, cognitive analysis *is* what Hume means by this passage should be clear to us from his general account of belief. Notice the similarity between this passage and Hume's summary statement of his general account of belief in the *Abstract*.

When the cause is presented, the mind, from habit, immediately passes to the conception and belief of the usual effect. This belief is something different from the conception. It does not, however, join any new idea to it. It only makes it be felt differently, and renders it stronger and more lively.[2]

We find in this passage the same reference to something being present to the mind, the same rejection of belief being just another perception. The reference to accompanying passions is consistent with the general nature of belief involving the addition of strength and liveliness.

There are other examples of present reflections and passions being occasioned by objects present to the mind. In *Treatise* II.II.VIII, Hume declares that there is "a general maxim, that no object is presented to the senses, nor image form'd in the fancy, but what is accompany'd with some emotion or movement of spirits proportion'd to it" (p. 373). He is there discussing such emotions as the admiration of large objects, lesser emotions coming with smaller objects. The degree of emotion that "commonly attends every magnitude of an object" influences our perception of the object: "when the emotion increases, we naturally imagine that the object has likewise increas'd" (p. 374). The transfer of the judgment of magnitude due to the accompanying emotion is just an instance of a general trait of applying "the judgments and conclusions of the understanding to the senses" (pp. 374-75). This general trait is disclosed by what Hume calls "the metaphysical part of optics" (p. 374). The factual part of optics tells us that the retinal image does not vary.

When an object augments or diminishes to the eye or imagination from a comparison with others, the image and idea of the object are still the same, and are equally extended in the *retina*, and in the brain or organ of perception. The eyes refract the rays of light, and the optic nerves convey the images to the brain in the very same manner, whether a great or small object has preceded; nor does even the imagination alter the dimensions of its object on account of a comparison with others. The question then is, how from the same impression and the same idea we can form such different judgments concerning the same object, and at one time admire its bulk, and at another despise its littleness. This variation in our judgments must certainly proceed from a variation in some perception; but as the variation lies not in the immediate impression or idea of the object, it must lie in some other impression, that accompanies it. (pp. 272-73)[3]

It is the impression of reflection to which Hume refers.

It is important to note that in these later passages Hume is relating the *sensing* of objects (retinal image, brain impression) to the *conceiving* or *judging* of objects. "Every part, then, of extension, and every unite of number has a separate emotion attending it, when conceiv'd by the mind" (p. 373). For an object to be present to the mind, it is not enough that an impression is made on the retina and conveyed to the brain. What is necessary in addition is that a judgment be made, a judgment which is then transferred (or, as Porterfield said, traced back) to the senses. Nor do we usually "judge of objects from their intrinsic value, but form our notions of them from a comparison with other objects" and from the emotion that "secretly attends every idea" (p. 375).

There are other places in the *Treatise* where Hume uses optics in order to show the difference between what is sensed and what is perceived or judged. He accepts Berkeley's claim in the *New Theory of Vision* that "our sight informs us not of distance or outness (so to speak) immediately and without a certain reasoning and experience" (p. 191). Earlier, Hume drew the same conclusion from the fact that "all bodies which discover themselves to the eye, appear as if painted on a plain surface, and that their different degrees of remoteness from ourselves are discover'd more by reason than by the senses" (p. 56). In other optical passages Hume shows that the phenomena, the appearances, do not justify some judgment. For example, that the idea of extension without visible or tangible objects standing between other objects (i.e., the idea of a vacuum) cannot be given from any of the usual distance clues.

The angles, which the rays of light flowing from them, form with each other; the motion that is requir'd in the eye, in its passage from one to the other; and the different parts of the organs, which are affected by them; these produce the only perceptions, from which we can judge of the distance. But as these perceptions are each of them simple and indivisible, they can never give us the idea of extension. (p. 58)

He offers here the examples of two luminous objects against a dark background, and the blue sky seen between my fingers when I hold up my hand, as possible cases from which the idea of empty space might be derived (pp. 56-58). He gives a careful analysis of these visual examples, and of some similar tangible ones, to show that the sensations experienced are the same whether visible objects are interposed between other objects (showing the distance between them, a filled distance) or not. In this way, Hume explains how "an invisible and intangible distance is converted into a visible and tangible one, without any change on the distant objects" (p. 59). Similarly, working from the information found in most optical treatises, about rays of light being reflected or refracted from points on the surfaces of objects and being collected in points on the retina, Hume argues that since "my senses convey to me only the impressions of colour'd points, dispos'd in a certain manner" (p. 34), our idea of extension "is nothing but a copy of these colour'd points, and of the manner of their appearance." He uses this account of our idea of extension to argue against infinite divisibility of matter and against mathematical points. As with his analysis of our idea of time, so with space and extension Hume wants to show what is and what is not conceivable, given the sensations and appearances we have. Color and tangibility are not only necessary for *sensation*, they are necessary for our *conceiving* of space and extension as well. "Upon the removal of the idea of these sensible qualities, they [the parts that make up our impressions of extension] are utterly annihilated to the thought or imagination" (pp. 38-39).

The same careful discussion of appearances, of our perceptions, is found in the "Scepticism with regard to the Senses" section. There, working from the ordinary belief that we see objects, that our perceptions are the objects, Hume wants to discover what it is about these perceptions that leads us to take them to be the objects, where objects are believed to be continuous and independent. To see or feel an external object is to have the object present to the mind. The object of course is not literally, formally, present to the mind. What then is the presence of objects to mind, what is it to see objects? Hume's answer is that an object is present to the mind, is seen or felt, when the perceptions that we take to be those objects are augmented by reflections and passions. The sorts of reflections necessary for externality are those involving continuity and independence. How, out of resemblance of perceptions, can we or do we conceive of continued existence when objects are not present to us? How is it that, given specific sensations and perceptions of knocks, footsteps, etc., we reach the idea of unseen doors, intervals of space, and time filled with unperceived objects? The phenomena of perceptions are, by themselves, insufficient for giving us the idea of externality, of independent objects being present to the mind. When Hume shows how we move from the constancy and coherence of our sense perceptions to the idea of external objects, he is showing what it must mean, on the vulgar view, for an object to become present to the mind "without some new creation of a perception or image." Just having more perceptions would not make *objects* present to the mind, would not, that is, enable the mind to conceive of objects. For perceptions by themselves are not objects; they lack the two important characteristics of continuity and independence.

Belief and Reason

Hume does not give as much attention as we might wish to elaborating his answer to the second, epistemic question about the presence of objects to the mind. That his analysis is in terms of his account of belief, that the belief in body (as belief in general) does not add new perceptions but is a way of conceiving some set of perceptions, and that this way of conceiving is due to the imagination are explicit in the passages I have cited. The belief in body was never in question. In his account of objects being present to us, given that in fact only perceptions are immediately present to the mind, Hume thinks he has described "the natural propensity of the imagination" (p. 210). The content of that belief is not, however, free of difficulty. The answer to the first question tried to conceive of perceptions as objects, as continued and independent of the mind. It takes only a little reflection, and a few simple experiments, to tell us that the "doctrine of the independent existence of our sensible perceptions is" in fact false, "contrary to the plainest experience." When philosophers reflect on phenomena such as double vision (from pressing the eyeball with a finger), they draw a distinction between "perceptions and objects, of which the former are suppos'd to be interrupted, and perishing, and different at every different return; the latter to be uninterrupted, and to preserve a continu'd existence and identity" (p. 211). Such a distinction between perceptions and objects is, however, only a temporary "palliative remedy." It does not cure the disease. The concept of an object not only distinct but different in nature from our perceptions is not intelligible. It is a desperate move made in the face of the phenomenological fact that perceptions are mind-dependent and are fleeting though similar. Hume thinks that this move would never be made were we not first convinced "that our perceptions are our only objects"; so the philosophical view of a double existence is an attempt to patch up the difficulties in the vulgar, single-existence view. But the notion of objects different in kind, specifically different, from perceptions is incoherent. Thus the philosophical, palliative remedy reduces to an arbitrary invention of "a new set of perceptions" to which the attributes of objects are ascribed (p. 218).[4] This double-existence view is not coherent.

The conflict between belief and reason is typical of Hume. What he is saying in these last passages is that no rational system can make sense of the belief in either a single or a double existence. The natural belief is in a double existence, internal and external. This belief can be explained, by reference to experience and the imagination, but there is no coherent concept that we can form of body distinct from perceptions: neither perceptions viewed as objects apart from mind, nor the invention of a second set of perceptions is intelligible. In ending his analysis of our belief in body with this examination of those philosophers who invented a second set of perceptions, Hume must have had Malebranche in mind. That way of formulating a double-existence view is given a full-scale analysis and rejection in a later section of the *Treatise*. There, this view is identified with the immaterialists, in the debate over the materiality or immateriality of the soul.[5]

This immaterialist philosophy says, Hume reminds us, that "no external object can make itself known to the mind immediately, and without the interposition of an image or perception" (p. 239). Perceptions, on this account, are properties of mind, either of finite mind or of an infinite mind. Mind was a substance, immaterial, simple, and indivisible. The rejection of this view is achieved by Hume's comparing it with the materialist account such as is found in Spinoza. These materialists talk of the system of objects. The immaterialists talk of the system of thoughts and ideas. Spinoza tells us that all the objects I observe—the sun, moon, stars, earth, seas, plants, humans, ships, houses—are not really objects (that is, are not really substances) but are only modes or modifications of a substance, a substance in which all these modes inhere, a substance which is simple, uncompounded, and indivisible. The other system, the system of thoughts, is, Hume says, a "system of beings, viz. the universe of thought, or my impressions and ideas" (p. 242). Impressions and ideas become real beings. When Hume examines this system of beings, what does he find? "There I observe another sun, moon, and stars; an earth, and seas, cover'd and inhabited by plants and animals; towns, houses, mountains, rivers; and in short, every thing I can discover or conceive in the first system" (p. 242).

We have seen that Malebranche accepted the maxim that the mind cannot know what is distant from it, that it can know only what is intimately united to the mind. In cognizing distant objects, then, we must see those objects where they are not located. What we see are other objects, other stars, moon, houses which are intimately united to our mind. There are, Malebranche said, "two sorts of beings," those that our mind sees immediately, and those that the mind knows only by means of the first sort of beings.[6] There were not many writers in Britain who took this extreme double-existence view. Hooke, as we have seen, suggested something like a double existence, without appealing to immaterial substances. Henry Grove and William Porterfield may also be taken as accepting such a view. Isaac Watts cited Malebranche's doctrine of intelligible sun, moon, and stars, and he held his own version of seeing things in the mind of God. The extreme version depicted by Hume reveals the inherent logic of the approach: thoughts, ideas, perceptions become modifications of one simple, uncompounded, and indivisible substance. There is an exact parallel, Hume wants us to note, with Spinoza's account of modes and one substance. These identical accounts, Hume remarks, have not been accorded the same reception. Spinoza's account is treated with "de-testation and scorn, and the second with applause and veneration" (p. 243). Both accounts are, Hume insists, equally unintelligible.

In his pursuit of some formulation of a double-existence view, Hume finds none that is satisfactory. Some are just incoherent: the ancient, general appeal to substance and accidents, the modern cor-puscular account with its separation of primary and secondary quali-ties. The immaterialist duplicate world of ideas or perceptions is more ridiculed than shown to be incoherent, but it is clearly rejected. One reason for its rejection is the way it is grounded in metaphysical and theological doctrine. The secular version of duplicate perceptions, presented by Hume as a response to the recognition of the false view of perceptions given by the imagination, is neither ridiculed nor found to be incoherent; it is, however, labeled 'monstrous' and hence is not satisfactory either.

Given that Hume finds fault in all these attempts to formulate a double-existence view, we might expect him at least to be tempted by a single-existence view. The imagination makes a valiant effort to preserve the single-existence view of the vulgar, but in doing so, it falsifies the nature of our perceptions, disguising the fact of their interruptedness and dependency. So the vulgar belief that our per-ceptions *are* the objects in the world cannot be accepted either. One option remains: to deny the external world entirely and to turn things into ideas. Hume recognized that such an alternative may seem a nat-ural consequence of the breakdown of the imagination's attempt to make ideas into things. But,

'tho we clearly perceive the dependence and interruption of our perceptions, we stop short in our career, and never upon that account reject the notion of an in-dependent and continu'd existence. That opinion has taken such deep root in the imagination, that 'tis impossible ever to eradicate it, nor will any strain'd metaphysical conviction of the dependence of our perceptions be sufficient for that purpose. (p. 214)

Only "a few extravagant sceptics" have ever tried to maintain this view, but they have managed to do so in words only, they "were never able to bring themselves sincerely to believe it" (p. 214; cf. pp. 215-16). The single-existence view is thus rejected; at least, it is not a pos-sible belief.

Hume makes one other attempt to find a way of thinking about an external world. Repeating his claim that we cannot conceive of "an object or external existence" specifically different from our percep-tions, he declares: "Whatever difference we may suppose betwixt them, 'tis still incomprehensible to us; and we are oblig'd either to conceive an external object merely as a relation without a relative, or to make it the very same with a perception or impression" (p. 241). The odd suggestion of conceiving "an external object merely as a relation without a relative" I take to mean that this alternative would be the concept of an object related to our perceptions (it occasions them); but we are unable to fill in any other content for that *relatum*. Such an alternative is not very acceptable, but the other route of making the object "the very same with a perception" is both unsatisfactory and false. The next paragraph in that passage even suggests that we may *suppose*, even if we cannot conceive, a specific difference between object and perception. It is because such a supposal is possible that "any conclusion we form concerning the connexion and repugnance of impressions, will not be known certainly to be applicable to objects" (p. 241). The supposal of a specific difference rules out moving from impression or perception to objects, because the conclusion we draw may be based upon just those ways in which objects differ from impressions. "'Tis still possible, that the object may differ from it in that particular" (p. 242). We can, however, go the other way: "whatever conclusion of this kind [of the connection or repugnance] we form concerning objects, will most certainly be applicable to impressions" (p. 241). Whatever reasoning or conclusion we reach about the object must be based upon our conception of the object, and that *conception* is, as we have seen, limited by being unable to go as far as our *supposal*.[7] The "quality of the object, upon which the argument is founded, must at least be conceiv'd by the mind" (p. 242). Even more interesting is Hume's remark in this passage about his attempts in I.IV.II to show how from the coherence of our perceptions we come to ascribe continuity and independence to those perceptions. Hume calls this attempt "an irregular kind of reasoning from experience." Thus Hume allows that it may not be true that "all true discoverable relations of impressions are common to objects."

With this last remark, Hume appears to allow for some specific difference between perceptions and objects. Conception still falls short of what we can suppose. Supposal (sometimes, another term for hypothesis), in a vague sort of way, supports our natural belief. That Hume believed in and defended a double-existence view, even though he was dissatisfied with all accounts of matter and the external world, is thus clear from his texts. Like most of his contemporaries, he thought knowledge was limited to experience, to the way the world appears to us. He did not think we could penetrate the secret springs and powers of nature, but that nature works in ways unavailable to us was a conviction Hume shared with most of his contemporaries. He took seriously the injunction of Locke and most other members of the Royal Society, to pay close attention to the observable features of the world. Hume's frequent reference to visual and tactual phenomena, in his account of space and time and in that on external objects, reveals both an acquaintance with optical writings and his concern to discover what we can and cannot say on the basis of the way the world appears to us. He was reluctant to claim that external objects *cause* perceptions (for reasons found in his phenomenological analysis of causal phenomena), but he was able to say that they *occasion* our perceptions. It is through the occasioning of sense perceptions that external objects become present to the mind, not sensorily present, but present to cognition. That explication in the *Treatise* which I have suggested reveals Hume's analysis of the meaning of 'present to the mind' for objects (through the thoughts and passions aroused by the sense perceptions occasioned by objects) is also found in a brief *Enquiry* passage. Excessive skepticism, Hume there says, is subverted by "the presence of the real objects, which actuate our passions and sentiments."[8] Real, external objects become present to the mind, not through the sense perceptions they occasion (though that is a necessary condition), but through the thoughts and feelings that accompany their perceptions.

Conclusion

For Hume, the question of how objects can be present to the mind is translated into the question of how we can conceive of objects. We cannot conceive of objects as being specifically different from ideas or perceptions. Thus the vulgar view is attractive: ideas *are* objects. But ideas lack the properties that even the vulgar give to objects: independence and continuity. Therefore, ideas or perceptions cannot *be* the objects. The imagination helps us think of perceptions as if they were objects by leading us to form the *belief* in the continuity and independent existence of our perceptions. This belief is not quite rational, but it gets as close as any account can to the basic truth that objects are as they appear to us in perceptual acquaintance. The objects we conceive are numerically distinct from our perceptions; there are perceptions *and* objects. Hume and Berkeley have reached the same conclusion.

Putting my reading of Hume and Berkeley together, the claims can be summarized as follows:

1. Both writers deny that they are rejecting the existence of an external world. Berkeley is especially emphatic in his account about not changing things into ideas, nor deviating from the ordinary view that I see objects.

2. Both formulate the ordinary view in much the same way, and both contrast that view with the philosopher's account, finding contradictions in that account.

3. In this chapter I have not argued that Hume's ideas are acts of awareness (that is done in chapter X), but I have indicated how this sense of 'idea' is found in Berkeley's writings. Ideas, in other words, are not entities, third things standing between perceiver and the world.

4. Moreover, Berkeley is very clear that ideas are not modes of mind, not properties of the perceiver, but are instead the very objects themselves, as cognitive contents. Hume characterizes the vulgar view in a similar way, adding to it his analysis of belief for the cognitive content.

5. The denial by Berkeley of ideas as modes of mind is a version of Descartes's discussion of objective reality, of the existence of objects in the mind.

6. 'Existence in the mind' for Berkeley turns out to mean 'known' or 'understood'. Hume offers a similar suggestion for 'present to mind'. The mind adds to my object-perceptions the belief in their continued existence.

7. Finally, both Berkeley and Hume insist that we cannot conceive of objects that are (on the substance and corpuscular views) *specifically* different (different in kind) from our ideas and perceptions. Hume is more emphatic in retaining a *numerical* distinction between ideas and objects, but Berkeley's twofold claim (that he has not denied the ordinary view of objects and that ideas are not modes of mind) indicates that he too distinguishes between ideas and objects.

The distinctions between ideas and objects which both Berkeley and Hume rejected were those that they identified with the ancient view (whereby objects were substances), the Lockean view (whereby matter is corpuscular and insensible), the Malebranchian view (whereby objects are ideas in God's mind), and, for Hume, the philosophical view (whereby objects are duplicate perceptions). The first two make objects specifically different from perceptions. The third view retains specific sameness, even identity between ideas and objects, but Hume ridicules it. Hume labels the fourth 'monstrous'.

Berkeley's objects are ideas as the things existing in the mind, as known or understood, whereas objects for Hume are ideas or perceptions conceived of and believed to be numerically different from the perceptions we actually experience.

Notes

1. There is a curious similarity between that passage from the *Treatise* and a passage from Arnauld's *Des vraies et des fausses idées* (1683). Arnauld is talking of Malebranche's representative beings, questioning the claim that they are united to the mind. How can such a being be united to my mind, Arnauld asks, without making a new modification of the mind, "that is, without the mind receiving any new perceptions"? (p. 223)

2. *An Abstract of A Treatise of Human Nature* (1740). References are to the 1965 reprint of the edition by J. M. Keynes and P. Sraffa (1938). A useful French edition of the text with introduction is Deleule's *Abrégé du Traité de la nature humaine* (1971).

3. R. F. Anderson uses this passage to argue for reading Hume's ideas as literally extended in the brain. See his "The Location, Extension, Shape, and Size of Hume's Perceptions," in *Hume: a Re-evaluation*, edited by Livingston and King (1976). I discuss Anderson's interpretation below in chapter X.

4. The discussion in the *Enquiry concerning Human Understanding* (the Selby-Bigge-Nidditch edition) of the single- and double-existence views is much less detailed but essentially the same. Men are said to be carried by instinct to trust their senses and to suppose an external universe, "which depends not on our perception." Men also always suppose "the very images, presented by the senses, to be the external object, and never entertain any suspicion, that the one are nothing but representations of the other." He cites as an example 'this very table'. But "the slightest philosophy . . . teaches us, that nothing can ever be present to the mind but an image or perception, and that the senses are only the inlets, through which these images are conveyed, without being able to produce any immediate intercourse between the mind and the object" (p. 152). Reason leads us to say that this house, this tree, "are nothing but perceptions in the mind, and fleeting copies or representations of other existences." This "pretended philosophical system" cannot, however, be justified because "the mind has never anything present to it but the perceptions, and cannot possibly reach any experience of their connexion with objects" (p. 153). The tensions between instinct and reason are no more resolved in the *Enquiry* than in the *Treatise*.

5. For a discussion of this section of the *Treatise*, see chapter III of my *Thinking Matter*.

6. In Berkeley's *New Theory of Vision*, he makes a similar remark, but about the ideas of sight and touch: "there are two sorts of objects apprehended by the eye, the one primarily and immediately, the other secondarily and by intervention of the former" (§ 50). Hume was not alone in finding Malebranche's doctrine a duplication of the world of ordinary objects. In his *Examination of Malebranche*, Locke questioned the same point, charging Malebranche with skepticism of real objects, with being unable to say there is a sun and stars in the sky. Arnauld also remarked that Malebranche's philosophy transports us into an unknown country, "where men no longer have true knowledge of each other, nor even of their own bodies, nor of the sun and stars which God has created." What we see instead are intelligible sun and stars, intelligible bodies. (*Des vraies et des fausses idées*, pp. 227-28)

7. This distinction between supposal and conception reminds us of Kant's distinction between knowing and knowledge, or the treatment given to the ideas of reason, ideas which go beyond the categories.

8. *Enquiry concerning Human Understanding*, p. 159.

Chapter IX

Hume on Imagination:
A Magical Faculty
of the Soul

In the eighteenth century there was an aesthetic response which Eric Rothstein has characterized as creating in the imagination aspects of scenes, parts of figures, not presented in the poetry or painting. Illusory realism, or what he tells us Lord Kames called 'ideal presence', was practiced by artists and poets: the spectator was expected to fill out what was only hinted or suggested. Rothstein quotes a remark by Jean Starobinski (*The Invention of Liberty*, 1964) that the eighteenth-century observer's pleasure "lay in completing mentally, in a complicity of the imagination, the work that the artist has abandoned." Using the art historian's notion of *nonfinito* — "a work which the artist *intended* to leave unfinished, like a torso or sketch" — Rothstein's analysis suggests some fascinating parallels to Hume's conception of imagination.[1] In the section on presence to mind which we examined in the previous chapter, we saw that the natural propensity of the imagination fills out and extends to what is present to us. It is as if nature has presented us with an unfinished sensory sketch which we are expected to complete. Nature has in fact also given us the natural inclination to complete that sketch.

When we trace all that the imagination does for Hume, we discover that its role in the skepticism section is by no means atypical. The imagination turns out to be the dominant — one could almost say, the only — faculty or operation of the understanding. That Hume intended to replace the usual three or four operations by one only, he explicitly indicates in a very important note in the *Treatise* (pp. 96-97). He there cites the usual three faculties to be found in all the current logics: conception (sometimes called simple apprehension), judgment, and reasoning. He levels certain criticisms against the latter two, concluding that

what we may in general affirm concerning these three acts of the understanding is, that taking them in a proper light, they all resolve themselves into the first, and are nothing but particular ways of conceiving our objects. Whether we consider a single object, or several; whether we dwell on these objects, or run from them to others; and in whatever form or order we survey them, the act of the mind exceeds not a simple conception . . .

The only act of the understanding is conception, an act which has various forms but which always consists in entertaining one or more ideas. Hume's note charts a radical departure from all other contemporary logics. The new, eighteenth-century British logics, together with the Port Royal and Crousaz logics, were, as we have seen, epistemic logics. They were all treatises of the human understanding. Hume's *Treatise*, book I, is his logic. Just as radical as his reduction of the faculties to a single operation of the understanding is his exposure of the impotence of reason. Reasoning is replaced by the smooth flow of the imagination along resembling ideas. The faculty of imagination is a faculty of conception; imagining is one form of conceiving. We can probably say that there are two basic forms of conception in Hume's logic, simple apprehension of what is present to the mind, and imagination which goes beyond what is present to simple apprehension. In detailing the workings of the imagination, Hume thought he was supplying what other eighteenth-century logics also claimed, a natural, as opposed to an artificial, logic.

We need to move through book I of the *Treatise*, noting what Hume says about the imagination: what it does, how it works, what principles control its operation. In this way, we shall come to appreciate the encompassing nature of the imagination in Hume's logic. Such a survey will also prepare us for our next task, a reconstruction of Hume's ideas.

The Universe of the Imagination

It is of interest that the imagination is not mentioned at all in the introduction to the *Treatise*. There, reason and reasoning are mentioned, and experience and observation are praised as the methods for building a science of human nature. Logic is even said to have as its sole end, "to explain the principles and operations of our reasoning faculty, and the nature of our ideas" (p. xix). Principles there are in the *Treatise*, but they are principles of the imagination, not of reason. Perhaps we should say, principles of conceiving, if we follow Hume's remark in that note.

The early pages of book I, section I set the stage for one of the main activities of the imagination: conceiving what is not present to the mind. "I can imagine to myself such a city as the *New Jerusalem*, whose pavement is gold and walls are rubies" (p. 3). A few pages later, we find the missing-shade-of-blue example: given a series of different shades of a color with a missing shade in the series, we can supply that missing shade from our imagination. We do this by raising up to ourselves the idea of that particular shade (p. 6). Impressions are also copied by the memory and imagination. Imagination is that faculty whereby we repeat our impressions but without any of the vivacity the impression had. The result is what Hume calls 'a perfect idea' (pp. 8-9). The imagination is not restrained by the order of the impressions. In this way, fables and romances are formed by the "liberty of the fancy" (p. 10). Hume announces a rule at this point: "Wherever the imagination perceives a difference among ideas, it can easily produce a separation." In such literary productions, "Nature there is totally confounded" (p. 10). The confounding of nature by the imagination is not, however, restricted to poets and romancers. We shall discover that it is a basic feature of the imagination.

The operation of the imagination in uniting ideas is governed by some universal principles, those of the relations of resemblance, contiguity, and cause and effect (p. 11). The association of ideas, in other words, is a function of these three relations and the faculty of the imagination. It is the imagination that runs from one idea to another, resembling idea. It is the imagination that, in conceiving of different objects, runs "along the parts of space and time." Connections are said to be in the fancy; objects are said to be connected there. The three relations are the principles of union or cohesion of ideas; they supply, in the imagination, "the place of the inseparable connexion, by which they are united in our memory." Hume refers to this connection of ideas as a kind of attraction (pp. 12-13). It is in the imagination that one idea naturally introduces another (p. 13). Hume also speaks of 'drawing out' in the imagination all the ideas associated with a word. Sometimes in these passages, it is the mind, rather than the imagination, that is given credit for these tasks. This may be a natural ambiguity, for later passages come close to identifying the mind with the imagination.

Hume speaks of the entrance in the imagination of individuals, although he must mean the *ideas* of individuals (p. 23). The imagination has a readiness to suggest its ideas. This is a very active faculty; it (he says 'fancy' here) "runs from one end of the universe to the other in collecting ideas, which belong to any subject" (p. 24). This collection is said to be done by a kind of magical faculty in the soul.

In discussing space and time, and the issue of infinite divisibility, Hume rejects the notion that the mind has an infinite capacity. One instance of this is the fact that the imagination "reaches a *minimum*" (p. 27). This means that the imagination can raise up an idea "of which it cannot conceive any sub-division, and which cannot be diminished without a total annihilation." He may be taken to draw a contrast between having a distinct *idea* of large numbers and forming the *images* that represent things. But he also moves back and forth between 'idea' and 'image', so we should be cautious when drawing an inference about such a contrast. He even occasionally speaks of images or impressions (p. 27), although this passage is concerned with showing the similarity between a sensible minimum and the minimum of the imagination. He asserts the mind's ability to form very tiny ideas, ideas of tiny objects, e.g., the idea of the smallest atom of the animal spirits (p. 28). "Nothing can be more minute, than some ideas, which we form in the fancy; and images which appear to the senses": an odd (perhaps an optical) use of 'image' in relation to the senses. The ability to imagine becomes the limits of the possible: "*nothing we imagine is absolutely impossible*" (p. 32). That it is the imagination that does the conceiving is indicated by Hume's question, "can time be conceived without our conceiving a succession of objects?" (p. 36) This is the same question as "can time alone form a distinct idea in the imagination?" When we think we can form such an idea, we are only using a fiction, as when we apply the idea of time to that which does not change (p. 37). It is this fictive role of the imagination that proves very important for Hume; it is similar to the confounding of nature.

Another example of conceivability is given on pp. 38-39: without color and tangibility, objects or qualities are not conceivable by the mind; they are annihilated "to the thought or imagination." In his discussion of extension and colored points, Hume suggests that we aid our fancy by conceiving these points to be of different colors. The ink-spot example is used: the imagination finds it difficult to break that spot into parts. There are also imaginary attempts by the mind, for example, in geometry. Another fiction of the mind appears here, that of an imaginary standard of equality (p. 48). This is a *natural* fiction: the mind carries on "even after the reason has ceas'd."

There are other similar examples of imaginary standards, in music, in painting. In each of these, the mind moves out beyond what it has experienced to a perfect tune, a perfect beauty (pp. 49-52). What nature does not supply to the senses, the imagination supplies to the mind in conception.

Another fictive idea is that of a vacuum, the idea of space without any objects. Such an idea is like the idea of time without any change of objects (p. 53). Not only does the imagination fill out and supply what is not given, it can break apart in conception what is in fact not separate: "every idea, that is distinguishable, is separable by the imagination," and every idea that is so separable by the imagination may be conceived to be separately existent (p. 54). Adding, subtracting, and even substituting are all acts of the imagination: "wherever there is a close relation betwixt two ideas, the mind is very apt to mistake them, and in all its discourse and reasoning to use the one for the other" (p. 60). There are some limits on what is conceivable, on what is imaginable: " 'tis impossible for us so much as to conceive or form an idea of any thing specifically different from ideas and impressions." We can "chace our imagination to the heavens, or to the utmost limits of the universe; we never really advance a step beyond ourselves, nor can conceive any kind of existence, but those perceptions, which have appear'd in that narrow compass" (pp. 67-68). The *universe of the imagination* is circumscribed in this way; the liberty of the imagination is bound by the *type* of existences present in our experience. It was this fact about the imagination which played so important a role in Hume's analysis of our conception of the external world. Being bound by the *type* of objects still leaves plenty of room for the imagination to roam over past and future experience, as well as over that which experience does not disclose. The imagination can conceive of an object coming into being without a cause (pp. 70-80); it can feign "any past scene of adventure," even invent new fictions. In all these activities, Hume's imagination is in the tradition of that close association between conception and the fancy which runs from Hobbes to Reid. Imagination is the conception of an absent object. The imagination fills out what the senses do not supply; it enables us to go beyond what is not present, although there is that ultimate limit on what is conceivable: it must be similar to what has been experienced.

The Reality Principle

In his analysis of natural belief, Hume speaks of *the mind* passing from an idea or impression of an object to the idea or belief of another object. In doing this, the mind is not determined by reason but by "certain principles, which associate together the ideas of these objects, and unite them in the imagination" (p. 92). This union is also said to take place in the fancy. There is also an association between words and ideas; it is the imagination again that supplies the associated idea upon hearing the word (p. 93). What is important for this last association is the stress Hume places on understanding the meaning of propositions. Even when propositions, which someone asserts, are false, even when belief does not attend my entertaining these propositions, "'tis evident, that notwithstanding my incredulity, I clearly understand his meaning, and form all the same ideas" (p. 95). Throughout this passage, conceiving goes along with the imagination, the imagination is described as a force for conceiving both sides of a question. The understanding or imagination is even described as drawing inferences from past experiences, but this turns out to be unconscious, unreflective movements of the mind (p. 104). It is the three relations of resemblance, contiguity, and cause and effect that are the "associating principles of thought"; these principles are capable of "conveying the imagination from one idea to another" (p. 107).

It was important for Hume to distinguish between reality and "mere fictions of the imagination," especially when characterizing belief (p. 108). He speaks to this distinction in an insert for p. 97. Assent to an idea "*feels* different from a fictitious idea, that the fancy alone presents to us" (p. 629). Belief, by means of the special manner of conceiving, is "that act of the mind, which renders realities more present to us than fictions." The imagination by itself can never reach belief. The reality principle for Hume is the cause-and-effect relation. The imagination does not always work with this principle.

The imagination has the command over all its ideas, and can join, and mix, and vary them in all the ways possible. It may set them, in a manner, before our eyes in their true colours, just as they might have existed. (p. 629)

Without the causal principle, the imagination cannot reach belief. The causal principle seems to introduce some controls into the normal activity of the imagination. The cause-and-effect principle enables us to "people the world" with those objects that "lie beyond the reach of the senses and memory" (p. 108). This extended world is painted in my imagination, as are any perceptions not immediately present to me, but the world of the imagination guided by cause and effect is distinguished from the mere offsprings of the imagination by its greater uniformity and its conformity with past uniformities of experience. The first two relations, of resemblance and contiguity, assist the third relation in giving us their realities, the system of realities; but when they operate on the imagination by themselves, the first two relations exert only a "very feeble and uncertain influence on the fancy" (p. 109).

One instance of the feigning of the imagination without the reality principle is found in poetry. When such feigning is done arbitrarily and "of our mere goodwill," it has little effect upon the mind. These fictions, based only on the resembling and contiguity relations, are "founded on so little reason, that nothing put pure *caprice* can determine the mind to form" them. They arise in the imagination "from a feign'd resemblance and contiguity" (p. 110). The cause-and-effect principle "is requisite to persuade us of any real existence" (p. 109). The imagination is at work in both cases, in working toward a system of realities on the basis of cause and effect, and in producing mere fictions, based on feigning and the other two relations. The proper effects of custom and cause and effect are contrasted with the "loose floating images of the fancy" (p. 116). Hume even refers to two kinds of custom, having in mind the false beliefs acquired in our youth: "Custom may lead us into some false comparison of ideas" (p. 116). The repetition of falsehoods can replace the impressions of sense and memory, leading our judgment or imagination to link other ideas (p. 117).

Truth and assent are even important for poetic productions. Judgment must give assent to the images presented to our fancy before we can take pleasure in literary discourses. For such assent, truth is necessary. Thus, even for entertainment, truth and reality are necessary. Hume recognizes that some ideas may influence and entertain the imagination from some other principles than those of truth and reality (p. 121), as in some poetical systems. Nevertheless, the poet or the dramatist does not ignore reality altogether. The tragedian may borrow names from history as a way of gaining easy reception in the imagination (p. 122). Comic poets use personages and incidents that are "the pure offspring of the fancy," and "belief must please the imagination." But equally, "a vigorous and strong imagination is of all talents the most proper to procure belief and authority" (p. 123). Without the reality principle in some way at work in such productions, there is a danger that "a lively imagination very often degenerates into madness or folly" (p. 123). Sometimes such madness has a physiological cause, as when the imagination is affected by some "extraordinary ferment of the blood and spirits" (p. 123). He tends to except the poet from folly, even though the poet works with "a counterfeit belief." There are, in Hume's brief treatment of literary uses of the imagination and counterfeit belief, three different cases of belief and imagination: the cases in which the imagination and belief work from truth and reality (gaining their force and vivacity from the reality principle); the arbitrary cases in which truth and reality are in part borrowed or feigned; and the cases in which the imagination degenerates into folly and madness.

Natural Logic and Normative Rules

The reality principle gives us a basis in past experience for our expectations of the future. What we believe will happen is a function of what has happened. Hume's analysis of probability, of what he calls 'the probability of causes', is done in terms of belief. The negation of causes, chance, leaves the imagination "perfectly indifferent" to consider the existence or nonexistence of some object. The "native situation" of the mind is that of indifference. In the case of throwing a die, our knowledge of gravity, of cubes, of solidity, etc., is brought to bear on our imagination, causing us to form certain expectations (p. 128). The difficulty we have in predicting which side will turn up is traced to the imagination. "The imagination passes from the cause, *viz.* the throwing of the die, to the effect, *viz.* the turning up one of the six sides; and feels a kind of impossibility both of stopping short in the way, and of forming any other idea" (p. 129). In another example—where it was observed in the past that of twenty ships leaving port, only nineteen returned—Hume speaks of images appearing to the mind. The way in which the various images of past observations unite renders the idea of the number of returning ships stronger and livelier, "not only than a mere fiction of the imagination, but also than any idea, which is supported by a lesser number of experiments" (p. 135).

The psychological conclusion that Hume draws from these examples is that an inference about the future cannot be merely drawn by the understanding. The transference of the past to future must be "some operation of the *fancy*" (p. 140). After we have become accustomed to seeing one object united to another, our imagination "passes from the first to the second, by a natural transition, which precedes reflection, and which cannot be prevented by it" (p. 147). Hume does remark that the imagination sometimes moves to the effect even though all it has to work with are the accidental or superfluous circumstances of cause and effect. This is a propensity to make the customary transition, but to do so too hastily, on inadequate grounds. This propensity can be corrected through reflection. The naturalness of the imagination in making such transitions, even when it functions on the basis of insufficient evidence, is contrasted with "the authentic operations of the understanding" (p. 150). What the authentic operations are, however, are the workings of the imagination under control of specific rules, normative rules for drawing conclusions about the future around the cause-effect relation. It should not be surprising to find some normative rules incorporated in a logic, even in a logic of the natural workings of the mind. But there is a tension in Hume's logic between the descriptive, natural features of the workings of the mind (especially of the imagination) and the normative regulations. The distinction between 'mere fictions' and fictions properly formed may fall outside the natural logic of the *Treatise*.

The prescriptive rules for drawing conclusions about cause and effect (pp. 173-75) are given much less attention than the descriptive accounts of the workings of the imagination. In addition to those passages we have already noted in his account of causal inferences, Hume remarks that the imagination, "in running from the present impression to the absent idea," does so more easily and also conceives of the object with greater force, when the connection is common and universal. Reasoning is also more convincing the less activity the imagination has to contribute (pp. 151, 153). Even when Hume does not use the term 'imagination' in his account of causal expectations or of the feeling of necessity (the feeling of passing or the propensity to pass from one object to its usual attendant), he describes the workings of the understanding under conditions that generate belief and the easy transition of the mind. As we have seen, these are the activities of imagination. His second definition of 'cause' makes it clear what role the imagination plays: "An object precedent and contiguous to another, and so united with it in the imagination, that the idea of the one determines the mind to form the idea of the other" (p. 172).

Suppositions and False Beliefs

The tension between the natural operations of the imagination and that faculty working under the guidance of normative controls surfaces in a more virulent form in part IV of the first book of the *Treatise*. We had a glimpse of the imagination at work in this context when we examined Hume's account of the single- and double-existence view. We saw Hume tracing the belief in a distinct and continued existence to the imagination: this belief arises from the concurrence of some of the qualities of our impressions (coherence and constancy) "with the qualities of the imagination" (p. 194). Such a belief is sometimes termed a 'supposition', a supposition which may seem similar to those conclusions drawn from cause and effect but which, Hume insists, arises from "the understanding, and from custom in an indirect and oblique manner" (p. 197). The supposition of a distinct and continued existence can never be "the direct and natural effect of the constant repetition and connexion," but must be the result of other principles. He then reminds us of the principle cited in I.II.IV (pp. 48, 50-51), that once set in train, the imagination "is apt to continue, even when its object fails it." He uses the galley-oars example as an analogy of the way the mind continues on even when impressions have stopped. He also refers back to his discussions of perfect standards (in mathematics, in art, in morals), as additional examples of this principle. The belief in a continued existence is thus a result of this quality of the imagination, together with the qualities of coherence and constancy of our sense impressions. This belief gives us another example of how the imagination confounds nature, forming or feigning fictions. The feigning in this case covers over real gaps in our impressions, acting as if there is a continuity. Our imagination supplies us with the notion of "a real existence, of which we are insensible" (p. 199).

It is by a similar deception that a succession of related objects puts the mind in the same disposition, "and is consider'd with the same smooth and uninterrupted progress of the imagination, as attends the view of the same invariable object." Our thought slides along the succession with as much facility as it does when it considers a single object. In this way, succession is confounded with identity. He gives the example of surveying his room, shutting his eyes, and then opening them. The new perceptions resemble the old ones. This resemblance connects the ideas of the interrupted perceptions. The mind is conveyed from one to another; the imagination makes an easy transition "along the ideas of these different and interrupted perceptions" (p. 204). The opinion "that any of our objects, or perceptions are identically the same after an interruption" is a result of the imagination being "seduced into such an opinion" (p. 209). The imagination is perverted. Both the fiction of a continued existence and the supposed identity are false. The natural propensity of the imagination leads to false beliefs (p. 210).

Hume goes on to say that there are "no principles of the understanding or fancy, which lead us directly to embrace" the double-existence view either. By its original tendency, the imagination would never be led to such an opinion. The only view that does have a direct recommendation to the imagination, which is in fact "the most natural of any," is the common view that our perceptions are our only objects and that they continue to exist when not perceived (p. 213). This view has a *primary* recommendation to the fancy. The double-existence view acquires its influence on the imagination from the common-sense view. Hume seems to conclude from the fact that the philosophic system does take hold of many minds that it must influence the imagination. The acceptance of any opinion or supposition is a function of the imagination. Hume gives the details on the functioning of the imagination in other modes of conceiving: in thinking, reflecting, reasoning (pp. 213-14). He presents the double-existence view of the philosophers as pleasing our reason, in the sense that it allows perceptions to be interrupted and different, while pleasing our imagination in giving a continued existence to something else. The imagination tells us "that our resembling perceptions have a continued and uninterrupted existence." But in doing so, our imagination already goes against the facts. Reflection tells us that even our resembling perceptions are interrupted and different. We elide the incompatibility of these two views by ascribing each of the qualities to different objects: the interruption to perceptions, the continuous existence to objects. The latter is a new fiction; we feign a double existence and then ascribe these qualities to different objects. The opinion that external objects resemble our perceptions is also derived from the fancy. From the fact that "we never can conceive any thing but perceptions," Hume concludes that it is the imagination which operates here (p. 216). The ideas of the existence of objects and perceptions are "united together in the fancy" by the relation of cause and effect, and we naturally add the resemblance notion as a way of completing the union. He cites the principle: "We have a strong propensity to compleat every union by joining new relations to those which we have before observ'd betwixt any ideas."

In his concluding paragraphs to this section on skepticism with regard to the senses, Hume reflects that he began this subject "with premising, that we ought to have an implicit faith in our senses" (p. 217). He now has "a quite contrary sentiment, and am more inclin'd to repose no faith at all in my senses, or rather imagination." Why the switch in mid-sentence, from 'senses' to 'imagination'? The answer would seem to be that the senses have been shown to be limited to the present, both in time and in space. It has been the imagination that has tried to go beyond the senses, but Hume confesses now that

"I cannot conceive how such trivial qualities of the fancy, conducted by such false suppositions, can ever lead to any solid and rational system." In the final paragraph of this section, he speaks only of reason and the senses, remarking that "'tis impossible upon any system to defend either our understanding or senses" (p. 218). Reference to the imagination disappears. No *rational* account of our belief in external existence has been produced. The double-existence view, in which the imagination has been seduced, is the one which he predicts we all have when we cease trying, by reason, to justify that view. Thus it would appear that the natural operation of the imagination which leads to this belief has been accounted for by Hume on the basis of a descriptive analysis of the workings of the imagination.

Imagination as the Judge of Philosophical Systems

In the next section, "Of the Antient Philosophy," Hume traces a number of false, even meaningless, concepts to the imagination. He says that the imagination readily takes one idea for another, where their influence on the mind is similar (p. 220). He speaks of the progress of thought and of those easy transitions that deceive the mind. Faced with contradictions of identity in change, "the imagination is apt to feign something unknown and invisible, which it supposes to continue the same under all these variations." Here, Hume is accounting for the notion of substance, a notion of the ancients which he rejects. What is interesting about his accounting for the origin of this idea is that he traces it to the imagination. It is generated in the same way as he has just said, in the previous section, the idea of perceptions that continue to exist is generated. Do both products of the imagination, then, have to be rejected? If not, how does he distinguish them? He gives a similar analysis for 'simplicity', where the fancy misses the compound, nonsimple nature of some objects and treats them as simple. This mistake is also traced to the imagination (p. 221). The whole of the ancient system of philosophy is, Hume asserts, based upon such fictions: substances, substantial forms, occult qualities are all "derived from principles as natural as any" (p. 222). Every "trivial propensity of the imagination" produces the peripatetic's sympathies and antipathies (p. 224).

Hume sees that he must find a way of drawing a distinction between those fictions of the imagination that are acceptable and those that are not. He confronts the question directly.

But here it may be objected, that the imagination, according to my own confession, being the ultimate judge of all systems of philosophy, I am unjust in blaming the ancient philosophers for making use of that faculty, and allowing themselves to be entirely guided by it in their reasonings. (p. 225)

It is important to notice Hume's statement that he makes the imagination the ultimate judge of all systems of philosophy, for this seems to confirm our reading of the final paragraph of the section on skepticism and the senses: it is the belief system of the imagination that wins out. Here, in answering the question about differentiating acceptable from unacceptable fictions of the imagination, he talks of two kinds of principles in the imagination. The one kind are "permanent, irresistible, and universal." He cites as an example, "the customary transition from causes to effects, and from effects to causes" (p. 225). The other kind of principles of the imagination are those "which are changeable, weak, and irregular," such as those leading the ancients to their fictions. What is important in this distinction is not whether Hume can defend it or not. What is important is to find him saying that the first kind of principles of the imagination "are the foundation of all our thoughts and actions." To remove or fail to follow these principles would be to undermine human nature: human nature would "perish and go to ruin." The other sort of principles are not necessary or useful. Both kinds of principles are natural, but the second kind are so only in the way that "a malady is said to be natural."

Hume is on safe ground in claiming that the principle governing the transition of our thought from customary uniformities in the past to expected uniformities in the future is the foundation for human nature, because we probably could not function in the world without a belief in the uniformity of nature, without the natural acceptance of such a belief. Does this principle govern only those causal inferences? Are those beliefs the only ones coming under this principle, are there in fact other *good* principles? Does Hume really want to say that the belief in objects *and* perceptions is no better than the ancient beliefs in substance, substantial forms, sympathies, and so on? It would seem not, since it is the belief in external and internal existences that we all have, and that is our basis for acting. But such a belief does not appear to be a product of causal inferences.

We may get some light on this problem from the next object of Hume's attack. Modern philosophy is no better than the ancients'. It too draws conclusions on the basis of the second sort of principles of the imagination, conclusions, e.g., about primary and secondary qualities. Hume concludes this section with the remark that our reason and our senses are in conflict. He reformulates the opposition as one between "those conclusions we form from cause and effect, and those that persuade us of the continu'd and independent existence of body" (p. 231). This conclusion seems to place the double-existence view on the same footing as the belief in substance or substantial forms.

The imagination continues to play its role as Hume goes into a discussion of the immateriality of the soul. Remarking on the principle that he sometimes assigns to the imagination—"we have a strong propensity to add some new relation" to unite objects "in order to compleat the union"—Hume traces to this principle our propensity to feign a conjunction in place when objects are contiguous in time (p. 238). This is a mistake, he tells us, so this is a propensity that Hume discredits. He gives as an instance of it "the *inclination* of our fancy by which we are determin'd to incorporate the taste with the extended object." In this case, Hume insists that reason prevails over the imagination, in order to convince us that the natural inclination leads us to a false conclusion.

Similarly with personal identity. What gives us so great a propensity to ascribe an identity to our successive perceptions? Before answering, he draws the distinction between personal identity "as it regards our thought or imagination" and as it "regards our passions" (p. 253). As he did earlier, he speaks of the action of the imagination "by which we consider the uninterrupted and invariable objects, and that by which we reflect on the succession of related objects." These two actions are "almost the same to the feeling" (p. 254). It is this smooth transition from related objects to taking them as one, which makes a substitute identity for related objects. He refers to this propensity as a mistake. We find it difficult, though, not to make this substitution, even when we are aware of the mistake of doing so. In order to justify to ourselves the making of this substitution, "we often feign some new and unintelligible principle." He instances as such feignings "the continu'd existence of the perceptions of our senses" (p. 254) (as a way of removing their real interruption) and the running together of 'soul', 'self', and 'substance' (to disguise the differences). He again speaks of fictions for these attempts. The fiction for identity is said to be "either of something invariable and uninterrupted, or of something mysterious and inexplicable" (p. 255). But the running together of diversity and identity is said to be the result of "an easy transition of the imagination" (p. 255).

When the changes in a series are considerable and obvious, we scruple to ascribe identity. By an artifice we may induce the imagination to advance a step farther. That artifice is to refer the changes to a common end, as in the repair of a ship. When we add a "*sympathy* of parts," as in plants and animals, this move of the imagination is even easier. But such ascriptions of identity are in strictness wrong. The same is true for personal identity. It too is fictitious, proceeding from "a like operation of the imagination" (p. 259). Hume then raises the question whether the identity we ascribe to the mind is a relation "that really binds our several perceptions together, or only associates their ideas in the imagination" (p. 259). Is it a real bond among perceptions, or the feeling of one among the ideas we form of the perceptions? It is the latter alternative that Hume asserts (p. 260). He then reaffirms that it is only the three relations of resemblance, contiguity, and cause and effect that "can give ideas an union in the imagination" (p. 260). These principles are characterized now as the uniting principles in *the ideal world*, the world of ideas.

Conclusion

It is tempting to read Hume as suggesting that the reality principle, the cause-effect relation, is also the test for meaningfulness. It is not easy to determine how many of the fictions of the imagination are traceable to the workings of this principle.

> Experience is a principle, which instructs me in the several conjunctions of objects for the past. Habit is another principle, which determines me to expect the same for the future; and both of them conspiring to operate upon the imagination, make me form certain ideas in a more intense and lively manner, than others, which are not attended with the same advantages. (p. 265)

Were some ideas not enlivened more than others, "we cou'd never assent to any argument, nor carry our view beyond those few objects, which are present to the senses" (ibid.). Moreover, without the activity of the imagination, we could never attribute any existence to the objects present to us except a sense-dependent existence. Without the imagination, we would have to limit our claims and our beliefs to the present.

> Nay farther, even with relation to that succession [of perceptions], we cou'd only admit of those perceptions, which are immediately present to our consciousness, nor cou'd those lively images, with which the memory presents us, be ever receiv'd as true pictures of past perceptions. (p. 265)

From these remarks, Hume concludes that the imagination (he refers to it as a faculty but also as a princple) must be followed, even though it is inconstant and fallacious. It leads us into errors, but they are errors we depend on if we are to escape something like a solipsism of the present moment. It is, after all, this principle of the imagination "which makes us reason from causes and effects; and 'tis the same principle, which convinces us of the continu'd existence of external objects, when absent from the senses" (p. 266). The difficulty for Hume is that the reality principle and the other two associative principles often lead the imagination into incompatible views. In the *Conclusion* to book I of the *Treatise*, Hume reflects on how best to deal with the incompatibilities of the imagination. That the imagination cannot be ignored is clear; the other operations of the mind depend upon it: "The memory, senses, and understanding are, therefore, all of them founded on the imagination, or the vivacity of our ideas" (p. 265).[2]

The imagination is a producer of fictions, of illusions. How far should we yield to these illusions? On the one hand, Hume says, we cannot assent to "every trivial suggestion of the fancy." The "flights of the imagination" are dangerous to reason. On the other hand, it is equally dangerous to "adhere to the understanding," or to what he seems to equate with the understanding, "the general and more establish'd properties of the imagination" (p. 267). The result of this latter course is full skepticism. We save ourselves from such total skepticism "only by means of that singular and seemingly trivial property of the fancy, by which we enter with difficulty into remote views of things" (p. 268).

Notes

1. See Eric Rothstein's article, "'Ideal Presence' and the 'Non Finito' in Eighteenth-Century Aesthetics," in *Eighteenth-century Studies* 9, no. 3 (Sept. 1976):307-32.

2. The *Abstract* also ends with a reference to "the empire of the imagination," maintaining that the imagination has "a great authority over our ideas" (p. 31).

Chapter X

Hume's Ideas

The accounts of perceptual acquaintance in eighteenth-century Britain were a mixture of optical and psychological analyses. To the extent that the optical analogy dominated, writers were pushed toward skepticism; the optical array becomes a screen obscuring the external world, or the question becomes one of discovering the conditions under which that array is located on the object. To the extent that writers were able to distinguish optical from psychological or cognitive language, the traditional questions about our knowledge of an external world were turned into questions of conception, of understanding. This latter move is closely related to perceptual optics, for our idea, our notion, our conception of the physical world is derived from the way that this world appears to us. Hume's analysis, like Berkeley's, was an attempt to determine what the appearances are and what we do with those appearances, how they enable us to make judgments. Appearances for Hume cover appearances to the eye, in the phenomenological sense of how we see objects under specific conditions, but his interest in the phenomenology of seeing was put to the service of his more fundamental interest in cognitive psychology. What both Hume and Alexander Pope called 'the anatomy of the mind' marks the growing attention paid to cognitive psychology during the century. This anatomy of the mind, like its medical counterpart, was dedicated to a detailed description of the parts and functional relations of the structures examined. Both anatomies had a curative, therapeutic goal as well: from an accurate account of the anatomical structures, cures could be effected; at least, some regimen rules could be extracted. The differences between the older, artificial logics and the newer, natural ones lay precisely there: the latter constructed the rules for the direction of the mind from an account of the natural workings of the mind. Another difference is that the newer logics were more dedicated to descriptive anatomy than to normative rules.[1]

It is in the descriptive account that Hume's analysis of our conceptualizations helps us understand the direction perceptual-acquaintance analyses were taking. Hume's account of the vulgar or ordinary belief in a single existence gave us an explication of 'present to the mind' in terms of further *thoughts* about the appearances to sense. From perceptions of a certain sort, the mind moves naturally and easily to the idea of external existence. Hume replaced the optical concerns about the location of images with the cognitive account of our ideas or conception of externality. Hume's reduction of all the operations of the mind to conception is less important, though radical, than what this reduction signals: that his logic is primarily concerned with psychology, the psychology of belief, of understanding, of awareness. As with the other new logics, and in the tradition of most of the writers using the way of ideas, Hume takes ideas to be the medium of conception. His logic is one of acts and contents. What can we say about the nature of those contents of the acts of conceiving?

Brain Impressions or Thoughts?

Commentators on Hume tend to take his ideas as images, staying close in their reading to visual, optical language. Hume's talk of ideas resembling or copying or as the faint images of impressions is seized upon (without much critical explication of 'image') to support such an interpretation. Most eighteenth-century critics of the way of ideas followed this reading. Reid grouped Hume with Descartes, Arnauld, and Locke, contending that they all took the term 'idea' in this way. Ideas as entities, as objects, was the easy reading of 'image'. There is another candidate for ideas as entities, the brain impression. In his early writings, Descartes coupled 'image' with 'idea' in this sense, an impression on the pineal gland. One recent forceful account of Hume argues that the hidden agenda in Hume's writings (not always hidden, either, he claims) is the acceptance of ideas and impressions as *brain* impressions.[2]

Anderson's interpretation is carefully and subtly constructed from a wide range of passages in Hume. Two main sources for his interpretation are (1) the many references by Hume to physiology and (2) Hume's explicit assertion that some ideas and impressions are extended. Like all the other writers, from Descartes to Reid, Hume accepted the current physiology of perception. He frequently offered physiological explanations of some cognitive process. Some eighteenth-century writers developed accounts of human nature and of our various conscious operations, accounts which pointed in the direction of mechanism and materialism. Hartley's 1749 *Observations on Man* was a natural and concerted application of these new developments. A few of these writers (e.g., Anthony Collins) even moved toward the claim of Joseph Priestley, at the end of the century, that thought is a property of the brain.[3] Hooke is clearly one writer who did try to make this identification. In several entries in his *Cyclopaedia* (1728), Chambers quotes liberally from a Dr. Astruc who, though he fails to make that identification, certainly traced highly specific correlations between physiology and mental operations. Chambers does not identify the work of Astruc from which he quotes, but there are two likely candidates, both published prior to Chambers's *Cyclopaedia*.[4] Under the entry 'Brain', Chambers writes:

From the Texture, Disposition, and tone of the Fibres of the *Brain*, Philosophers ordinarily account for the Phaenomena of *Sensation* and *Imagination*; which see. Dr. *Astruc* goes further, and from the Analogy between the Fibres of the *Brain*, and those of Musical Instruments, solves the Phaenomena of Judgment and Reasoning, and the Defects and Perfections of both. He lays it down as an Axiom, that every simple idea is produc'd by the Oscillation of one determinate Fibre; that the greater or less degree of Evidence follows the greater or less Force wherewith the Fibre oscillates. He hence proceeds to show, that the Affirmation or Negation of any Proposition, consists in the equal or unequal Number of Vibrations, which the Moving Fibres, representing the two Parts of the Proposition, *viz.* the Subject, make in the same Time.

These correlations are much more specific than those usually found in the many other appeals to physiology by writers before and after Hume, but a great number of writers did recognize the underlying physiology. Charles Bonnet, who was often compared with Hartley, gives many details on the physiology of awareness, but he is always careful to say he does not confuse brain movement with ideas.[5] Although Hartley also might be thought to have come close to making such an identification, he maintained that sensations and ideas are "of a mental Nature," whereas vibrations of nerve fibers are corporeal.[6]

Hume apparently did not hesitate, in the section on the immateriality of the soul, to identify ideas with brain impressions. At least, he seems to be serious when he speaks of some ideas being extended. Hume may be following Hooke. In a recent article, Anderson makes a strong case for this reading of that section.[7] When, in that section and in some other passages, Hume talks of perceptions having parts, and of the idea of extension being itself extended and located, we are hard pressed to know how to interpret such talk if we do not follow Anderson's lead. On the other hand, writers did frequently distinguish two senses of 'extension', applying that term to body and to space. Even mind was said by many to be extended, but not in the way body is. These writers struggled to find a sense of 'place' also which would be consistent with that dictum about all things being in a place and acting from a place, but which would not corporealize mind. It is precisely the issue that Hume discusses in his section on the immateriality of the soul. There he rejects this dictum on the grounds that it holds only for *some* things. It does apply, he says, to the ideas of sight and touch. Are these ideas located in a place and extended in the way body is or in the way that some writers said mind is?

We need to place this way of talking about some ideas in the total context of Hume's cognitive psychology. That he, like everyone else, recognizes the physiological foundations for all psychological processes, is clear. That he reduced the latter to the former, or even that he had such a program in mind, is not fully supported by the texts. The reduction of all acts of the mind to conception is a reduction *within* psychological operations. If we think Anderson is correct in his interpretation of the ideas of sight and touch, ideas for Hume must range from being located in the brain to being the meanings of words. His language of the mind includes both *physical* and *conceptual* talk. Ideas as thoughts and ideas as brain impressions: this would be the range. Before deciding how broad the range is, we need to survey the uses of the term 'idea' throughout the various sections of the *Treatise*. But before starting such a survey, it may be useful to remind ourselves of the language employed by Hume in his two rewritings of portions of the *Treatise*.

The term 'thought' is often used in place of 'idea' in the *Abstract*. There Hume speaks of "all our ideas or thoughts" being derived from "our impressions" (p. 22). The list of perceptions making up the system or train that is the soul ("as far as we can conceive it") includes "thoughts and sensations" (p. 25). Similarly, "it is by means of thought only that any thing operates upon our passions" (p. 32). The

Enquiry concerning Human Understanding describes the science of human nature as "mental geography," and it speaks of the "mental powers" of the mind (pp. 13-14). When he goes on to talk about the origin of ideas, Hume uses the phrase "the perceptions of the mind" (p. 17), and says that *thoughts* copy objects: "When we reflect on our past sentiments and affections, our thought is a faithful mirror, and copies its object truly" (pp. 17-18). When we divide perceptions into two categories, "the less forceable and lively are commonly denominated *Thoughts* or ideas" (p. 18). Hume continues to use the term 'thought' in many passages in the *Enquiry*, where the *Treatise* employed 'idea': e.g., "the thought of man" (p. 18), "our thoughts or ideas" (pp. 19, 23), "any particular thought" or "a succession of thoughts" (p. 23), "the principle which binds the different thoughts to each other" (p. 24), ideas occurring "to our thoughts" (p. 50).

In finding it easy to use 'thoughts' and 'ideas' interchangeably, Hume is illustrating for us his place in the way of ideas, for we have seen that earlier writers followed the same practice. Will a detailed examination of the behavior of the word 'idea' in the *Treatise* support the cognitive nature of ideas for Hume and of his "mental geography"?

Images?

The *Treatise* begins by dividing all perceptions of the human mind into two categories. Impressions and ideas differ in the degree of force and liveliness "with which they strike upon the mind." Even though the language of 'force' and 'liveliness' may be borrowed from physical talk, it is the *mind*, not the *brain*, on which perception strikes. The examples of impressions are sensations, passions, and emotions. Ideas are said to be the faint images of these impressions in thinking and reasoning. The term 'image' throughout the eighteenth century is never clearly explicated. Its inheritance from optical treatises always hangs about it. We should look to the example cited by Hume, in order to see whether we can construct a meaning for that term when used in these psychological contexts. Let us look first at his very first example of 'ideas': "all the perceptions excited by the present discourse" (p. 1). He explicitly excludes from these perceptions those "which arise from the sight and touch," as well as "the immediate pleasure or uneasiness" his discourse may excite in us. The perceptions that are thus excluded are sensations and emotions, the impressions he has just distinguished. The only candidate left for ideas would seem to be what this discourse says, our thoughts about it, my understanding of what it says.[8] The distinction is not one that Hume thinks is difficult to follow: "Every one of himself will readily perceive the difference betwixt feeling and thinking" (pp. 1-2). Last week I was sad; today I recall that feeling of sadness — the difference between being sad and remembering that I was sad. Hume gives a different example: the perceptions formed when I shut my eyes and *think of* my room (p. 3). Here we are often tempted to say I *image* my room, the objects in it, and their position. I may well do that, although I do not think it clear what such images are. But I can also *think about* my room, even the objects in it, without any attempt at imaging: I *know that* there is a typewriter, a desk, a black and white floor, and so on. My recalling each of the objects in my room, including their relative position, is what Hume would say is an "exact representation of the impressions" I have with my eyes open. 'Exact representation' need not be 'image' or 'picture'. An exact representation in thought gets it right, is the knowledge that the room is made up of these objects and these relations.

Another way of avoiding the too easy but unclear notion that ideas are images of impressions is to ask whether sensations, passions, and emotions are picturable or imageable? What is the image of pride or love? Hume also uses 'correspond' and 'resemble' for this relation. He remarks that for some complex ideas, there never are corresponding impressions. As examples of ideas never fully copied from impressions, he offers the idea of the New Jerusalem, or the idea of the Paris I have seen. In the latter case, I cannot form an idea that will "perfectly represent all its streets" and houses; I cannot think of all the streets and how they are related (p. 3). For every *simple* idea, he thinks, there is a corresponding simple impression that 'resembles it'; but again, we should be cautious in reading 'resemble' in any picture sense.[9] The example he offers here is the idea of red that we form in the dark: it differs from "that impression, which strikes our eyes in sunshine" only in degree. Can we say more about the impression of red, the visual sensation? Is it picturable? What is the idea that we form of red when we are in the dark, when we think of it after we have seen it? Hume gives the example of teaching a child the idea of scarlet or orange, sweet or bitter (p. 5). To do so, we present him with the relevant objects, we "convey to him these impressions." To have an idea of sweet would seem to be to know that taste, to be able to recognize it. The notion of imaging the taste hardly seems to make sense. He speaks of perceiving a color and of feeling a sensation, contrasting these perceivings and feelings with *thinking about* them.

Impressions are divided into those of sensation and those of reflection. The former are said to arise in the soul (not in the brain) from unknown causes. The latter are derived from ideas. He speaks of impressions striking the senses, making us perceive heat or cold, thirst or hunger (p. 7). The mind then makes a copy of that impression. The copy remains when the impression ceases. It is an idea. We must ask again, what is the *copy* of a sensation of hunger, heat, or pleasure?[10] When I think of the pleasure or pain I experienced before, am I not just recalling the fact of my feeling? Hume wants to say also that, when these ideas return again upon the soul, a new impression is formed: of desire and aversion, hope and fear. These are the impressions of reflection. Like all perceptions, they are *present to the mind* (p. 8). A little later, he contrasts the *mental* with the *natural* world (p. 12).

Hume uses the traditional classification of relations, modes, and substances, characterizing the idea of substance as "that of a collection of particular qualities." The idea of gold is given a particularly Lockean rendering (p. 16). Examples of modes are the idea of a dance, the idea of beauty (p. 17). When talking of abstract ideas, he speaks of conceiving a quantity or quality, and of forming a notion of degrees of these. He also cites the ideas of the length of a line, or the idea of a precise degree of any quantity or quality (pp. 18-19). Ideas are said to be joined in the conception. These ideas have their appearance *in the mind* (p. 19). Another example of the copying of impressions by ideas is given: what is absurd in fact and reality is absurd in idea also. Throughout these pages, both ideas and impressions are said to be present to the mind. The way to avoid talking nonsense is to look for repugnancies among our ideas, another stress on the close link between ideas and meaning.

A number of points emerge from this survey of book I, part I of the *Treatise*.

1. Hume never mentions the brain and the physiological processes. It is the mind or the soul which considers, conceives, imagines, remembers, thinks. It is also the mind or soul to which ideas and impressions are present.

2. The ultimate causes of the workings of the mind—"of our mental actions" (p. 22)—cannot be explained or known, unless by anatomists.

3. There is a mental *and* a natural world.

Ideas as the Medium of Conception

Hume starts the next part of the *Treatise* with a consideration of the mind's ability to conceive infinity. This discussion is meant to be introductory to the account of our ideas of space and time. There were debates over the question of whether space and time have parts, and whether these parts can be infinitely divided. Locke refers to one of the standard definitions of extension as *partes extra partes*. Mathematicians were involved in some of these debates. In the background there was, as well, a view of matter as corpuscular, as made up of insensible particles. Hume's discussion in this part is dense and difficult. It is not easy for us to discern in what he says all the issues and debates around which he wrote. Someone needs to fit this part of the *Treatise* into the eighteenth-century mathematical disputes. All I am trying to do here is to listen to Hume talking about the nature of ideas.

Hume deals in this part with several mathematical concepts: number, infinite divisibility, space, extension, time. Two features stand out in Hume's discussion of how the mind conceives of or forms ideas of these concepts: the various acts of the mind involved in forming these ideas, and the contrast between the appearances and their causes. The difficulties of interpretation arise from Hume's application of quantitative terms to ideas: size, parts, divisibility. We have to balance this quantitative language of ideas with Hume's ascription of logical properties to ideas: truth, contradiction, possibility. When he speaks of ideas 'representing' things, to which language does 'representation' belong: to the quantitative or to the logical language?

Hume begins the discussion in this part with a consideration of one dominant view about the mind's ability to conceive of infinity. A "full and adequate conception of infinity" would require, according to this view, an infinite capacity of the mind (pp. 26-27). Such a capacity would enable us to divide the idea of some quality infinitely. Any idea, no matter how complex, can "by proper distinction and separation" be divided into simple ideas that are no further divisible. Thus Hume disagrees with those who claim the possibility of and the need for infinite divisibility. He gives several examples to establish his claim that we end with simples. His first example is from the faculty of imagination: "the imagination reaches a *minimum*, and may raise up to itself an idea, of which it cannot conceive any subdivision, and which cannot be diminished without a total annihilation" (p. 27). Seemingly distinguishing between ideas and images, Hume says that he has a distinct idea of large numbers and of the relations between them (e.g., "the thousandth and ten-thousandth part of a grain of sand"), but the images that represent these numbers "are nothing different from each other, nor inferior to that image, by which I represent the grain of sand itself, which is suppos'd so vastly to exceed them." 'Having an idea of' may mean 'understand'. The use of 'image' in this passage is not made clear, but Hume's conclusion is firm: "But whatever we may imagine of the thing, the idea of a grain of sand is not distinguishable, nor separable into twenty, much less into a thousand, ten thousand, or an infinite number of different ideas."

A similar conclusion is drawn about the impressions of the senses. Fixing my gaze on a spot of ink on this paper, then backing off until I lose sight of the spot, "'tis plain, that the moment before it vanish'd, the image or impression was perfectly indivisible" (p. 27). Hume is careful in this case to remark that this is a report about appearances, not a function of a lack of light rays "striking the eyes." He is giving a phenomenological report, just as in the image case of the imagination he is giving an introspective report. Having argued from such reports that neither the image of the imagination nor the phenomenal impressions of sense can be infinitely divided, Hume goes on to argue against the notion that the mind is limited by these facts. Our ideas of small objects are *adequate* to those objects, without those ideas mirroring the size of such objects. In an extravagant passage, Hume supports this claim by saying that it is certain that "we can form ideas, which shall be no greater than the smallest atom of the animal spirits of an insect a thousand times less than a mite" (p. 28). We should be cautious in seizing upon the 'size' terms in this remark. If the image that represents the ten-thousandth part of a grain of sand is 'not inferior to' the image by which I represent the grain itself, presumably the same would be true of the idea by which I represent an atom of an animal spirit and that spirit itself; that is, the latter is not inferior to the one that represents the smaller object. Can we say that Hume means that the images in these two instances are the same size? Or is his point that size is not the means by which we represent objects to ourselves?

In the mite example, Hume goes on to say that what is important is whether we can enlarge our *conceptions* "so much as to form a just notion of a mite" (p. 28). A just notion requires a "distinct idea representing every part of them," of the objects. Such a representation is not possible if there is infinite divisibility, nor is it very easy according to the notion of "indivisible parts or atoms" because of "that vast number and multiplicity of these parts." 'Representation' seems to be the important word in these passages. If representation is not a matching of the size of ideas with the size of objects, how does representation occur? One form of representation (though it may not be the only form) resides in the logical properties of our ideas. Asserting that "our ideas are adequate representations of the most minute parts of extension," it is the logical relations that are said to do the representing: "the relations, contradictions and agreements of the ideas are all applicable to the objects" (p. 29).[11] Hume uses this representation of ideas as a way of showing the impossibility of infinite divisibility. The reasoning to his *reductio* is not important for my purposes, other than to remind us that a consideration of ideas of extension is used as a way of concluding that no "finite extension is infinitely divisible" (p. 30). The *reductio* form of argument is used throughout the rest of this section, to reach the conclusion that time "must be compos'd of indivisble moments" (p. 31) and that it is impossible for there to be mathematical points (p. 33). Thus, at least in this section, to say that ideas adequately represent objects is to say that by considering our ideas and their relations we can determine whether certain claims about space and time are possible or impossible.

Section III of the same part tells us how we acquire the idea of extension: open our eyes, turn toward the surrounding objects, perceive many visible bodies, shut our eyes, and *consider* "the distance betwixt these bodies" (p. 33). It is by the process of considering what I have seen that I acquire the idea of extension. The mental act of considering plays an important role in the formation of all abstract ideas. The example used in this passage is the move from the optical array of colored points disposed in a certain manner on our eyes to the idea of extension as colored points in a specific order (p. 34). From that idea we go on to realize that the color of the points is not important; it is the ordering that is important. We take some specific idea of extension and generalize it by considering it in a certain light.

Just as it is "from the disposition of visible and tangible objects" that "we receive the idea of space," by considering the appearances to sense in a certain way, so the idea of time is tied down to specific impressions. Time alone, disconnected from appearing objects, cannot give rise to the idea of time. We form the idea of time from the succession of ideas and impressions (p. 35). In this example, Hume writes indifferently of ideas, perceptions, and thoughts.[12] It is some perceivable succession on which our idea of time depends; at least the *first* appearance of time to the mind so depends upon a succession of objects.[13] Perhaps we are able to *conceive* of time "without our conceiving any succession of objects"? Time cannot, however, be even conceived without succession, since it is an idea that is a function of the manner, the order, of appearances. In this case, conception cannot go beyond experience, just as we cannot conceive of extension without color or touch sensations (pp. 36, 38).

The *idea* of extension must preserve the color and tangible qualities of the sensory experience. What form does that preservation take? Is the color of the sensed point actually transferred (formally, as Descartes would say) to the idea? Or does the idea preserve the color objectively? The actual color is necessary for the sensory simples to be *discovered* by the senses. The preservation in idea is necessary for the *comprehension* of those simples by the imagination. Sensory discovery is not the same as imaginative conception, i.e., understanding. We must *consider* the simples as colored or tangible; otherwise they "can convey to us no idea" (p. 39). So far, Hume seems to me to be keeping quite distinct the real, actual colored points affecting our senses and our ideas of such colored points. In order for me to form an idea of extension (an adequate idea), I must think of the sensory points as being colored. But this reading is clouded over when Hume goes on to speak of our idea of extension having parts, and then tells us that the idea of extension must also "be consider'd as colour'd and tangible." It looks as if he means for us to think of our idea itself being colored, at least its parts are colored. Still, if *considering* is a nonsensory process (as it seems clearly to be), then even considering our ideas to be colored would not mean they are in fact colored.

That there is some looseness in Hume's discussion is suggested by two features of this passage. First, consider the sentence, "We have therefore no idea of space or extension, but when we regard it as an object either of our sight or feeling" (p. 39). The 'it' looks as if it should refer to 'idea', yet I find it hard to believe Hume means to say *ideas* are objects of sight or touch. Second, the very next paragraph in this section applies a similar line of thought to time as he has just used for space, yet he does not say our ideas of time are in time. *Of course* they are, the succession of our ideas or perceptions is an equal partner with successively appearing objects in forming the idea of time. One would think that in drawing a parallel reasoning on the idea of time, Hume would have made this point: the idea of time is itself composed of successive parts, and the idea of space is itself composed of colored parts. The parallel reasoning Hume cites for *time* is not for the *idea* of time: "The same reasoning will prove, that the indivisible moments of time must be fill'd with some real object or existence, whose succession forms the duration, and makes it be conceivable by the mind" (p. 39).

Hume's stress is on what we need in order to have the thought of, to conceive of space and time. "The ideas of space and time are therefore no separate or distinct ideas, but merely those of the manner or order, in which objects exist" (pp. 39-40). We cannot conceive of a vacuum or of extension without something being ordered in a certain way. Similarly, time requires change and succession. Time consists of noncoexisting parts; space consists of coexisting parts. These facts about space and time (or about our sensory impressions underlying our experience of space and time) must be preserved in our ideas, our conceptions, our understanding of space and time. Hume is not saying, I am suggesting, that our thoughts of space are themselves colored, but that we must *think of* space as consisting of colored points in a certain order. Thinking of time as successive parts may be easier, since succession *is* a literal property of our thoughts. Time is more pervasive than space, as Kant was later to emphasize.

In these sections, as in the rest of this part, Hume goes into great detail to show how ideas are formed on the basis of or concomitantly with specific appearances and sensory impressions. Just as belief is always built upon a present impression and the manner of appearances to us, so the ideas Hume considers in part II of book I of the *Treatise* involve the same combination of sensory appearances and specific sorts of mental acts made on the basis of those appearances. Some of the more radical aspects of this part are, I suspect, Hume's careful account of how geometrical concepts are also intimately based upon sensory appearances: concepts of equality, line, surface, right angle, all are functions of appearances. Just as mathematical points are nonentities, so the claim for some standard of equality or of right-angularity that escapes sensory experience is erroneous. These concepts or ideas have a physiological causal foundation (see the example of dissection of the brain, pp. 60-61) and a psychological component. The psychological component is marked by the various mental acts that the mind engages in, in forming certain ideas. The act of *considering* is but one such act cited in several passages. There are others. Hume speaks of the mind *revolving over* all its ideas of sensation, such 're-volving over' is said to be a *contemplation. Taking notice* is another mental operation as well as *arriving at* a conception, or *regarding*. In speaking of the ability of the mind to determine whether one body is greater, less, or equal to another, he speaks of our *judgments*, of *reviewing* and *reflecting* upon that judgment (p. 47). Here, as in other cases, the mind works from the appearances to the eye. The mind also discovers and reasons, sometimes mistaking one idea for another (p. 60).

Acts of the Mind

With his stress upon the psychological components in the formation of the abstract ideas of geometry, which continues the part I use of the same mental acts, it should come as no surprise to discover that the discussion of knowledge and belief in part III is pervaded by the role of mental acts. The seven philosophical relations, around which this part is constructed, depend "entirely on the ideas, which we compare together," such comparing of ideas in knowledge being again firmly in the Lockean tradition (p. 69). For Locke also, all certainty arises from the comparison of ideas. Besides comparing, Hume speaks of abstract reasoning and of reflection (p. 69). He also cites 'considering' as a way of thinking about ideas (p. 71). Comparison, in the case of the nondemonstrative probable relations (identity, time and place, causation), works with objects or, as I presume he must mean, with the appearances of objects. "All kinds of reasoning consist in nothing but a *comparison*, and a discovery of those relations, either constant or inconstant, which two or more objects bear to each other" (p. 73). We can make such a comparison when both objects are present to the senses, or when neither is present, or when only one is present. When both are present, this is perception. In this case, there is no "exercise of the thought," only a "mere passive admission of the impressions thro' the organs of sensation." (ibid.)

In reasoning, *remembering* is another important mental act. Historical reasoning also requires that we understand evidence, such evidence being "certain characters and letters present either to our memory or senses; which characters we likewise remember to have been us'd as the signs of certain ideas" (p. 83). The interpretation of signs, understanding the meaning of words (even when I disbelieve what is said) is an important cognitive process (p. 95). In discussing causal inferences generally, Hume appeals to the logical properties of ideas again, in this case to their coherence: "We may draw inferences from the coherence of our perceptions, whether they be true or false; whether they represent nature justly or be mere illusions of the senses" (p. 84). Again, 'representation' is linked with logical relations. *Assenting* to ideas is another cognitive operation, one characterizing belief (pp. 94ff.). The language of the standard eighteenth-century logics also appears, when Hume speaks of the "simple conception of any thing" (p. 94). Such simple conception contrasts with the mingling, uniting, separating, and confounding of our ideas cited later (p. 96). That my interpretation of the very first example of 'idea' in the *Treatise* is correct is supported by a reference in this part to reading a book. This passage is offered as an illustration of how understanding the meaning of words is not tied to our believing what is said.

If one person sits down to read a book as a romance, and another as a true history, they plainly receive the same ideas, and in the same order; nor does the incredulity of the one, and the belief of the other hinder them from putting the very same sense upon their author. His words produce the same ideas in both; tho' his testimony has not the same influence on them. (p. 98)

What the words as characters and signs produce in their readers are not brain impressions; the shapes of the letters may do that.[14] Just as words produce ideas, so pictures of persons 'convey our thoughts' to the person pictured (p. 99). Hume also speaks of *thinking on* an object and of contemplating by "an intellectual view" (p. 100). We are also said to think on our past thoughts (p. 106).

In later passages 'thought' appears instead of 'idea'. We are said to have "a determination to carry our thoughts from one object to another" (p. 165); necessity is considered to be a "determination of the thought to pass from causes to effects and from effects to causes" (p. 166). Hume refers also to the act of the understanding that is considering or comparing (pp. 156, 166). The mind conceives and comprehends (pp. 161, 162); conception or having ideas precedes understanding (pp. 164, 168). All these various operations are what Hume calls "the actions of the mind" (p. 177). Detailing these actions, showing how they function in thinking, constitutes Hume's psychology or his epistemic logic. Such actions are a function of the "intellectual faculties of the mind" (p. 138), although of course the physiological functions play a role too. Together, the faculties and the actions make up the subject matter of what Hume called, in the *Enquiry*, mental geography (p. 13). In that work, Hume praised the results of "an accurate scrutiny into the powers and faculties of human nature," but he remarked as well upon the difficulties of such a study.

It is remarkable concerning the operations of the mind, that, though most intimately present to us, yet, whenever they become the object of reflexion, they seem involved in obscurity; nor can the eye readily find those lines and boundaries, which discriminate and distinguish them. The objects are too fine to remain long in the same aspect or situation; and must be apprehended in an instant, by a superior penetration, derived from nature, and improved by habit and reflexion.[15]

The program for such a science of human nature is to "know the different operations of the mind, to separate them from each other, to class them under their proper heads, and to correct all that seeming disorder, in which they lie involved, when made the object of reflexion and enquiry" (ibid.). Hume's contribution to such mental geography was massive, not so much in a direct cataloguing and classifying of the powers, faculties, and acts of the mind (although there is considerable contribution there), as in his careful account of how the mind comes to have certain ideas, how it forms its beliefs, what principles and faculties are at work in particular areas of concern. In pursuing this analysis, Hume was also very careful to distinguish what can be discovered by diligent reflection and attention from the speculations about the causes of the phenomenological facts so discovered. He was, in the *Enquiry*, guarded in his hopes for the discovery of "the secret springs and principles, by which the human mind is actuated in its operations" (p. 14). The *Treatise* cautioned that any such explanation must be based upon experience.

Logical Properties or Extended Parts

What our brief look at book I, part III of the *Treatise* discloses is that, as Hume started analyzing specific questions, the role and nature of ideas became much less important in acquiring ideas than the operations of the mind. The very nature of those acts of the mind, being cognitive and mental, should be indication enough that ideas for Hume are not brain impressions. While Hume accepted the current notion that the mind can influence the physiology by affecting the animal spirits, what the mind associated, compared, compounded, divided, reflected upon, etc., are mental contents, thoughts. This conclusion, as well as the claim that it is the acts of the mind that became more important in the body of the *Treatise* than the way of ideas, is further supported by an examination of part IV in book I. This part also contains one puzzling, seeming counterexample to my claim that ideas are mental contents.

Section I of this part is concerned with reason and reasoning. Discussion of 'faculty' and of acts of the mind looms large. Demonstrative reasoning is distinguished from the reasoning in common life (p. 180). Reflection is cited, considering appears, and assent also (pp. 180-83). Judging is characterized as natural: nature "by an absolute and uncontrollable necessity" determines us "to judge as well as breathe and feel" (p. 183). Nature implants the faculty of judging in our minds, just as nature has given us the faculty of seeing bodies. Reasoning and believing are said to be "some sensation or peculiar manner of conception," illustrating again Hume's reduction to one type of mental operation (p. 184). He also speaks of a question being proposed to him and of his carrying his thoughts from those impressions to the objects. The product of these mental acts is a strong conception, which forms his decision on the question. We find throughout this section a wide variety of mental activities, of acts of the mind: decisions, principles of judgment, balancing of opposite causes, imagination, thought, conception of ideas, feeling a sensation, common judgments, comprehending, an effort of thought, the operation of our sentiments. The animal spirits of his physiology also appear here (pp. 185-86). All these remarks presuppose a rather complex account of the workings of the mind. Hume also speaks in these pages of the regular flow of the passions and sentiments and of the straining of the imagination.

In the next section, discussion of 'faculty' persists: he is concerned to trace our idea of body to one particular faculty. We find him talking of inferring and of supposing, also of suggesting (p. 189). He speaks of the actions and sensations of the mind: these are known to us by consciousness (p. 190). As he moves into the details of this complex section, inferring, regarding, and supposing reappear. Conception is seen to be important, since the belief in continued existence "consists in the force and vivacity of the conception" (p. 199). We also find 'idea' linked with 'meaning': the idea expressed by the word 'object' must have a meaning different from 'ourselves' (p. 200). The mind is here said to pronounce and to consider. Comprehension, opinion, belief, perceiving, assent, conceiving, notion, representation: the whole apparatus of his cognitive psychology runs throughout this section.

We then come to the apparent counterexample. This example is contained in that curious section on the immateriality of the soul. Part IV of this book of the *Treatise* as a whole, and the immateriality section in particular, have a dialectical structure: opposing views on some claim are discussed; a possible resolution is suggested. This section has another trait which makes its interpretation difficult: it is a clever satire on a controversy that raged throughout the eighteenth century, the controversy over the question, "could matter think?" A lesser claim was that matter and motion were the sole causes of thought. Hume's discussion of these issues is, as I have shown in *Thinking Matter*, redolent with the echoes of many writers and doctrines in that debate. He announces, and this is the heart of the satire, that he will show that immaterialism, not materialism, is an atheism. One of the arguments used by the opponents of materialism was that thought and extension differ fundamentally, belong to different kinds of substances, and that therefore they are incompatible properties, they cannot belong to the same substance. In the background of much of this debate was the principle (with, as we now know, an acceptance wider than the context of this debate) that 'no thing can be or act where it is not'. Hume makes the proper point that the conjunction of properties need not be local or spatial conjunction: coexistence does not entail *spatial* coexistence; the being or existence of anything (where 'thing' must be taken to include substances as well as qualities) does not always require spatial location. Another way of making the same point is to say that extension is not a property of all that exists.

In referring to the idea or notion of space or extension (Hume, like other writers, tended to think of both body and space as extended), Hume repeats what he said in part II: that idea is derived from sight and feeling (p. 235). What is extended must have some shape. Shape does not 'agree with' such properties as desire, a statement seemingly meaning that shape is incompatible with desire, that a desire cannot be shaped. Hume adds that shape does not agree with "any impression or idea, except" those of the senses of sight and feeling, apparently meaning that shape *is* compatible with those impressions. Similarly, his denial of the dictum 'no thing can be where it is not' carries an excepting clause: the claim that something can exist and be nowhere is true, he says, for "all our perceptions and objects, except those of the sight and feeling" (p. 236). Hume's main concern in these sentences is to press the point that most perceptions are not located or extended, apparently leaving open the possibility that some *are* located or extended. The crucial passage that explicitly makes this assertion is found on pp. 239-40. There, he returns to the 'agreement' talk of p. 235. He begins by saying that no external object can be known to the mind immediately. An image or perception interposes between us and such objects. The table that appears to me is only a perception. The qualities of that table are, then, qualities of a perception. That perception has parts. The parts of that perception give us the notion of distance and extension. The idea of extension is copied from an impression and perfectly *agrees with* that impression. Therefore, to say the idea of extension agrees with anything is to say the *idea* is itself extended.

In working his way to this conclusion, Hume uses the language of complex ideas having parts. The tradition stemming from Locke — whereby the language of whole and parts is applied to ideas, and compound ideas are made up of combinations of other, simple ideas — lends itself to an ambiguity of the term 'part'. One meaning of that term is as an *analogy* with, not literally the same as, physical parts. Locke's abstract and complex ideas follow this sense of the term. The other meaning of that term is the literal one, where (as Hume ends by making them) the 'parts' seem to become literal, physical parts. The slide from the one to the other meaning of 'part' is explicit in Priestley's writings, published later in the century. Priestley openly argues for a materialism, albeit for a materialism in which matter is force and activity rather than corpuscles that are passive and inert. Priestley remarks that "the idea of a *man*, for instance, could in no sense correspond to a man, which is the architype of it, and therefore could not be the idea of a man, if it did not consist of the ideas of his *head, arms, trunk, legs*, etc."[16] The 'idea of head, arms, trunk, etc.' is not yet an idea with physical size and shape. Nor do we have physical parts when Priestley says that, since the idea of 'man' consists of parts, it consequently is 'divisible'. But his next remark moves us toward physical division: "And how is it possible that a thing (be the *nature* of it what it may) that is *divisible*, should be contained in a substance, be the nature of it likewise what it may, that is *indivisible*" (pp. 37-38). He then draws a firm conclusion, reminiscent of Hume's argument that the idea of extension is itself extended.

If the architypes of ideas have extension, the ideas which are expressive of them, and are actually produced by them, according to certain mechanical laws, must have extension likewise; and therefore the mind in which they exist, whether it be material or immaterial, must have extension also. I am therefore obliged to conclude, that the sentient principle in man, containing ideas which certainly have parts, and are divisible, and consequently must have extension, cannot be that simple, indivisible, and immaterial substance that some have imagined it to be; but something that has real *extension*, and therefore may have the other properties of matter. (p. 38)

We cannot ignore the fact that Hume's conclusion about extended ideas occurs in the section that discusses the very issue that Priestley took up in 1777: the materiality or immateriality of the soul. It would not be surprising to find Hume defending in 1740 a conclusion that the soul is not immaterial: he would not have been alone at that time in so arguing. Thus we cannot lightly dismiss his talk of some ideas being extended either as analogy or as the result of the satire at work in that section. In his 1976 article, Anderson links this paragraph in the *Treatise* about extended ideas with a later one in which Hume uses some optical language.

When an object augments or diminishes to the eye or imagination from a comparison with others, the image and idea of the object are still the same, and are equally extended in the *retina*, and in the brain or organ of perception. The eyes refract the rays of light, and the optic nerves convey the images to the brain in the very same manner, whether a great or small object has preceded . . . (p. 372)

Anderson's conclusion is as follows:

The extension of our perceptions of extended objects, then, appears to result from the physics of light and the physiology of visual perception. . . . The impression or idea of the extended object apparently is quite literally an image of that object, and hence, resembles it in that sense.[17] (p. 166)

Anderson assumes that Hume does accept a world of objects, even though our only access to that world is by way of our perceptions. But Anderson thinks our perceptions, our impressions, copy objects, where 'copy' is taken in the literal sense. Just as bodies are extended and located in space, so some of our ideas of bodies are extended and located in space, i.e., in the brain. Without the assumption that my visual and tactual impressions do literally copy or mirror the shape of objects, the ascription of shape to my ideas of extension is not so straightforwardly materialist. If the table that I see is only a perception, the sense in which that perception is extended is just that it takes up space in my visual or tactual field. The perception-table is a phenomenological table. Hence, to ascribe space or shape to it is not to ascribe a shape in the way that a brain impression (which is not a phenomenological event) has a shape and a location. In other words, if we interpret Hume's perception-table in a phenomenal sense, we cannot consider his talk of extension as being the materialist's extension. On a phenomenological reading, the way the world appears to me just is that some of my perceptions are extended and located, others are not; but since space and extension are also phenomenological, Hume has not ascribed to visual and tactual perceptions a location in the brain.

Conclusion

I am not entirely happy with this phenomenological reading of Hume's perception-table, because I think the 'scepticism with regard to the senses' section tried to avoid a strict identification of ideas with objects. There is a numerical but not a specific difference between ideas and objects. The phenomenological reading does not, of course, violate this numerical difference, since the object may be the way it appears to be without being identical with that appearance. In that way, this reading is consistent with my reading of the skepticism in the senses section. Moreover, if Hume is, in the immateriality section, going to be effective in arguing for and against materialism, it would seem that he must mean by 'extension' what the materialists mean. On the other hand, Hume does resolve the libertarian-necessitarian dispute by applying *his* account of 'necessity' and 'cause' to that controversy: there is the same sort of uniformity between motives and actions as there is between events in nature; therefore, actions are just as much caused or determined as are natural events.[18] So it may be that in the materialist-immaterialist controversy, Hume seeks a resolution in terms of *his* analysis of our knowledge of the external world.[19] That analysis, close to a direct realism, does make an appeal to the appearances, to our experiences. Taste sensations are not experienced as being extended. If we find ourselves thinking of the taste being in the object, a little reflection convinces us that this is an absurdity and an impossible notion (p. 238). There is no absurdity in conceiving of our shape perceptions being extended and located; that is how they are experienced, and no absurdity results. They are visually and tactually extended in our perceptual field.

Hume's appeal to absurdity and impossibility in the taste-location example is, I think, revealing. We saw earlier, in part II, how 'represent' and 'preserve' were translated in logical terms. While Anderson cites this use in part II of the logical properties of ideas as a basis for reaching a conclusion about objects, he does not pause to ask how such logical properties lead to his reading of 'copy' as 'literal resemblance'. Hume uses the same logical language about ideas in the immateriality section, shortly after the paragraph with the apparent counterexample. Pointing out that we are led to believe that the table before us is a perception because we are unable to conceive of an object *specifically* different from our perception (p. 241), he then discusses the inferences we can make around the "connexion and repugnance" of our impressions. In this passage, he argues that we cannot know for certain that these relations of ideas apply to objects, but we can know that "whatever conclusions of this kind we form concerning objects, will most certainly be applicable to impressions" (p. 241). Hume's reason for running the logical move in this way is bound up with the satire he is constructing. The details of that reason and of that satire need not detain us. What we need to note is that "connexion and repugnance" was and would be recognized as being, in the eighteenth century, a Lockean use of logical relations: 'repugnance' meant 'contradiction'. The relations between objects and impressions, on the basis of which we can make inferences from one to the other, are logical. In the very voice in which Hume says, "We have no idea of any quality in an object, which does not agree to, and may not represent a quality in an impression," he goes on to speak of finding, or failing to find, any repugnancies: "Every idea of a quality in an object passes thro' an impression; and therefore every *perceivable* relation, whether of connexion or repugnance, must be common both to objects and impressions" (p. 243). Once again, 'agree with' and 'represent' are closely linked with those logical properties.

The logical reading of 'representation' and 'agree with' may not be the only way Hume intended those terms, but the frequent use of logical relations between ideas in his discussion of specific problems reminds us again that Hume's *Treatise* is a logic in the eighteenth-century sense, of an account of the workings of the mind. One of the activities of the understanding is to draw inferences around logical relations. Such inferences are just one of many mental acts Hume details. Whatever we make of his assertions in part IV that perceptions are located and extended, we cannot ignore the pervasive application of psychological language, both to acts of the mind and to ideas, to the contents of the mind.[20]

Notes

1. Hume was more concerned with the details of the workings of the mind than was Pope. Pope may have foreseen those dilemmas that Hume got into by undue attention to the details, dilemmas about our ideas of external existence, of cause, of personal identity. "It is therefore in the Anatomy of the Mind as in that of the Body; more good will accrue to mankind by attending to the large, open, and perceptible parts, than by studying too much such finer nerves and vessels, the conformations and uses of which will for ever escape our observation. The *disputes* are all upon these last, and, I will venture to say, they have less sharpened the *wits* than the *hearts* of men against each other . . ." ("An Essay on Man," Epistle). Like Hume, Pope constructed a morality on the basis of this anatomy. That the use made of this metaphor by Hume is modeled after Pope's use is strongly suggested by the closing passage of book III of the *Treatise*: "The anatomist ought never to emulate the painter: nor in his accurate dissections and portraitures of the smaller parts of the human body, pretend to give his figures any graceful and engaging attitude or expression. There is even something hideous, or at least minute in the views of things, which he presents; and 'tis necessary the objects shou'd be set more at a distance, and be more cover'd up from sight, to make them engaging to the eye and imagination. An anatomist, however, is admirably fitted to give advice to a painter; and 'tis even impracticable to excel in the latter art, without the assistance of the former. We must have an exact knowledge of the parts, their situation and connexion, before we can design with any elegance or correctness. And thus the most abstract speculations concerning human nature, however cold and unentertaining, become subservient to *practical morality*; and may render this latter science more correct in its precepts, and more persuasive in its exhortations" (pp. 620-21). Hume did send Pope a copy of the *Treatise*. The metaphor also occurs in Thomas Reid, *An Inquiry into the Human Mind*, Introduction.

2. See Anderson, R. F., *Hume's First Principles* (1966).

3. Ideas are also called brain impressions in an entry in Voltaire's *Dictionnaire*. Under 'idée', he says that an idea is "an image which is painted in my brain." The details on the development of materialism in eighteenth-century Britain, and on the physiology of thinking and acting are given in my *Thinking Matter*. The analysis of Hume's ideas needs to be placed in that context, especially in the context of Hume's role in the debate over materialism and immaterialism.

4. Jean Astruc published a work entitled *Quaestio medica de naturali et praeternaturali judicii exercitio* (1720). In 1719, he gave an oral dissertation, *De sensatione*. Astruc was

most famed for his work on venereal disease, *De morbis venereis*, first published in 1736. I am indebted to John Wright for these references to Astruc.

5. See Bonnet's *Essai analytique sur les facultés de l'ame* (1760), p. 45, where he says that "ideas are attached to the movement of certain fibres" but goes on to insist that "an idea is a mode of mind."

6. *Observations on Man* (1749), p. 34.

7. "The Location, Extension, Shape, and Size of Hume's Perceptions," in *Hume, A Re-evaluation* (1976), edited by D. W. Livingston and J. T. King, pp. 153-71.

8. That ideas are linked with meanings is indicated in the *Enquiry*: "When we entertain . . . any suspicion that a philosophical term is employed without any meaning or idea . . ." (p. 22).

9. In the *Enquiry*, the principle about ideas copying impressions is expressed as follows: "It is impossible for us to *think of* any thing, which we have not antecedently *felt*, either by our external or internal senses" (p. 62).

10. Hume remarks that "the examination of our sensations belongs more to anatomists and natural philosophers than to moral" (p. 8). Does this remark enable us to say that sensations are physiological? Certainly he recognized that the account of how they arise in the soul is a function of physiology and hence is a task for anatomy or natural philosophy.

11. With a clear echo of Locke's definition of knowledge, Hume adds that, in these relations, contradictions and agreements are "the foundation of all human knowledge." Earlier, he ran the relation between ideas and objects backward: if something "be absurd in *fact and reality*, it must also be absurd in *idea*" (p. 19).

12. "A man in a sound sleep, or strongly occupy'd with one thought, is insensible of time; and according as his perceptions succeed each other with greater or less rapidity, the same duration appears longer or shorter to his imagination" (p. 35).

13. Once again, Hume uses phenomenological examples. "If you wheel about a burning coal with rapidity, it will present to the senses an image of a circle of fire; nor will there seem to be any interval of time betwixt its revolutions" (p. 35).

14. Hume is always aware of the background that physiology provides for our conscious perceptions, even for our interpretation of signs. (See, e.g., the physiological example on pp. 98-99.) Anderson presents many other examples of physiology in his book. Meaning also appears in Hume's discussion of necessary connection: he remarks that when we attempt to use terms like 'energy' or 'efficacy', "we have really no distinct meaning, and make use only of common words, without any clear and determinate ideas" (p. 162).

15. *Enquiry*, p. 13. Cf. *Treatise*, p. 105: "I must not conclude this subject without observing that 'tis very difficult to talk of the operations of the mind with perfect propriety and exactness; because common language has seldom made any very nice distinctions among them, but has generally call'd by the same term all such as nearly resemble each other."

16. Joseph Priestley, *Disquisitions relating to Matter and Spirit* (1777), vol. I, p. 37.

17. It is difficult not to think of the early scientific treatises of Descartes in which he too used 'idea' as 'brain impression'.

18. *Enquiry*, p. 88.

19. In the immateriality section, Hume resolves the question about matter causing thought by invoking his uniformity account of cause: "we find by the comparing their ideas, that thought and motion are different from each other, and by experience, that they are constantly united; which being all the circumstances, that enter into the idea of cause and effect, when apply'd to the operations of matter, we may certainly conclude, that motion may be, and actually is, the cause of thought and perception" (p. 248).

20. I briefly remarked above on the dialectical and satirical nature of the immateriality section. Thomas Reid makes an interesting suggestion about Hume's talk of extended perception which fits into the spirit of that section. Early in that section, Hume had argued

against the idea of substance, saying that it was a meaningless idea. Either it is without meaning, or, on the standard definition of substance, everything is a substance (p. 233). Reid read Hume as saying there are no substances, including mind substance. In an obvious reference to the immateriality section, Reid says that "the author of the *Treatise of Human Nature*" tries to prove "that the mind either is no substance, or that it is an extended and divisible substance; because the ideas of extension cannot be in a subject which is indivisible and unextended." A few sentences later, Reid puts the point again: "He takes it for granted that there are ideas of extension in the mind; and thence infers, that if it is at all a substance, it must be an extended and divisible substance." (*Enquiry into the Human Mind*, ed. T. Duggan, p. 170.)

Chapter XI

Sense and Meaning

Thomas Reid identified a natural prejudice of humans:

> to conceive of the mind as having some similitude to body in its operations. Hence men have been prone to imagine, that as bodies are put in motion by some impulse or impression made upon them by contiguous bodies; so the mind is made to think and to perceive by some impressions made upon it, or some impulse given to it by contiguous objects.[1]

The same natural prejudice leads us to conceive "that what is an immediate object of thought, and affects the mind, must be in contact with it" (p. 56). The next step is easy, Reid thinks: what is present to the mind are "certain images or species" of objects, not the objects themselves. Hence we do not perceive external objects immediately (p. 110). Such quasi-literal accounts of perceptual awareness are reinforced by the dictum that no thing can be or act where it is not.[2]

The natural prejudice that leads to these results seems, on Reid's account, to be found among philosophers, not among the vulgar. Reid might better have called it a philosophical prejudice, because, on his account, it does not seem to be natural to all men. In their common use, 'to perceive', 'to remember', 'to conceive', and 'to imagine' signify different operations of the mind, operations which are not analogous to the working of the body (p. 9). Precisely what these mental-operation words mean or designate Reid does not elucidate. In fact, "when we lay aside those [physical] analogies, and reflect attentively upon our perception of the object of sense, we must acknowledge, that, though we are conscious of perceiving objects, we are altogether ignorant how it is brought about; and know as little how we perceive objects as how we were made" (p. 245).

The examination in the previous chapters of the accounts of perceptual acquaintance has revealed a persistent appeal to the notion of 'presence to mind'. As I show in *Thinking Matter*, that notion also played a significant role in the development of materialism in Britain. The analogy with body commented upon by Reid, together with use of physiological explanations, led to a tendency to locate awareness in the nerves or brain. While Reid misses, in the very authors he cites as being trapped in the language of body, the steady recognition of the cognitive content of ideas, he may have noted another language used by those authors which also leads to some misconceptions of what they were saying. The presence of optical language and optical examples may have misled some in this way, although I tend to think that that language and those examples mislead us more than they did the authors who used them. But Reid could have claimed this language also as a factor leading to the hated skepticism which he saw in all the users of the way of ideas.

As we have seen, the use of optical models encouraged writers to use visual-perception language in locating images on or near objects. In some cases, the use of these models even led to the conclusion that we perceive only images. The *camera obscura* controlled much of the discussion about perceptual awareness, and it was used in three different ways.

(a) Early in the seventeenth century, Chanet asserted that we peer out the holes of our eyes at the passing scene. The *camera obscura* is, as it were, turned inside out. There are no images to locate or see on the inside of the box; real things replace those images and are seen through the hole in the perspective box of our body. Late in the eighteenth century, we encounter the same notion in an anonymous work, *A Theological Survey of the Human Understanding* (1776): the senses are said to be windows through which the soul discerns objects (p. 52).

(b) Hooke and Locke employed the *camera obscura* model in the usual fashion. Locke's comparison is with the understanding. On his view, rays of light from outside leave pictures or images on the inside of the box. The comparison is never drawn out in detail, but there is the suggestion that the perceiver is like the perspective box because images of objects are imprinted on his insides. Then it is as if we can also peer at those images in our box. Reid reached this conclusion in his account of his predecessors only by noting the wax impression model: what we see, according to Reid's reading of the way of ideas, are impressions on the brain. Reid took literally his predecessors' assertions that the brain was the seat of the soul. The optical model has the advantage, over the wax impression one, of drawing similarities between seeing the picture on the opaque surface of the box and seeing real objects. Vision, whether dealt with by opticians or by philosophers, requires images produced by light rays. The production of the images by the rays of light retains the external rooting of perception, whether or not the conclusion of the optical model for the understanding is that we know objects, not just the images of them.

(c) If we pressed the *camera obscura* model in one direction, we might come to deny or claim as unknowable the external reference. Henry Grove's self-enclosed, percipient globe with its lovely painted pictures of birds, trees, etc., might then result. Grove insisted that certain characteristics of those pictures nevertheless carry a mark of external parentage, but it would be easy enough to become trapped in his globe model, concluding (as did the object of Grove's attack, Arthur Collier) that not only do we not see objects, but we have no basis for believing that there are objects other than the images we see.

It is just such a conclusion that Reid was convinced Berkeley reached. At least Reid claims that this is the conclusion to which Berkeley's principles lead. Perhaps it should not be surprising that, even with the advantage of his position late in the century, Reid sees Berkeley with no more understanding than did those closer in time to Berkeley. Berkeley's denial of a *material* world, the world of the corpuscularians, Reid took as a denial of "heaven and earth, and body and spirit."[3] Reid comes back repeatedly to this characterization of Berkeley—Bishop Berkeley's Ideal System[4]—both in his *Inquiry* and in his *Essays*. In the former, Berkeley's system is said to hold that

extension and figure, and hardness and motion; that land, and sea, and houses, and our own bodies, as well as those of our wives, and children, and friends, are nothing but ideas of the mind; and that there is nothing in nature, but minds and ideas (p. 110).

A similar passage occurs in the *Essays*: Berkeley maintains that "there is no such thing as matter in the universe: That sun, moon, and stars, the earth which we inhabit, our own bodies, and those of our friends, are only ideas in our minds" (p. 70; cf. p. 183). Reid's equating of 'matter' with the ordinary objects of our experience misses entirely Berkeley's careful and labored distinction between them.

Because he failed to make this distinction, Reid did not realize that Berkeley would agree with him in saying it is "a perfect lunacy to call in question the existence of external objects" (*Essays*, p. 165). Reid's tracing of the history of the way of ideas convinced him that such a denial as he thought Berkeley and Hume made of an external world was due to their making ideas into things, not the ordinary objects of our experience but special objects in addition to the ordinary ones.

Thus, in the perception of an external object, all languages distinguish three things, the *mind* that perceives, the operation of that mind, which is called *perception*, and the *object* perceived. Nothing appears more evident to a mind untutored by philosophy, than that these three are distinct things, which, though related, ought never to be confounded. The structure of all languages supposes this distinction, and is built upon it. Philosophers have introduced a fourth thing in this process, which they call the *idea* of the object, which is supposed to be an image, or representative of the object, and is said to be the immediate object. (*Essays*, p. 222)

Reid's account of the way of ideas is hardly supported by a close examination of the writings of those I have discussed in this study. With respect to Berkeley, Reid misses two fundamental features: the translating of 'exist in' by such cognitive terms as 'perceive' and 'understand', and the denial that ideas are modes of mind. This second feature carries, as we have seen, the positive assertion that objects are present to us in the form of ideas. In terms of the above-quoted passage from Reid, Berkeley espouses a view very close to that which Reid says is embedded in all languages. As I have suggested earlier, this remark about ideas not being modes of mind is strongly reminiscent of Descartes's discussion of objective reality: both writers were struggling to find a way of articulating our perceptual acquaintance with objects. That articulation borrowed from scholastic terminology but went on to stress the meaning or significatory aspect of sensory awareness.

Tipton's discussion of Berkeley helps us understand Berkeley in this way, although Tipton does not in the end believe this was Berkeley's final view. Reid's reading of all those who followed the way of ideas is identical with Berkeley's characterization of the materialists (corpuscularians). What the mind perceives, according to the materialists, is "only the impressions made upon its brain or rather the ideas attending those impressions."[5] Berkeley argues that we never do perceive the external objects of these materialists, objects which (to use Hume's language) differ specifically, not just numerically, from the ideas of which we are aware.[6] Tipton points out that

Berkeley was "himself convinced that as he looked around he saw the fields, woods, groves, rivers and springs, the things themselves."[7] Berkeley insisted that the real world is sensible, available to us through sensation—just what the materialists denied. What we know or perceive are the things themselves. We do not have to resort to inference to claim knowledge of those things.

What is it to perceive the things themselves? In his account of those who deny such perception, Tipton speaks of being "in a quite straightforward sense, acquainted with the things 'out there'" (p. 20). At other times, he uses the locution, being acquainted with "tables, chairs, and other ordinary objects" in a "straight-forward sense" (p. 22), and that of knowing, or not knowing, things immediately (p. 49). The only meaning Tipton seems to give to these locutions is that we know things 'out there' without the help of other entities 'inside the mind'. In discussing more recent appeals to the 'scientific causal theory' (which is supposed to yield the conclusion that what we know are our own sensations), Tipton observes: "The way out of the difficulty is not to deny the propriety of scientific accounts of perception in terms of processes but rather to resist the temptation to reify sensations" (pp. 23-24). Later, in discussing the distinction between primary and secondary qualities, Tipton remarks that if we decide "that the table is not *really* brown," there is no need for us to say "that we see something—an idea-thing—which is brown" (p. 35). Later still, writing about the causal theory of perception, he identifies as the basic error in that theory, "supposing that the end result of the process described by the scientist must be the perception of an entity quite distinct from the causal object" (p. 66). Tipton also cites Jessop's remark: "The sensed is itself the real corporeal world, perception interposing no screen, whether opaque or diaphanous, of mental entities between us and it" (p. 82).[8] Tipton insists that we can accept the causal account of perception without accepting the usual conclusion, that the product of that process is an *entity*. He still does not explain what it is to be acquainted with objects in a quite straightforward sense, but what is interesting in his remark is his recognition that it is the reification of sensations that makes for indirectness. One of the two concepts of ideas that we have found in some writings of the period just examined (ideas as entities) Tipton identifies as leading to the indirectness and skepticism against which Reid wrote. Reid found skepticism in the way of ideas because he thought (wrongly) that the only concept of ideas, or the dominant concept, was *that* one.

Reid thought it important to distinguish "the appearance of

objects to the eye, from the judgment which we form by sight" (*Inquiry*, p. 95). He praised Berkeley for recognizing "that the visible appearance of objects is a kind of language used by nature, to inform us of their distance" (p. 94). The "visible appearance of objects is," Reid believed, "hardly ever regarded by us," it is not made "an object of thought or reflection" (p. 93). Tipton is convinced that Berkeley "does want us to think of the appearance as itself a thing" (p. 187). The difficulty for Tipton comes in understanding what he takes to be Berkeley's single-existence view, for that view requires us to say that the very things we see and touch are the things themselves, that these appearances (the immediate objects of perception) "are themselves the basic things in the sensible world" (p. 191). Tipton cannot find a way of understanding this move in the single-existence view without, after all, turning the appearances into special things: Berkeley does "really . . . hold that each sense datum is an entity" (p. 185).

Not worried about equating Berkeley's 'ideas' with the much more modern term 'sense-data', Tipton does nevertheless reach this conclusion reluctantly, for he elsewhere recognizes that Berkeley took the claim that "we perceive only ideas" as "asserting that the physical world is something we are acquainted with in sense experience" (p. 85). He recognizes that for Berkeley "there is only one world, a world which our senses inform us of and which is made up of ideas, and that this world is the real world" (p. 53). The difficulty with this last remark is that the phrase, the one world 'is made up of ideas', sounds as if ideas are ontic building blocks. It is as if the atomic corpuscular doctrine has been replaced by an atomistic mental-entity doctrine. But we have seen that the dominant concept of idea employed by the writers examined in this study is the one that treats ideas as the same as thoughts, or as the cognitive content of awareness. Reid misses this important fact. Tipton comes close to an appreciation of this way of understanding the term 'idea', but he ends by viewing Berkeley's ideas as ontic building blocks and as numerically identical with objects. Tipton fails to see that Berkeley holds to a double-existence view, in which the distinction between cognitive content and objects in the world is not a distinction between two different kinds of objects.

Tipton's analysis of Berkeley's account takes seriously the ontological tone of the *esse est percipi* principle, despite his recognition that there are some passages (he cites Principle 48) where 'exist in' clearly means 'be perceived by' (p. 87). As we have seen, a number of other passages give the same translation of the notion of existing in a mind. If we take that translation seriously, the mind-dependency principle would lose its apparent ontic sting. Moreover, if, as Berkeley insists, ideas are things and not modes of mind, then the notion of ideas as supposed *mental* entities would disappear from his account. 'To perceive an idea' would be equivalent with 'to perceive an object or thing'. Tipton thinks that this is a too generous reading of Berkeley's mind-dependency principle (pp. 94-95). What I believe we must all admit now is that, however we deal with this principle in Berkeley's account of perceptual awareness, Thomas Reid's route to the Ideal System (and to its consequent skepticism) is built upon a feature that does not apply to that system: the claim that ideas are mental things. Ideas for Berkeley, as for Arnauld, can be viewed in two ways: as perceptions or as the things perceived. Berkeley comes out of and belongs to that tradition. The dependency principle probably has a theological motive; it provides an account of the dependency of the world on God. That principle also recognizes the point made later by Hume, that perceptions are interrupted and discontinuous. The fact that the dependency of ideas or perceptions is cognitive and not causal is itself symptomatic of changes in the eighteenth century, changes which Ian Hacking has recently surveyed.[9]

Certainly for human knowledge, that ideal of a deductive knowledge from necessary connections which was present in, even detailed but rejected by Locke was displaced by the attentive systematic construction of natural histories. Such histories were an account of coexistences. An account of systematic coexistences became the foundation for the science of nature, a science based upon discovering uniformities. This change, of course, was begun before Locke by Bacon, Hobbes, and others. It is also present in Descartes, alongside the older model of knowledge. But Locke marks the watershed for this change. He portrays in great detail what the structure and content of a deductive science of nature would be, from real essences and real necessary connections, but he also shows that such a knowledge is not possible for humans, urging us to be good observers instead.[10] The belief in real causes, in the secret springs and causes in nature, is present in Hume, especially in his *Enquiry concerning Human Understanding*, but he too was convinced that all claims to penetrate nature's real causes were chimerical. Berkeley's *De Motu* contained a strong warning against assuming that Newton's gravitational force was a principle of nature disclosing real forces. Hacking cites section 35 of that work: "It is not, however, in fact the business of physics or mechanics to establish efficient causes, but only the rules of impulsions or attractions, and, in a word, the laws of motions, and from the established laws to assign the solutions, not the efficient cause, of particular phenomena." In his *Principles* and his *Dialogues* too, Berkeley replaced causal language with the language of uniformities, taking those uniformities to provide us, when we learned how to do so, with signs and significations. Nature as the language of God was the eventual form this substitution of signs for causes took in Berkeley's writings.

The notion of the book of nature is older than Berkeley. It is found in Paracelsus and alchemists, reappearing in different forms down to Berkeley's time. The major difference between Berkeley's use of this metaphor and the earlier uses of it seems to be that the earlier users believed we could gain access to the real workings of the world by deciphering the signs in which the book of nature was written, whereas Berkeley limited us to making predictions from one bit of experience to future uniformities of experience.[11] It is precisely this change from searching for causes to making predictions within experience, which turns our attention away from the world specifically different from our perceptions in order to concentrate upon the uniformities of our perceptions. This change is paralleled by, if not the same as, the change in the concept of meaning. The older sixteenth- and early seventeenth-century views found meaning in the world. Even language was part of the world, either in its Adamic form (where Adam read the signs and signatures on things) or in the quest for a universal language that, as with Wilkins, would recapture what had been lost from the Adamic language: universal signs revealing the nature of things. Here also, Locke was at the heart of change, for as Murray Cohen has observed, the notion of naming expressed by Locke's Adam "was not distinguished by an essential connection between word and thing, but by a correspondence between the order of ideas (the pattern of his thoughts) and the grammar of language."[12] In the passage cited by Cohen (*Essay*, 3.6.51), Adam conforms to Locke's account of naming: Adam's making of complex ideas was tied down to the "pattern of his own thoughts," and, Locke adds, the same has been true for all men ever since.

Foucault's analysis of the change in the concept of meaning in the eighteenth century shows how theories of signs turned away from the world, in upon themselves. There is a suggestion in Foucault's account that such inward turning tended to trap sign-users inside the sign system.[13] In this shift in theory of signs, there are some interesting possible similarities with skepticism—or, better, supporting tendencies toward skepticism. Reid may after all (it might seem) be right, but for the wrong reasons. If the theory of signs does reinforce the theory of perception, we can say that Berkeley was located at the intersection of both theories. The problem then is: is it possible to distinguish meaning from referent, idea from thing?[14]

Present throughout the various appeals to ideas in the accounts of perceptual acquaintance we have examined is the theme of meaning and signification. The alternative to ideas as entities was ideas as meaningful contents. The alternative to assimilating cognition to viewing the images in a *camera obscura* was the stress upon understanding and intelligibility. The language of sign and signification was interwoven with optical language and with the language of objects. All the writers we have examined stress the importance of understanding and meaning in the account of perception. Descartes's analysis of beeswax set the direction for this stress. He had in mind knowledge, not perceptual acquaintance, of bodies. Knowledge was of the essential features, not of the sensory appearances of body. Malebranche's appeal to intelligible extension was a similar stress on the need for augmenting perception with understanding. In Britain, Mayne thought conceptual understanding was such an important ingredient in the perception of objects that he insisted upon the distinction between notions and ideas. Crousaz made a similar point, as did Burthogge earlier. It is not clear whether Mayne thought the sensory content of perception had no meaning: it was for him an image that waits to be understood. The image as he understood it may have been something between a brain impression and a cognitive content. He very likely considered it to be a conscious mental content and hence cognitive, but too weak to bear the weight of perceptual knowledge. The categories in terms of which he viewed such knowledge—substance, existence, unity, cause—were ones also used by Locke. What Mayne missed in Locke's account was that sensory ideas are signs and hence for Locke carry meaning. Such ideas, together with those nonsensory categorial ideas of substance, cause, etc., are the contents in terms of which we perceive and know the world.

The distinction between knowing and perceiving was not so much a distinction of kind as it was one dealing with different features of the world. The accounts of sense-perception, of perceptual acquaintance, in the two centuries examined in this study assumed that such acquaintance was cognitive, that it involved understanding. Locke's doctrine of idea-signs is an account of meaningful mental contents that arise in the mind by, in most cases, the joint operation of bodies acting by impulse on our body and the operations of our mind in attending, considering, supposing, concluding, and so on. Locke's sensory ideas are our cognition of appearances, of coexisting qualities.

With respect to these ideas, we could say that Locke is working with a single-existence notion. Those ideas are not things, but ways of knowing, of being perceptually acquainted with objects as groups of experienced qualities. But calling this a single-existence notion is not to say that Locke fails to distinguish between the experience and what is experienced. Keeping the cognitive perceptual content and the qualities perceived distinct is not always easy, Locke frequently runs them together. But he does make a threefold distinction between the thing itself, as a group of insensible, cohering particles; the appearances or coexisting qualities as perceived; and the ideas or mental contents of those appearing qualities. The difficulty of maintaining this distinction is perhaps compounded by the distinction Locke drew between primary and secondary qualities, for the latter seem to have a different status in appearance from the former. That this difference is only apparent is a suggestion I have made elsewhere.[15] When, in Locke's account, we talk of the coexisting qualities as they constitute what we call one thing, the ideas we have are of the very things themselves. Sensory ideas are not signs of the corpuscular structure, but signs in terms of which we know or are acquainted with appearances.

In Berkeley's writing, we find that this aspect of ideas as signs, as the basis for our knowledge of the world, is developed into an account of scientific knowledge. The search for causes has been replaced by the close examination of the uniformities and regularities in our world. Reid praises Berkeley, as we saw, for considering the visible appearances of objects as a kind of language "used by nature, to inform us of their distance, magnitude, and size" (*Inquiry*, p. 94). Mastering the language of nature gives us predictive powers: one mental content can serve as the basis for others, either as between vision and touch, or as between present and future experiences. We discover these sign-signified connections through custom and experience. Reid makes this point by saying that this sign-signified relation is "established by nature, but discovered only by experience" (p. 65). As far as we know, Reid says, no necessary connections exist in nature, but the significatory relations are adequate for our needs. Such signs are for Reid one of three kinds of *natural* signs. The second kind are those that are established by nature and discovered by us through natural principles of our nature, without reasoning, e.g., facial gestures, smiles, tears. The third kind are natural signs which, although we have not been aware of their signification, have been signifying for us nevertheless. An example is that sensations signify a sentient being (p. 66).

Earlier in the *Inquiry*, Reid spoke of natural suggestions:

sensation suggests the notion of present existence, and the belief that what we perceive or feel, does now exist; that memory suggests the notion of past existence, and the belief that what we remember did exist in time past; and that our sensations and thoughts do also suggest the notion of a mind, and the belief of its existence, and of its relation to our thoughts. (pp. 38-39)

The belief that accompanies these experiences arises through the original constitution of our nature (p. 45). While sensation suggests and makes us believe in the existence of external objects, Reid does not pretend to know how it works: it happens "by a law of our nature" (p. 85). Another example of this third kind of natural sign is that certain sensations signify or suggest hardness in bodies (p. 67), sensations of touch "suggest to us extension, solidity, and motion" (p. 38). The sensations experienced when we press our hand against a table "both suggest to the mind the conception of hardness and create the belief of it" (p. 62). This suggestion or significatory relation is triggered "by the material impression upon the organ of which we are not conscious" (p. 119). Nor do we seem to be aware of the sensation that is the natural sign: "we pass from the sign to the thing signified, with ease, and by natural impulse," without being aware of the sign (p. 121). To discover the specific sensory sign that suggests some specific quality "is a work of labour and difficulty" (ibid.). This sign function of sensation is compared to language: "The sensations of smell, taste, sound, and colour are of infinitely more importance as signs or indications, than they are upon their own account; like the words of a language, wherein we do not attend to the sound, but to the sense" (pp. 45-46).

These natural signs of Reid are descendents of the signs instituted by nature of which Descartes mentioned the possibility and Cudworth and Bonnet elaborated some details. A later passage in Reid's *Inquiry* makes this connection more apparent.

Nature hath established a real connection between the signs and the things signified; and nature hath also taught us the inter-representation of the signs; so that, previous to experience the sign suggests the thing signified, and creates the belief in it. (p. 235)

Some sensations or perceptions are natural and original, others are acquired. Both for Reid are the language of nature, for it is by their means that we learn about nature (p. 233).[16] In acquired perception,

the signs are either sensations, or things which we perceive by means of sensations. The connection between the sign and the thing signified, is established by nature: and we discover this connection by experience; but not without the aid of our original perceptions, or of those which we have already acquired. After this connection is discovered, the sign, in like manner as in original perception, always suggests the things signified, and creates the belief of it. (p. 236)

Reid's acquired perceptions play the same role as Berkeley's natural signs, enabling us to link vision with touch or present with future experience. Reid's natural perceptions, with their original sensations, which are unconscious signs for us of object properties, echo another aspect of Berkeley's visual language of God: the way in which ideas are God's means of informing us about qualities of objects. For Berkeley, the ideas that are our sensory contents and the sensible qualities in the world are run together. Or, we can say, no distinction can be drawn between them. The world as known *is* the world of ideas, of significatory content. It is a manifest contradiction to attempt to apprehend a world that is not conceived. To think of a world unexperienced is to attempt to think of a world in nonperceptual, noncognitive terms. Hume makes the same point when he says it is "impossible for us so much as to conceive or form an idea of any thing specifically different from ideas and impressions" (*Treatise*, p. 67). From this conceptual and factual point (and it *is* both), it does not follow that our conceptions of objects are not *of* objects. Our ideas have objective as well as formal reality.

It is this Cartesian notion of objective reality, with its roots in scholastic theory, which sets the theme for the analysis of our knowledge of bodies during the two centuries. If we can understand how ideas must have objective reality, what it means to use that vocabulary, we shall comprehend what many accounts of perceptual acquaintance were saying. That notion was difficult for most of Descartes's contemporaries to grasp. We have noted earlier the problems Caterus had with that notion. Olivier Bloch points out Gassendi's objections to it also. Besides denying that ideas as modalities could represent substances, and besides denying that ideas can ever have a reality of their own, the more important objection raised by Gassendi is, as Bloch expresses it, simply that the so-called objective reality of ideas cannot be the measure of the formal reality of things. The objective reality can capture the awareness we have of things, not the things: "the objective reality of an idea is reduced to a relation . . . and it is only an extrinsic denomination in relation to the idea itself."[17] There is nothing in the idea itself that is analogous to the formal reality of the object.

The relation between that supposed objective reality of the idea and the formal reality of the thing is in effect of the same sort as the relation between myself and the image of me in a mirror or in a picture; in both cases the objective reality invoked by Descartes is itself nothing other than the way in which the image represents me; that is, the relation of parts of the mirror or picture to each other in the way that my parts are related. In other words, the relation is a *mode* of the formal reality of the image.[18]

Because what is seen is seen in or by means of a mirror, I see the object only as it is in relation to that medium. Because what is seen or perceptually known is seen by means of ideas, I see or am perceptually aware of the object only as it is mediated by ideas. Seeing the object direct, rather than by means of a mirror, knowing the object direct, rather than by means of ideas: these are the conditions that some writers believe must be met for direct, nonmediated perception. If, to paraphrase Arnauld, 'perception by means of ideas' means 'perception by means of special entities', the distancing of the object from the perceiver follows easily. The skepticism in this move noted by Reid was also stressed by Arnauld. But, if those who speak of ideas mean by that term the perceptual contents of awareness, Arnauld seems to be right in saying the demand for idea-less direct perception is in effect a demand that we perceive without perceiving, "because it is clearer than the day that we are able to see, perceive, or know only by the perceptions we have" of things.[19]

Another way of making Arnauld's point might be to remark with Bloch that the scholastic-Aristotelian theory "makes of vision, and in general of perception, an essentially metaphysical phenomenon: the intentional species is an accident of substance, having with it a metaphysical connection which is in some way a connection of *signification* by means of which the species translates or expresses the meaning of the *thing*."[20] Take this significatory translation which expresses the meaning of objects, and cut the species loose from any ontic status; then you have made the point: perceiving will and must yield, if it is to be conscious, a meaningful, significant content. The mirror does not, by some magic, produce an image unrelated to the object; nor does the perceiver create perceptual content unrelated to the world. The discourse between the world and the perceiver is not causal, it is significant.

In a recent interesting article, A. C. Danto recognizes that there are "two sorts of liaison between ideas and whatever it may be, external to themselves, upon which their truth depends when and if they are true: what we may term a *semantical liaison*, and a causal one."[21] But in his elaboration of the way of ideas in Descartes, Danto tends to ignore the semantical connection; he tends to appeal to the causal one when it is the semantical one he should be using. Danto's mistake may prove useful. He is concerned with the conditions that, for Descartes, justify me in affirming an idea (p. 292). Affirming is asserting, claiming that an idea is true. His answer is that I am justified in affirming some idea when I am "caused to have it by the object O which satisfies that idea's truth-condition." In other words, "it must be ultimately with reference to O that I explain the fact that I have the ideas of it to begin with." *Being caused by O* and *with reference to O* are not the same, however. These two phrases should be correlated with the two liaisons identified by Danto, the *with reference to O* indicating the *semantical connection*. In searching for the conditions under which "I may be wrong in affirming truth," Danto lists three: (a) when the idea I affirm has no denotation in the world; (b) "when the idea has a denotation, but it fails to satisfy the further truth-conditions of the idea, as when I affirm that there are purple goats"; and (c) "when I am caused to have the idea by something other than anything which may satisfy its truth-conditions, as when I am caused to have an idea of goats in a dream by having eaten too much fondue" (p. 292). In pursuing the third of these conditions Danto begins to use the causal connection incorrectly. He suggests that Descartes's account of the causation of true ideas is that "the object must activate the right nerves in the right way" (ibid.). Such physical and physiological causation is necessary for perceptual acquaintance, but it is not, as Danto seems to believe, sufficient. The necessary and sufficient conditions for having a true idea are (a) that the physiology be linked causally with the object and (b) that the idea acquire the reality of the object objectively. For the latter condition, physical causation is impotent.

In trying to explicate the causal liaison, Danto uses the example of a photograph. What are the conditions for a photograph being *of* a particular object? Whether the likeness is close or not, something "is a photograph of X just if caused by X, and if caused by something other than X, it is not of X. In brief, the representational characterization of a snapshot, viz. as *of* X, always implies a causal condition which, if not satisfied, renders false the representational characterization" (p. 294). The comparison between ideas and photographs is, however, misleading, because the representational property of the latter is dependent only upon its having been physically caused by the object. The representational property of Cartesian ideas is not only dependent upon the physical causal process. The difference lies in the fact that for cognition, but not for photography, representation is dependent as well upon those cognitive, psychological features of meaning and significance. The semantical feature of representation is not divorced from the causal features, although in Descartes's doctrine of degrees of reality, the causation of some ideas need not be linked to only one object. That is, it is not true that, as Danto claims, "Every idea licenses an ontological argument" (p. 295), for as an immaterial substance, I am capable of being the cause of the idea of a material substance; it is even easier for me to be the cause of the idea of a quality. Causation in Descartes's chain-of-being ontology requires that the cause have at least as much reality as the effect. It may have more.

Nevertheless, let us set aside these possible causes of ideas of body. Let us take those cases of normal perception in which I have the idea of a stone, a book, a table. Two modes of causation, it may seem, are involved in the genesis of such an idea. One mode of causation is formal to formal. The formal cause of my idea of the stone is I myself, my mind. Ideas are modes of mind. But the formal cause of this idea does not account for its content, for the fact that it is the idea of a stone, a book, a table. The second mode of causation in the production of this idea is formal to objective. The content of this idea is linked with the object; the idea contains that object objectively. What this last phrase means, as used by Descartes, Arnauld, Locke, Berkeley, Hume, and others in the period we are studying, is simply that the object is perceived, known, apprehended, understood. What is the nature of the causation that results in understanding? It cannot be physical or physiological because, while such causation is necessary for awareness, and for the specific awareness of that stone, the idea as conscious content of awareness must result from cognitive processes. We do not have ready to hand any concept of causation that makes sense of, or that explains, the formal to objective liaison.

Throughout, I have suggested that this relation not be viewed as causal, that instead of placing the emphasis on formal objects as the initiators of the perceptual responses, we give that emphasis to the perceptual response. A response is usually thought of as caused by some event or object, and perceptual acquaintance for the way of ideas *is* a response to events occurring in the environment and in our physiology. Perceptual acquaintance is a significatory response to natural signs. Instead of two modes of causation, it is better to talk of two kinds of relation or connection. In Danto's language, the signified liaison augments the cause-effect liaison. Perceptual acquaintance involves two liaisons: a semantical and a causal connection.

In his discussion of Locke, Duchesneau recognizes the same two relations.[22] Locke identifies two kinds of signs, words and ideas. There are some similarities between sentences and complex ideas as signs: meaning is a function of the relation of the components, of words in the one case and of simple ideas in the other. The analysis of language was for Locke intimately linked with the analysis of knowledge. Duchesneau makes the point that linguistic meaning was for Locke dependent upon epistemic meaning. Words signify ideas, but the relation between words is not a sufficient condition for knowledge of the world; that relation depends upon and even implies "the relation of the idea to a real producing cause" (p. 200). Simple ideas for Locke are rooted in reality. Duchesneau cites *Essay* 4.4.4 as a reminder:

From whence it follows that *simple* ideas *are not fictions of* our fancies, but the natural and regular productions of things without us, really operating upon us, and so carry with them all the conformity which is intended or which our state requires; for they represent to us things under those appearances which they are fitted to produce in us: whereby we are enabled to distinguish the sorts of particular substances, to discern the states they are in, and so to take them for our necessities and apply them to our uses.

In the language of truth, Duchesneau remarks, "the word-idea correlation is true only when it functions in conformity with the data of experience" (p. 200).

Elsewhere, Duchesneau calls attention to the same two relations in Locke's discussion of primary and secondary qualities. Duchesneau distinguishes in *Essay* 2.8 "the semiotic argument" and "the argument taken from physical theory."[23] The latter argument is Locke's appeal to the corpuscular theory as a causal explanation of the genesis of ideas. The semiotic or semantic argument (the argument from meaning) refers to the stress Locke places upon what we can conceive about primary qualities, those qualities that the mind finds as part of its conception of matter whatever form it takes. Duchesneau also reminds us of Locke's characterization of the science of signs, "to consider the nature of signs the mind makes use of for the understanding of things" (4.21.4). 'Understanding' is the important word here. Duchesneau suggests that "the fundamental thesis of the *Essay* is that the empirical presentation of the object is the moment of its conceptualization."[24] With his recognition of the centrality in Locke of the concept of meaning and understanding, Duchesneau goes on to make the point that, instead of 'copy', "the relation of representation must be interpreted according to the model of the relation of signification."[25] The representation of objects by ideas is rooted in the origin of simple ideas: in actually receiving ideas of sense, the reception of those ideas carries the sense of their external, causal origin. Even in the case of the ideas of secondary qualities, their 'objectivity' does not make them phantasms:

There is an *objective* relation of signification, excluding resemblance, between the perception of colors, smells, . . . and the real properties of things. That relation is grounded in the certitude of *sensitive knowledge*, since the ideas of sensible qualities in the actual experience of sensing, tell us of the real existence of a corresponding object.[26]

In the genesis of ideas on Locke's account, two processes occur. One process is that of corpuscles acting on sense organs and of impulses being transmitted to nerves and brain. The other process is psychological, involving the same mental operations as we noticed in Hume's account: attending, considering, conceiving, inferring. Where Locke is silent is on the intersection of these two processes. Locke's silence on this point is not unique; we have not found many of the writers in the two centuries addressing this intersection. Almost all the writers we have examined recognized the role of meaning in perceptual acquaintance. Most settled for concomitance: concurrently with the physical causal process there occurs the cognitive one. This was Descartes's account in the *Regulae*; Malebranche accepted it while adding God's intervention in our awareness; Locke stays with that concomitance while attending to the details of the significance-relation captured by ideas. Duchesneau catches Locke's acceptance of the concurrence of causal and cognitive processes in that phrase cited above: when the object is given in sensation, the perceiver's reaction is one of conceptualization—the significatory response to physical processes. Duchesneau's expression could stand as a characterization for most of those in the way-of-ideas tradition.

We can distinguish two versions of the stress on the semantic connection. One version is that suggested by Descartes, elaborated by Cudworth and Bonnet, and touched upon by Reid: cognitive awareness is viewed as a significatory response to unconscious signs. The other and more common version is the view of ideas as signs, as the intelligible contents of awareness, where these idea-signs are the cognitive translation of objects, the meaning of things, the intelligibility of the real. It is this view of ideas, and of the perceptual process, that survives the optical metaphors and the spatial language. The talk of being *present to* the mind, of existing *in* the mind, was not always as carefully translated as it was by Locke in a few passages, by Berkeley generally, and most clearly and firmly by Arnauld. Arnaud never gave up trying to show Malebranche the sense of these phrases, even as with Berkeley later, the sense of 'in the mind of God'. Noting St. Thomas's remark (*Summa Theo.*, I, Q.15) that "the idea of the thing to be produced is in the mind of the producer as that which is understood, and not as the likeness whereby he understands," Arnauld went on to make the comment, which Berkeley was to echo in the eighteenth century, that "a thing is able to be objectively in God, that is, to be known by God."[27]

When we sort out the various concepts of idea, when we follow Arnauld's lead in drawing a careful distinction between spatial and cognitive language, and when we then place Hume's mental geography, his anatomy of the mind, in this context, we are able to thread our way through the tradition from Descartes to Reid and arrive at a more accurate history of the way of ideas. One of the more fascinating aspects of this tradition is the way the discussion starts and ends with the same issue. Just as Reid charged the way of ideas with skepticism, because, as he thought, the writers in that mode took ideas as separately existing entities, so Arnauld made the same charge against Malebranche, because Malebranche's ideas were separately existing entities.

It was the ontologizing of ideas which, in large part, resulted in the standard interpretation of the representative theory and of those seventeenth- and eighteenth-century philosophers who were supposed to have held that theory. It may have been the Cartesian notion of objective reality (read as Malebranche, not as Arnauld, did) which gave impetus to ontologizing ideas, or to viewing them so. When this notion is combined with that of representation, ideas could be taken as representative *beings*. The de-ontologizing of ideas, which our examination of the literature from Descartes to Reid has revealed to be a prominent feature throughout, was due to two moves. One move was to indicate that having ideas was the same as perceiving. The second de-ontologizing move was the translating of the metaphor 'exist in the mind' as 'perceived, conceived, understood or known'. Both moves point to the conscious, cognitive, and semantic features of perceptual awareness. 'Representation' may still be a term to apply to such awareness, to the contents of that awareness, but that label, 'the representative theory of perception', or 'representative realism', should no longer carry the association of that other metaphor, 'the veil of perception'. If the skepticism about the external world which Reid saw in the way-of-ideas tradition was traced, as he did, to ideas being proxy objects, third things, then, in revising the standard reading of that tradition in the light of what we have discovered, such skepticism should also disappear. Attention can then be directed toward the more important component in accounts of perceptual acquaintance, the meaning and significatory response. Attention can also be given to the cognitive processes that were so prevalent in this tradition, to what Hume characterized as 'acts of the mind'.

Once we appreciate these components of the cognitive psychology found in the way of ideas, we can also say that, despite a heavy use of and even some influence by the optical treatises, the majority of seventeenth- and eighteenth-century writers did not consider the mind to be a mirror of nature.[28] The correction that this study makes to the standard accounts of these philosophers will be no more palatable to Richard Rorty than the mirror-of-nature reading which he accepts, for the writers in the way of ideas firmly held the belief in a world of objects with which we interact. We find that world meaningful as well as useful. Talk of such a world is not just a convenient way of talking and believing. Perceptual acquaintance leads, so these writers believed, to knowledge (or at least, probability) of that world. Rorty is too quick to find foundationalism and incorrigibility in that account of knowledge, but the main fault he finds with that account is that it claims to be knowledge of a world. Many of the writers we have examined took such knowledge to be direct, in the sense that our cognitive responses are to objects, not in the sense that objects are in some mysterious, mystical way absorbed by, incorporated into the mind. There are lessons to be learned from Arnauld, from Berkeley, and from Hume about what is and is not, about what can and cannot be direct awareness of objects. Before we can profit from those writers, we must correct the long misunderstanding of their doctrines.

Notes

1. *Essays on the Intellectual Powers of Man* (Edinburgh, 1785); the quotation appears in vol. I, pp. 107-8 of the Dublin edition of 1786. Page references in the text are to the Dublin edition.
2. For Reid's discussion of the dictum, see ibid., pp. 240-44.
3. *An Inquiry into the Human Mind* (1764); the quotation is found on p. 32 of the modern edition by T. J. Duggan (Chicago, 1970). Page references in the text are to the modern edition.
4. Ibid., p. 143.
5. Berkeley's *Philosophical Commentaries*, entry 74 in Notebook B.
6. See I. C. Tipton, *Berkeley, the Philosophy of Immaterialism* (1974), p. 40.
7. Ibid., p. 81.
8. Later in this work, Tipton quotes another contemporary writer, Don Locke, making a similar point about the sense-datum theory. "Sense data are what we immediately perceive. But this does not mean that sense data form some special class of objects which are perceived in some special way. Sense data are not, on a Realist interpretation, objects at all." (pp. 184-85 in Tipton, from p. 179 of Locke's *Perception and Our Knowledge of the External World*, 1967).
9. Ian Hacking, *The Emergence of Probability* (1975). Hacking traces the notion and use of signs instead of causes through a variety of writers: physicians, magicians, alchemists,

and philosophers. The link between signs and evidence for belief and probable knowledge is carefully explored by Hacking.

10. For a discussion of these two types of science of nature, see my *Locke and the Compass of Human Understanding* (1970), chapters 3 and 4.

11. These differences have been traced by Foucault, *Les Mots et les choses* (1966), chapter 11. There is a useful discussion of the book-of-nature notion in relation to printing. the dissemination of knowledge, and science in Elizabeth Eisenstein, *The Printing Press as an Agent of Change* (1979), part 3, chapter 5.

12. Murray Cohen, *Sensible Words: Linguistic Practice in England, 1640-1785* (1977), p. 40.

13. Foucault, *Les Mots et les choses*, pp. 76-80.

14. I chart some of the similarities in the question of the reality of knowledge and the reality of language in *Locke and the Compass*, chapter 5.

15. *Locke and the Compass*, pp. 122-24.

16. Reid notes another similarity between the two languages: "as in human languages, ambiguities are often found, so this language of nature in our acquired perceptions is not exempted from them. We have seen, in vision particularly, that the same appearance to the eye, may, in different circumstances, indicate different things. Therefore, when the circumstances are known upon which the interpretation of the signs depends, their meaning must be ambiguous; and when the circumstances are mistaken, the meaning of the signs must also be mistaken" (p. 233). In the next century, Mill uses the language of natural signs for sensations, in explaining, against Bailey, Berkeley's account of visual and tactual impressions: the mind does not attend to the sign but "runs on to the thing signified." ("Bailey on Berkeley's Theory of Vision" [1842] in *Essays on Philosophy and the Classics*, ed. J. M. Robson, in the edition of Mill's works published by the University of Toronto Press, vol. 11, p. 259.)

17. Olivier René Bloch, *La Philosophie de Gassendi* (1971), p. 128.

18. Arnauld's conclusion from a similar mirror example is quite different: people believe mistakenly that it is not the bodies themselves that are seen in mirrors, but only their images. Arnauld insists that we see both the image and the body. (*Des vraies et des fausses idées*, p. 190.)

19. Ibid., p. 210.

20. Bloch, *La Philosophie de Gassendi*, pp. 20-21.

21. "The Representational Character of Ideas and the Problem of the External World," in *Descartes: Critical and Interpretive Essays* (1978), ed. Michael Hooker, p. 291.

22. François Duchesneau, *L'Empirisme de Locke* (1973).

23. "L'Analyse d'idées selon Locke," in *Les Études philosophiques* 1977, no. 1, pp. 67-94.

24. Ibid., p. 72.

25. Ibid., p. 70.

26. Ibid., p. 89.

27. Arnauld, *Des vraies et des fausses idées*, p. 246.

28. This is the reading given to this period by Richard Rorty in his recent study. *Philosophy and the Mirror of Nature* (1979). For a discussion of this book, see my review in *Philosophical Books*, July 1981.

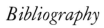

Bibliography

Bibliography

Primary Sources

[Aldrich,Henry.] *Artis Logicae Compendium*. Oxonii: E Theatro Sheldoniano, 1691. 99 p.

[Applegarth, Robert.]*A Theological Survey of the Human Understanding; Intended as an Antidote against Modern Deism*. Salisbury: J. Hodson, 1776. 276 p.

Aristotle. "De anima (on the Soul)." In *The Basic Works of Aristotle*, edited with an Introduction by Richard McKeon, pp. 535-603. New York: Random House, 1941.

Arnauld, Antoine. *Des vraies et des fausses idées, contre ce qu'enseigne l'auteur De la recherche de la vérité* [N. Malebranche]. À Cologne: Chez N. Schouten, 1683. 339 pp. Also published in *Oeuvres de Messire Antoine Arnauld*. Paris: Chez S. D'Arnay, 1775-83. Vol. 38, pp. 177-362.

———. *Défense de Mr. Arnauld . . . contre la Réponse au livre, Des vraies et des fausses idées . . .* Cologne: N. Schouten, 1684. 623 pp.

———, and Pierre Nicole. *Logic; or, The Art of Thinking . . . Translated into English by Several Hands*. London: Printed by T. B. for H. Sawbridge, 1685. 2 vols. (250, 247 pp.)

Astruc, Jean. *De Morbis Venereis Libri Sex . . .* [Paris]: Apud G. Cavelier, 1736. xxiv, 600 pp.

———. *Dissertatio Medica de Sensatione*. Montpellier, 1720. 54 pp. Listed in A. L. J. Bayle and A. Thillaye, *Biographie médicale, par ordre chronologique . . .* Paris, 1885. Vol. 2, pp. 215-19. See also Janet Doe's article, "Jean Astruc (1684-1766): A Biographical and Bibliographical Study." *Journal of the History of Medicine* 15 (April 1960): 84-197.

———. *Quaestio Medica de Naturali et Praeternaturali Judicii Exercitio*. Monspelii, 1718. 41 pp.

Barron, William. *Lectures on Belles Lettres and Logic*. London: Longman, Hurst, Rees and Orme, 1806. 2 vols.

[Baxter, Andrew.] *An Enquiry into the Nature of the Human Soul; Wherein the Immateriality of the Soul is Evinced from the Principles of Reason and Philosophy*. London: Printed for J. Bettenham, [1733] 376 pp.

Bayle, Pierre. *Oeuvres diverses*. À la Haye: Chez P. Husson [et al.], 1727. 4 vols.

_____. *Dictionnaire historique et critique*. 3d ed. Rotterdam: Chez M. Bohm, 1720. 4 vols.

Beasley, Frederick. *A Search of Truth in the Science of the Human Mind. Part the First.* Philadelphia: S. Potter & Co., 1822. 5, 561 pp. No more published.

Bentham, Edward. *An Introduction to Logick, Scholastick and Rational.* Oxford: Printed by J. Jackson and J. Lister, 1773. 129 pp. Facsim. reprint: Menston, Eng.: Scolar Press, 1969.

_____. *Reflexions upon Logick*. 2d ed. Oxford: Printed for J. Fletcher and Sold by J. & J. Rivington, London, 1755. 56 pp.

_____. *Reflexions upon the Nature and Usefulness of Logick, As It Has Been Commonly Taught in the Schools.* Oxford: Printed at the Theatre, and Sold by M. Fletcher, 1740. 33 pp.

Berkeley, George. *Works*. Edited by A. A. Luce and T. E. Jessop. Bibliotheca Britannica Philosophica. London: Nelson, 1948-57. 9 vols.

_____. *An Essay towards a New Theory of Vision*. Dublin: Printed by A. Rhames for J. Pepyat, 1709. xiv, 187 pp. Also published in *Works* (1948-57), vol. 1, pp. 141-239.

_____. *Philosophical Commentaries*. In *Works* (1948-57), vol. 1, pp. 7-139.

_____. *Three Dialogues between Hylas and Philonous*. In *Works* (1948-57), vol. 2, pp. 147-263.

_____. *A Treatise concerning the Principles of Human Knowledge. Part I. Wherein the Chief Causes of Error and Difficulty in the Sciences, with the Grounds of Scepticism, Atheism, and Irreligion, are inquir'd into.* Dublin: Printed by A. Rhames for J. Pepyat, 1710. iii, 214 pp. No more published. The *Treatise* is published in *Works* (1948-57), vol. 2, pp. 1-113.

Blakey, Robert, *Historical Sketch of Logic, from the Earliest Times to the Present Day*. London: H. Baillière, 1851. xxxii, 524 pp.

Bonnet, Charles. *Essai analytique sur les facultés de l'ame*. À Copenhague: Chez C. & A. Philibert, 1760. xxxii, 552 pp.

_____. *Essai de psychologie; ou, Considerations sur les operations de l'ame, sur l'habitude et sur l'education*. À Leyde: Chez E. Luzac, 1754.

Broughton, John. *Psychologia; or, An Account of the Nature of the Rational Soul. In Two Parts. The First, Being an Essay Towards Establishing the Received Doctrine of an Immaterial and . . . Immortal Substance, United to Human Body. The Second, A Vindication of That . . . Doctrine, against a late Book, call'd Second Thoughts, &c.* [by William Coward]. London: Printed by W. B. for T. Bennet, 1703. 19 prelim leaves, 418, 14 pp.

Brown, Thomas. *Lectures on the Philosophy of the Mind*. Edinburgh: W. and C. Tait, 1820. 4 vols.

[Browne, Peter.] *The Procedure, Extent, and Limits of Human Understanding*. London: Printed for W. Innys, 1728. 477 pp.

Buffier, Claude. *Traité de premières vérités, et de la source de nos jugemens, où l'on examine le sentiment des philophes* [!] *de ce temps, sur les premières notions des choses.* À Paris: Chez la Veuve Maugé, 1724. x, 290 pp.

Burthogge, Richard. *An Essay upon Reason, and the Nature of Spirits*. London: Printed for J. Dunton, 1694. 280 pp.

_____. *Organon Vetus & Novum; or, A Discourse of Reason and Truth. Wherein the Natural Logick Common to Mankinde Is Briefly and Plainly Described* . . . London: Printed for S. Crouch, 1679. 73 pp.

Chambers, Ephraim. *Cyclopaedia; or, An Universal Dictionary of Arts and Sciences* . . . London: Printed for J. and J. Knapton [et al.], 1728. 2 vols.

Chanet, Pierre. *Eclaircissement de quelques difficultez touchant la connoissance de l'imagination*. La Rochelle: T. de Gouy, 1648. 120 pp.

————. *Traité de l'esprit de l'homme et ses fonctions*. Paris: Chez la Veuve J. Camusat et P. LePetit, 1649. xiv, 349 pp.

Cheyne, George. *The English Malady; or, A Treatise of Nervous Diseases of All Kinds . . .* London: Printed for G. Strahan, 1733. xxxii, 370 pp.

Clarke, Samuel. *A Collection of Papers, Which Passed between the Late Learned Mr. Leibnitz and Dr. Clarke, in the Years 1715 and 1716; Relating to the Principles of Natural Philosophy and Religion. With an Appendix. To which are added, Letters to Dr. Clarke concerning Liberty and Necessity, from a Gentleman of the University of Cambridge* [Richard Bulkeley]; *with the Doctor's Answers to Them. Also, Remarks upon a Book, Entituled, A Philosophical Enquiry concerning Human Liberty* [by Anthony Collins] *. . .* London: Printed for J. Knapton, 1717. xiii, 416, 46 pp. French and English texts are on facing pages of the correspondence (pp. 2-399); Bulkeley's work occupies pp. 401-16; and the "Remarks" on Collins's work are given on the 46 pp. at the end.

————. *A Demonstration of the Being and Attributes of God; More Particularly in Answer to Mr. Hobbs, Spinoza, and Their Followers. Wherein the Notion of Liberty is Stated, and the Possibility and Certainty of It Proved, in Opposition to Necessity and Fate. Being the Substance of Eight Sermons Preach'd at the Cathedral-Church of St. Paul, in the Year 1704, at the Lecture Founded by Robert Boyle*. London: Printed for J. Knapton, 1705. [16], 264 pp.

[Clayton, Robert.] *An Essay on Spirit*. Dublin: Printed by S. Powell, 1750. lxv, 171 pp.

Coke, Zachary. *The Art of Logick; or, The Entire Body of Logick in English*. London: Printed by R. White for G. Calvert, 1654. 12 prelim. leaves, 222 pp.

Collier, Arthur. *Clavis Universalis; or, A New Inquiry after Truth. Being a Demonstration of the Non-Existence or Impossibility of an External World*. London: Printed for R. Gosling, 1713. 148 pp.

"Concerning the Perceptive Faculty." In *The Annual Register . . . for the Year 1763*, pp. 182-85. Signed: A. B.

Crousaz, Jean Pierre de. *A New Treatise of the Art of Thinking; or, A Compleat System of Reflections, concerning the Conduct and Improvement of the Mind. Illustrated with Variety of Characters and Examples Drawn from the Ordinary Occurrences of Life . . . Done into English*. London: Printed for T. Woodward, 1724. 2 vols.

Cudworth, Ralph. *A Treatise concerning Eternal and Immutable Morality. With a Preface by . . . Edward* [Chandler] *Lord Bishop of Durham*. London: Printed for J. and J. Knapton, 1731. xii, 303 pp.

Cumberland, Richard. *De Legibus Naturae Disquisitio Philosophica, in qua Earum Forma, Summa Capita, Ordo, Promulgatio & Obligatio è Rerum Naturae Investigantur; quinetiam Elementa Philosophiae Hobbianae cùm Moralis tum Civilis Considerantur & Refutantur*. Londini: Typis E. Flesher, prostat verò apud N. Hooke, 1672. 32 prelim. leaves, 421 pp.

————. *A Treatise on the Laws of Nature. Made English from the Latin by John Maxwell . . . To which is prefix'd, An Introduction concerning the Mistaken Notions Which the Heathens Had of the Deity, and the Defects in Their Morality, Whence the Usefulness of Revelation May Appear. At the end is subjoin'd, An Appendix, containing Two Discourses, 1. Concerning the Immateriality of Thinking Substance. 2. Concerning the Obligation, Promulgation, and Observance of the Law of Nature, by the Translator*. London: Printed by R. Phillips, and Sold by J. Knapton [et al., Pref. 1727]. 13 prelim leaves, clxviii, 377, 167, [24], xxviii pp.

Cureau de la Chambre, Marin. *Le Système de l'ame*. Paris: Chez I. d'Allin 1665. 554 pp.

Descartes, René. *Oeuvres de Descartes, publiées par Charles Adam & Paul Tannéry, sous les auspices du Ministère de l'instruction publique.* Paris: L. Cerf, 1897-1910. 12 vols.

_____. *Oeuvres philosophiques. Textes établis, présentés et annotés par Ferdinand Alquié.* Paris: Garnier Frères, 1963-73. 3 vols.

_____. *The Philosophical Works. Rendered into English by Elizabeth S. Haldane and G. R. T. Ross.* Cambridge: University Press, 1911-12. 2 vols.

_____. *Discours de la méthode. Avec introduction et notes par Étienne Gilson.* Paris: J. Vrin, 1970. 146 pp.

_____. *Treatise of Man.* French text, with translation and commentary by Thomas Steele Hall. Cambridge: Harvard University Press, 1972. xlviii, 115 pp.; facsim.: 107 pp.; 227-32 pp. Facsimile is of the First French edition of *De homine.*

[Desgabets, Robert.] *Critique de la Critique de la Recherche de la vérité; où l'on découvre le chemin qui conduit aux connoissances solides. Pour servir de reponse à la lettre d'un academicien* [S. Foucher]. Paris: Chez J. Du Puis, 1675. 216 pp.

Ditton, Humphrey. *A Discourse concerning the Resurrection of Jesus Christ. In Three Parts . . . Together with an Appendix containing the Impossible Production of Thought, from Matter and Motion: the Nature of Humane Souls, and of Brutes: the Anima Mundi, and the Hypothesis of the τό πᾶν; as also, concerning Divine Providence, the Origin of Evil, and the Universe in General.* London: Printed by J. Darby, and Sold by A. Bell, 1712. xvi, 568 pp.

Doddridge, Philip. *A Course of Lectures on the Principal Subjects in Pneumatology, Ethics, and Divinity; with References to the Most Considerable Authors on Each Subject.* London: Printed by Assignment from the Author's Widow, for J. Buckland [et al.], 1763. 10 prelim. leaves, 595 pp.

Dodsley, Robert. *The Preceptor; Containing a General Course of Education. Wherein the First Principles of Polite Learning Are Laid Down in a Way Most Suitable for Trying the Genius and Advancing the Instruction of Youth . . .* London: Printed for R. Dodsley, 1748. 2 vols. Vol. 2 includes William Duncan's *Elements of Logic.*

Drummond, Sir William. *Academical Questions.* Volume I. London: Printed by W. Bulmer and Co., 1805. xv, 412 pp. No more published.

Duncan, William. *The Elements of Logick. In Four Books.* London: Printed for R. Dodsley, 1748. iv, 363 pp.

[Ellis, John, D. D.] *Some Brief Considerations upon Mr. Locke's Hypothesis That the Knowledge of God Is Attainable by Ideas of Reflexion. Wherein Is Demonstrated, Upon His Own Principles, That the Knowledge of God Is Not Attainable by Ideas of Reflexion. Being an Addition to a Book Lately Publish'd, entitled, The Knowledge of Divine Things from Revelation, Not from Nature or Reason.* London: Printed by J. Watts, and Sold by B. Dod [et al.], 1743. 51 pp.

Encyclopaedia Britannica; or, A Dictionary of Arts and Sciences. Compiled upon a New Plan . . . By a Society of Gentlemen in Scotland. Edinburgh: Printed for A. Bell and C. Macfarquhar, 1771 [i.e. 1768-71]. 3 vols.

[Fédé, René.] *Meditations metaphysiques, de l'origine de l'âme, sa nature, sa béatitude, son devoir, son desordre, et sa restauration.* [Amsterdam?], 1683. 72 pp.

[Foucher, Simon.] *Critique de la Recherche de la vérité* [par N. Malebranche]; *où l'on examine en même-tems une une* [sic] *partie des principes de Mr. Descartes. Lettre par un academicien.* Paris: Chez M. Coustelier, 1675. 7, 124 pp.

Gerdil, Giacinto Sigismondo, Cardinal. *Defense du Sentiment du P. Malebranche sur la nature & l'origine des idées, contre l'examen de M. Locke . . .* À Turin: De l'imprimerie royale, 1748. 8 prelim. leaves, xxxix, 246 pp., 10 leaves.

Glanvill, Joseph. *Essays on Several Important Subjects in Philosophy and Religion . . .* Imprimatur, Martii 27, 1675, Thomas Tomkins. London: Printed by J. D. for John

Baker and Henry Mortlock, 1676. 8 prelim. leaves, 66, 56, 43, 28, 61, 58 pp. Seven essays; most are separately paged.

_____. *Scepsis scientifica: or, Confest Ignorance, the Way to Science; in an Essay on the
Vanity of Dogmatizing, and Confident Opinion. With a Reply to the Exceptions of the
Learned Thomas Albus* [i.e. White]. London: Printed by E. Cotes for H. Eversden, 1665.
184 pp.

_____. *The Vanity of Dogmatizing: or, Confidence in Opinions Manifested in a Discourse
of the Shortness and Uncertainty of Our Knowledge and Its Causes; with Some Reflexions on Peripateticism; and An Apology for Philosophy* . . . London: Printed by E. C.
for H. Eversden, 1661. 16 prelim. leaves, 250 pp.

Grove, Henry. *An Essay towards a Demonstration of the Soul's Immateriality*. London:
Printed for J. Clark, 1718. 88 pp.

Hartley, David. *Observations on Man, His Frame, His Duty, and His Expectations. In Two
Parts*. London: Printed by S. Richardson; for J. Leake [et al.], 1749. 2 vols.

Hobbes, Thomas. *The English Works. Now first collected and edited by Sir William Molesworth*. London: J. Bohn, 1839-45. 11 vols.

_____. *De Homine = Traité de l'homme*. Traduction et commentaire par Paul-Marie
Maurin. Préface par Vasco Ronchi. Paris: A. Blanchard, 1974. 204 pp.

Hooke, Robert. "Lectures of Light, Explicating Its Nature, Properties, and Effects, &c."
In *The Posthumous Works . . . Containing his Cutlerian Lectures, and Other Discourses, Read at the Meetings of the Illustrious Royal Society . . . Published by Richard
Waller* . . . , pp. 71-148. London: Printed by S. Smith and B. Walford, 1705. There is a
facsimile reprint of this volume, called a second edition, by F. Cass, London, 1971.

Hume, David. *An Abstract of a Treatise of Human Nature, 1740; a Pamphlet Hitherto Unknown*. Reprinted with an Introduction by J. M. Keynes and P. Sraffa. Cambridge: University Press, 1938. xxxii, 32 pp. Reprinted in Hamden, Conn. by Archon Books, 1965.

_____. *Abrégé du Traité de la nature humaine*. Texte original avec présentation, traduc-
tion et notes par Didier Daleule. La Philosophie en poch. Paris: A. Montaigne [1971].
126 pp.

_____. *A Treatise of Human Nature; Being an Attempt to Introduce the Experimental
Method of Reasoning into Moral Subjects* . . . London: Printed for J. Noon, 1739. 2
vols.

Jackson, John. *A Dissertation on Matter and Spirit. With Some Remarks on a Book, Entitled, An Enquiry into the Nature of the Humane Soul* [by Andrew Baxter]. London:
Printed for J. Noon, 1735. xiii, 56 pp.

_____. *The Existence and Unity of God; Proved from His Nature and Attributes. Being a
Vindication of Dr. Clarke's Demonstration of the Being and Attributes of God. To which
is added, An Appendix, Wherein is Considered, the Ground and Obligation of Morality*.
London: Printed for J., J., and P. Knapton, 1734. viii, 159 pp.

King, William. *De Origine Mali*. Dublinii: A. Crook, 1702. 2 prelim. leaves, 214 pp., 13
leaves.

_____. *An Essay concerning the Origin of Evil. Translated from the Latin, with Large
Notes; Tending to Explain and Vindicate Some of the Author's Principles against the
Objections of Bayle, Leibnitz, the Author of a Philosophical Enquiry concerning Human
Liberty* [i.e. Anthony Collins]; *and Others. To which is prefix'd, A Dissertation concerning the Fundamental Principle and Immediate Criterion of Virtue. As also, The Obligation to and Approbation of It. With Some Account of the Origin of the Passions and Affections*. London: Printed for W. Thurlbourn, Bookseller in Cambridge; and Sold by R.
Knaplock [et al.], London, 1731. lvi, 330 pp. The "Dissertation" is John Gay; the
translation and notes by Edmund Law.

La Chambre, Marin Cureau de, *see* Cureau de la Chambre, Marin

[La Mettrie, Julien Offray de.] *L'homme-machine*. Leyde: De l'imprimerie d'E. Luzac Fils, 1748. 10 prelim. leaves, 109 pp.

————. *L'Homme Machine: A Study in the Origins of an Idea*. Critical Edition, with an Introductory Monograph and Notes by Aram Vartarian. Princeton: Princeton University Press, 1960. 264 pp.

Le Ramée. Pierre de. *See* Ramus, Peter.

Law, Edmund. *An Enquiry into the Ideas of Space, Time, Immensity, and Eternity; as also the Self-Existence, Necessary Existence, and Unity of the Divine Nature. In Answer to a Book lately Publish'd, by Mr. Jackson, entitled, The Existence and Unity of God Proved from His Nature and Attributes . . . To which is added, A Dissertation upon the Argument A Priori for Proving the Existence of a First Cause, by a Learned Hand* [i.e. Daniel Waterland]. Cambridge: Printed for W. Thurlbourn, 1734. 196, 98 pp.

[Layton, Henry.] *Observations upon a Treatise, Intitl'd Psychologia: Or, An Account of the Nature of the Rational Soul* [by John Broughton. 1703]. 132 pp. Published without title page.

LeClerc, Jean. *Logica; sive, Ars ratiocinandi*. Londini: Impensis A. & J. Churchill, 1692. 2 vols. in one.

Lectures on Locke; or, The Principles of Logic, Designed for the Use of Students in the University. London: T. Cadell, 1840. 240 pp.

Lee, Henry. *Anti-Scepticism; or, Notes upon Each Chapter of Mr. Lock's Essay concerning Humane Understanding. With an Explication of All the Particulars of Which He Treats, and in the Same Order. In Four Books*. London: Printed for R. Clavel and C. Harper, 1702. 15 prelim. leaves, 140, 201-342 pp.

Le Grand, Antoine. *An Entire Body of Philosophy, according to the Principles of the Famous Renate des Cartes, in Three Books: I. The Institution, in X. Parts . . . II. The History of Nature, Which Illustrates The Institution, and Consists of Great Variety of Experiments Relating Thereto, and Explained by the Same Principles, in IX. Parts . . . III. A Dissertation of the Want of Sense and Knowledge in Brute Animals, in II. Parts . . . Written Originally in Latin . . . Now Carefully Translated from the Last Corrections of the Author, Never Yet Published . . . by Richard Blome*. London: Printed by S. Roycroft, and Sold by R. Blome, 1694. 15 prelim. leaves, 403, 263 pp.

Leibniz, Gottfried Wilhelm. *A Collection of Papers. See* Clarke, Samuel.

Locke, John. *An Essay concerning Human Understanding*. Edited, with an Introduction, by John W. Yolton. Everyman's Library, 332, 984. London: J. M. Dent, 1961 (revised printing, 1965). 2 vols.

————. *An Examination of P. Malebranche's Opinion of Seeing All Things in God*. In *Works, A New Edition, Corrected*. London: Printed for T. Tegg [et al.], 1823. Vol. 9, pp. 211-54.

————. "Locke's First Reply to John Norris. Edited by Richard Acworth." *The Locke Newsletter* 2 (summer 1971):7-11.

Malebranche, Nicolas. *Oeuvres complètes de Malebranche*. 20 vols. and index. Direction: André Robinet. Paris: J. Vrin, 1958-70. Some vols. in revised editions. Vols. 1-2 contain *De la recherche de la vérité*; vol. 3, its *Eclaircissements*; all three vols. edited by Geneviève Rodis-Lewis. *Eclaircissement* X is "sur la nature des idées"; XVI, "sur la lumière et les couleurs." Vol. 6 contains *Réponse au livre Des vraies et des fausses idées*, and *Trois Lettres touchant la défense de M. Arnauld*, both edited by Robinet. Vol. 12 is *Entretiens sur la métaphysique et sur la religion*, also edited by Robinet.

————. *Dialogue: on Metaphysics and Religion. See* Secondary Sources, below.

————. *The Search after Truth*. Translated from the French by Thomas M. Lennon and Paul J. Olscamp. *Elucidations of the Search after Truth*. Translated from the French by Thomas M. Lennon. Philosophical Commentary by Thomas M. Lennon. Columbus: Ohio State University Press, 1980. xxxii, 861 pp.

Maxwell, John. *A Treatise of the Laws of Nature. See* Cumberland, Richard.

[Mayne, Zachary.] *Two Dissertations concerning Sense and the Imagination. With an Essay on Consciousness.* London: Printed for J. Tonson, 1728. 4 prelim. leaves, 231 pp. Authorship attribution is very doubtful.

Mill, John Stuart. "Bailey on Berkeley's Theory of Vision." In *Collected Works of John Stuart Mill,* vol. 11. *Essays on Philosophy and the Classics,* edited by J. M. Robson, pp. 245-69. Toronto: University of Toronto Press, 1978.

Monboddo, James Burnett, Lord. *Antient Metaphysics; or, The Science of Universals.* Edinburgh: Printed for T. Cadell, London, and J. Balfour, 1779-99. 6 vols.

Morgan, Thomas. *Physico-Theology; or, A Philosophico-Moral Disquisition concerning Human Nature, Free Agency, Moral Government, and Divine Providence.* London: Printed by T. Cox, 1741. vii, 353 pp., 8 leaves.

Newton, Isaac. *The Mathematical Principles of Natural Philosophy. Translated into English by Andrew Motte. To which are added, Newton's System of the World; a Short Comment on, and Defence of the Principia, by William Emerson . . . A New Edition (with a Life of the Author . . .) Carefully Revised and Corrected by William Davis.* London: Printed for Sherwood, Neely and Jones [et al.], 1819. 3 vols.

_____. *Opticks; or, A Treatise of the Reflections, Refractions, Influxions, and Colours of Light. Also, Two Treatises of the Species and Magnitude of Curvilinear Figures.* London: Printed for S. Smith and B. Walford, 1704. 144, 211 pp.

Norris, John. *Cursory Reflections upon a Book, call'd An Essay concerning Human Understanding . . . In a Letter to a Friend.* London: Printed for S. Manship, 1690. 44 pp. Published, with its own title page, at the end of his *Christian Blessedness* (1690).

_____. *An Essay towards the Theory of the Ideal or Intelligible World. Design'd for Two Parts. The First, Considering It Absolutely in It Self, and the Second, in Relation to the Human Understanding.* London: Printed for S. Manship [et al.], 1701-04. 2 vols.

A Philosophick Essay concerning Ideas, according to Dr. Sherlock's Principles. Wherein His Notion of Them is Stated, and His Reasonings Thereupon Examin'd. In a Letter to a Friend. London: Printed, and . . . to be Sold by B. Bragg, 1705. 24 pp.

Plotinus. *The Enneads.* Translated from the Greek by Stephen Mackenna. The Library of Philosophical Translations. London: Medici Society, 1917-30. 6 vols.

Pope, Alexander. *An Essay on Man.* Edited by Maynard Mack. London: Methuen, 1951. 186 pp. The Twickenham Edition of the Poems of Alexander Pope, vol. 3, part 1.

Porterfield, William. "An Essay concerning the Motions of the Eyes." In *Medical Essays and Observations of the Philosophical Society of Edinburgh.* 2d edition, corrected (1737-38), vol. 3.

_____. *A Treatise on the Eye, the Manner and Phaenomena of Vision.* Edinburgh: Printed for A. Millar at London, and for G. Hamilton and J. Balfour at Edinburgh, 1759. 2 vols.

Priestley, Joseph. *Disquisitions relating to Matter and Spirit. To which is added, The History of the Philosophical Doctrine concerning the Origin of the Soul, and the Nature of Matter; with Its Influence on Christianity, Especially with Respect to the Doctrine of the Preexistence of Christ.* London: Printed for J. Johnson, 1777. xxxix, 336 pp. An Appendix, usually considered vol. 2 of this work, is entitled *The Doctrine of Philosophical Necessity.*

_____. *A Free Discussion of the Doctrines of Materialism, and Philosophical Necessity; in a Correspondence between Dr. Price and Dr. Priestley. To which are added, by Dr. Priestley, An Introduction, Explaining the Nature of the Controversy, and Letters to Several Writers Who Have Animadverted on his Disquisitions relating to Matter and Spirit, or his Treatise on Necessity . . .* London: Printed for J. Johnson and T. Cadell, 1778, xliv, 428 pp.

Ramus, Peter. *The Logike of the most excellent philosopher P. Ramus, Martyr. Newly translated, and in diuers places corrected, after the mynde of the Author. Per M. Roll. Makylmenaeum* . . . London: Imprinted by T. Vautroullier, 1574. 101 pp.

Reid, Thomas. *The Works, Now Fully Collected. With Selections from His Unpublished Letters.* Preface, Notes, and Supplementary Dissertations, by Sir William Hamilton. Edinburgh, 1846. 2 vols.

_____. *An Inquiry into the Human Mind.* Edited with an Introduction by Timothy Duggan. Chicago: University of Chicago Press, 1970. li, 279 pp.

_____. *Essays on the Intellectual Powers of Man.* Edinburgh: Printed for J. Bell [et al.], 1785. xii, 766 pp.

[Sanderson, Robert.] *Logicae Artis Compendium.* Oxonii: Excudebat Ios. Barnesius, 1615.

Smith, Norman Kemp. *Studies in the Cartesian Philosophy.* London and New York: Macmillan, 1902. xiv, 276 pp.

Stewart, Dugald. *Elements of Philosophy of the Human Mind.* London: Printed for A. Strahan and T. Cadell, 1792. xii, 566 pp.

A Theological Survey of the Human Understanding. See Applegarth, Robert

Thomas Aquinas, Saint. *The Basic Writings of Saint Thomas Aquinas.* Edited and Annotated with an Introduction by Anton C. Pegis. New York: Random House, 1945. 2 vols.

Voltaire, François Marie Arouet de. *Dictionnaire philosophique, portatif.* Londres, 1764. viii, 344 pp.

_____. *Letters concerning the English Nation.* London: Printed for C. Davis and A. Lyon, 1733. 253 pp.

Watts, Isaac. *Logick; or, The Right Use of Reason in the Enquiry after Truth. With a Variety of Rules to Guard against Error, in the Affairs of Religion and Human Life, as well as in the Sciences.* London: Printed for J. Clark and R. Hett, 1725. vi, 534 pp.

_____. *Philosophical Essays on Various Subjects, Viz. Space, Substance, Body, Spirit, the Operations of the Soul in Union with the Body, Innate Ideas, Perceptual Consciousness, Place and Motion of Spirits, the Departing Soul, the Resurrection of the Body, the Production and Operations of Plants and Animals. With Some Remarks on Mr. Locke's Essay on the Human Understanding. To which is subjoined, A Brief Scheme of Ontology; or, The Science of Being in general, with its Affections. By. I. W.* London: Printed for R. Ford [et al.], 1733, xii, 403 pp.

Wilkins, John. *Of the Principles and Duties of Natural Religion, Two Books.* London: Printed by A. Maxwell for T. Basset [et al.], 1675. 9 prelim. leaves, 410 pp.

Witty, John. *The First Principles of Modern Deism Confuted. In a Demonstration of the Immateriality, Natural Eternity, and Immortality of Thinking Substances in General; and in Particular, of Human Souls; Even from the Supposition that We Are Intirely Ignorant of the Intrinsic Natures of the Essences of Things.* London: Printed for J. Wyatt, 1707. xxii, 301 pp.

Periodicals

Memoirs for the Ingenious. Containing Several Curious Observations in Philosophy, Mathematicks, Physicks, History, Philology, and Other Arts and Sciences. In Miscellaneous Letters. By J. de La Crose. Vol. 1, no. 1-12; Jan.-Dec. 1693. London: Printed for H. Rhodes and J. Harris, 1693. 389, 13 pp.

Nouvelles de la Republique des Lettres. Tomes 1-40; mars 1684-mai/juin 1718. Amsterdam: H. Desbordes, 1684-1718. Founded by Pierre Bayle, and edited by him until February 1687.

The Spectator. [By Joseph Addison, Sir Richard Steele, and others.] Mar. 1, 1711-Dec. 6, 1712; June 18-Sept. 29, 1714. London. Reprinted in many editions.

Secondary Sources

Aaron, Richard I. *John Locke.* 3d ed. Oxford: Clarendon Press, 1971. xiv, 383 pp.

Acworth, Richard, *see* Primary Sources, under Locke, John

Alquié, Ferdinand. *Le Cartésianisme de Malebranche.* Bibliothèque d'histoire de la philosophie. Paris: J. Vrin, 1974. 555 pp.

————. *La Découverte métaphysique de l'homme chez Descartes.* Bibliothèque de philosophie contemporaine. Paris: Presses universitaires de France, 1950. 384 pp.

Anderson, Robert F. *Hume's First Principles.* Lincoln: University of Nebraska Press [1966]. xv, 189 pp.

————. "The Location, Extension, Shape, and Size of Hume's Perceptions." In *Hume: A Re-evaluation,* edited by Donald A. Livingston and James T. King, pp. 153-71. New York: Fordham University Press, 1976.

Aquila, Richard E. "Brentano, Descartes, and Hume on Awareness." *Philosophy and Phenomenological Research,* 35, no. 2 (Dec. 1974):223-39.

Bennett, Jonathan. *Locke, Berkeley, Hume: Central Themes.* Oxford: Clarendon Press, 1971. x, 361 pp.

Bloch, Olivier René. *La Philosophie de Gassendi: nominalisme, matérialisme, et métaphysique.* Archives internationales d'histoire des idées, 38. La Haye: M. Nijhoff, 1971. xxx, 525 pp.

Boyer, C. "Réflexions sur la connaissance sensible selon Saint Thomas." *Archives de philosophie* 3, cahier 2 (1925).

Cohen, Murray. *Sensible Words: Linguistic Practice in England, 1640-1785.* Baltimore: Johns Hopkins University Press, 1977. xxv, 188 pp.

Cook, Monte. "Arnauld's Alleged Representationalism." *Journal of the History of Philosophy* 12, no. 1 (Jan. 1974):53-62.

Dalbiez, R. "Les Sources scolastiques de la théorie cartésienne de l'être objectif (à propos du 'Descartes' de M. Gilson)." *Revue d'histoire de la philosophie* 3 (1929):464-72.

Danto, Arthur C. "The Representational Character of Ideas and the Problem of the External World." In *Descartes: Critical and Interpretive Essays,* edited by Michael Hooker, pp. 287-97. Baltimore: Johns Hopkins University Press, 1978.

Duchesneau, François. "L'analyse d'idées selon Locke." *Les Études philosophiques* 1 (1977):67-94.

————. *L'Empirisme de Locke.* Archives internationales d'histoire des idées, 57. La Haye: M. Nijhoff, 1973. xv, 261 pp.

Eisenstein, Elizabeth L. *The Printing Press as an Agent of Change: Communication and Cultural Transformations in Early-Modern Europe.* Cambridge: University Press, 1979. 2 vols.

Foucault, Michel. *Les mots et les choses; une archéologie des sciences humaines.* Bibliothèque des sciences humaines. Paris: Gallimard, 1966. 400 pp.

Garin, Pierre. *La Théorie de l'idée suivant l'école thomiste; études d'après les textes.* Paris: Desclée de Brouwer [1932] 2 vols. (1260 pp.)

Gaukroger, Stephen, editor. *Descartes: Philosophy, Mathematics, and Physics.* Brighton, Sussex: Harvester Press, 1980. xi, 329 pp.

Gérando, J. M. de. *Histoire de la philosophie moderne, à partir de la renaissance des lettres, jusqu'à la fin de la dix-huitième siecle.* Paris: A. Delahays, 1848. 4 vols.

Gilson, Étienne. *Études sur le rôle de la pensée médiévale dans la formation du système cartesien.* Rev. ed. Études de philosophie mediévales, 13. Paris: J. Vrin, 1951. 342 pp.

Ginsberg, Morris. *See* Malebranche, Nicolas, below

Hacking, Ian. *The Emergence of Probability: A Philosophical Study of Early Ideas about*

Probability, Induction, and Statistical Inference. Cambridge: University Press [1975]. 209 pp.

Howell, Wilbur Samuel. *Eighteenth-Century British Logic and Rhetoric.* Princeton: Princeton University Press, 1971. xi, 742 pp.

Kenney, W. Henry. "John Locke and the Oxford Training in Logic and Metaphysics." Ph.D. thesis, St. Louis University, 1959. 309 pp.

Kenny, A. J. P. *Descartes: A Study of His Philosophy.* New York: Random House, 1968. 242 pp.

Knight, William Angus. *Lord Monboddo and Some of His Contemporaries.* London: J. Murray, 1900. xv, 314 pp. Contains selections from Monboddo's correspondence.

Laird, John. "The 'Legend' of Arnauld's Realism." *Mind* 33, no. 130 (April 1924):176-79.

Larmore, Charles. "Descartes' Empirical Epistemology." In Gaukroger, S. (q.v.), pp. 6-22.

Lennon, Thomas M. "The Inference Pattern and Descartes' Ideas." *Journal of the History of Philosophy* 12, no. 1 (Jan. 1974):43-52.

_____. "Representationalism, Judgment, and Perception of Distance: Further to Yolton and McRae." *Dialogue* 19, no. 1 (Mar. 1980):151-62.

Locke, Don. *Perception and Our Knowledge of the External World.* Muirhead Library of Philosophy. London: Allen & Unwin; New York: Humanities Press, 1967. 243 pp.

Lovejoy, A. O. "'Representative Ideas' in Malebranche and Arnauld." *Mind* 32, no. 128 (Oct. 1923):449-61.

Mackie, J. L. *Problems from Locke.* Oxford: Clarendon Press, 1976. ix, 237 pp.

McRae, R. F. "On Being Present to the Mind: A Reply." *Dialogue* 14, no. 4 (Dec. 1975): 664-66.

Malebranche, Nicolas. *Dialogue on Metaphysics and Religion.* Translated by Morris Ginsberg. Muirhead Library of Philosophy. London: Allen & Unwin, [1923]. 374 pp. Useful for the translator's notes.

Marin, Louis. *La Critique du discours sur la "Logique de Port-Royal" et les "Pensées" de Pascal.* Le Sense commun. Paris: Editions du Minuit, [1975]. 438 pp.

Maull, Nancy L. "Cartesian Optics and the Geometrization of Nature." In Gaukroger, S. (q.v.), pp. 23-40.

Maurin, Paul-Marie, *see* Primary Sources, under Hobbes, Thomas

Noel, Léon. *Notes d'épistémologie thomiste.* Louvain: Institut supérieur de philosophie, 1925. 242 pp.

O'Neil, Brian. *Epistemological Direct Realism in Descartes' Philosophy.* Albuquerque: Univeristy of New Mexico Press, [1974]. 112 pp.

Picard, Gabriel. "Essai sur la connaissance sensible d'après les scolastiques." *Archives de philosophie* 4, cahier 1 (1926):1-93.

Popkin, Richard. "Berkeley and Pyrrhonism." *Review of Metaphysics* 5, no. 2 (Dec. 1951): 223-46.

Radner, Daisie. "Representationalism in Arnauld's Act Theory of Perception." *Journal of the History of Philosophy* 14, no. 1 (Jan. 1976):96-98.

Rescher, Nicholas. *Conceptual Idealism.* Oxford: B. Blackwell, 1973. xiii, 204 pp.

Rodis-Lewis, Geneviève. "Le Domaine propre de l'homme chez les cartésiens." *Journal of the History of Philosophy* 2 no. 2 (Oct. 1964):157-88.

_____. "Langage humain et signes naturels dans le cartésianisme." *Le langage; actes du 13. Congrès des sociétés de philosophie de langue française.* Neuchatel: La Baconnière, 1966. Vol. 2, pp. 132-36. Congress held at Geneva, August 2-6, 1966.

_____. *Nicolas Malebranche.* Les Grands penseurs. Paris: Presses universitaires de France, 1963. 357 pp.

Ronchi, Vasco. *L'Optique, science de la vision.* Paris: Masson, 1966. 158 pp.

_____.*Traité de l'homme. See* Primary Sources, under Hobbes, Thomas

Rorty, Richard. *Philosophy and the Mirror of Nature.* Princeton: Princeton University Press, 1979. xv, 401 pp.

Rothstein, Eric. "'Ideal Presence' and the 'Non Finito' in Eighteenth-Century Aesthetics." *Eighteenth-Century Studies* 9, no. 3 (Sept. 1976):307-32.

Ryle, Gilbert. "John Locke on Human Understanding." In *Tercentenary Addresses on John Locke,* edited by J. L. Stocks, pp. 15-28. London: Oxford University Press, 1933.

Sabra, A. I. *Theories of Light; from Descartes to Newton.* London: Oldbourne, [1967]. 363 pp.

Singer, B. R. "Robert Hooke on Memory, Association, and Time Perception." *Notes and Records of the Royal Society* 31 (1976):115-31.

Stewart, M. A. "Locke's Mental Atomism and the Classification of Ideas." *The Locke Newsletter* 10 (1979):53-82; and 11 (1980):25-75.

Thackray, Arnold. *Atoms and Powers; an Essay on Newtonian Matter-Theory and the Development of Chemistry.* Harvard Monographs in the History of Science. Cambridge: Harvard University Press, 1970. xxiii, 326 pp.

Tipton, I. C. *Berkeley, the Philosophy of Immaterialism.* London: Methuen, 1974. viii, 397 pp.

Yolton, John W. "As in a Looking-Glass: Perceptual Acquaintance in Eighteenth-Century Britain." *Journal of the History of Ideas* 40 no. 2 (April-June 1979):207-34.

_____. "Hume's Ideas." *Hume Studies* 6, no. 1 (April 1980):1-25.

_____. "Ideas and Knowledge in Seventeenth-Century Philosophy." *Journal of the History of Philosophy* 13, no. 2 (April 1975):145-66.

_____. "Locke and Malebranche: Two Concepts of Ideas." In *John Locke: Symposium Wolfenbüttel 1979,* edited by Reinhard Brandt, pp. 208-24. Berlin: W. de Gruyter, 1981.

_____. "On Being Present to the Mind: A Sketch for the History of an Idea." *Dialogue* 14, no. 3 (Sept. 1975):373-88.

_____. "Phenomenology and Pragmatism." [Review of Rorty's *Philosophy and the Mirror of Nature;* with a reply by R. Rorty.] *Philosphical Books* 22, no. 3 (July 1981): 129-35.

_____. "Pragmatism Revisited: An Examination of Professor Rescher's Conceptual Idealism." *Idealistic Studies* 6, no. 3 (Sept. 1976):218-38.

Index

Index

Aaron, R. I., 4, 16
Acworth, Richard, 103
Adam, Charles, 39
Aldrich, Henry, 114
Alexander, H. G., 86
Alquié, F., 24, 26, 33-34, 39, 41, 53, 56, 58, 72-73, 74
Anderson, R. F., 164, 182-83, 184, 198-99, 200, 202
animal spirits, 9, 24, 25, 43, 45, 71, 93, 155, 168, 171, 189, 195, 196
Annual Register, The, 83, 87
Aquila, Richard E., 41
Aristotle, 6-7, 8, 37, 48, 71, 89, 97, 123, 134, 216
Armstrong, D. M., 104
Arnauld, Antoine: his account of ideas, 8-9, 13, 14, 35, 37-38, 39, 41, 46, 61-68, 90, 93, 95, 96, 98-104 passim, 106, 107, 109, 115, 117, 120, 121, 138, 182, 210, 216; his cognitive psychology, 16, 76; and direct realism, 64; his doctrine of cognitive presence, 15, 69, 84, 85, 86, 89; the exchange with Malebranche, 8-10, 14, 35, 53, 55, 56, 62-68, 72-73, 164, 192; and existence in the mind, 142, 153, 218, 220-21; Laird and Lovejoy on, 69-70; and mirrors, 145, 223; his objections against Descartes, 33; and the Port Royal *Logic*, 112. *See also* objective reality
Astruc, Jean, 183, 201-2
atheism, 196
Augustine, Saint, 95

Bacon, Francis, 210
Bailey, Samuel, 17, 223
Barron, William, 123
Barrow, Isaac, 10, 133
Baxter, Andrew, 82, 97, 140
Bayle, Pierre, 86-87, 95, 122, 142
Beasley, Frederick, 100
Belief(s) or opinion, 170, 192, 193, 195, 210, 214: false, 173-76; natural, 152, 158, 161, 169; psychology of, 182; Reid's account of, 119-20; its (their) relation to the imagination, 172, 177; about the world, 3, 55, 130-38, 140, 148-49, 152-54, 157-63
Bennett, Jonathan, 4-5, 16
Bentham, Edward, 118-19, 122
Berkeley, George, Bishop: and belief, 152;

and direct realism, 121, 136, 142, 162, 163, 222; and distance perception, 96, 209; and existence in the mind, 14, 86, 134-37, 153, 209-10, 218, 220; and idealism, 130; and the language of God, 13, 211, 213, 215; and materialism, 146, 206, 207, 208; and the nature of ideas, 99, 109, 136-39, 148-51, 207-10, 213; and the representative theory, 4-5, 136; and secondary qualities, 83; his theory of vision, 17, 132-38, 147, 156, 164, 181, 223; and visible points, 10

Blakey, Robert, 123

Bloch, Olivier, 215-16, 223

Bonnet, Charles, 13, 29-30, 183, 202, 214, 220

Boyer, C., 16

Boyle Lectures, 81

brain, 39, 84, 85, 96, 100, 105, 107, 108, 120, 185, 192, 194, 195, 198: fantasy located in, 20; figures or impressions traced on, 25, 27, 28, 40, 155, 201; ideas extended in, 164; impressions, 122, 126, 127; impulses in, 24; as locus of mind, 40; motions in, 21, 26-30, 37, 40, 42, 50, 56, 92, 183; motor force of, 21; and the nerves, 84, 205, 220; physiology of, 39, 187; pictures or images in, 10, 25, 26, 45, 49, 77, 78, 106; pores of, 24; its role in cognitive activity, 26; sensations as properties of, 141; and the soul, 79. See also mind

Brentano, F., 41

Broughton, John, 108

Brown, Thomas, 99

Browne, Peter, 109

Brunschvicg, Léon, 56

Buffier, Claude, 121

Burnet, Thomas, 103

Burthogge, Richard, 106-7, 113, 114, 212

camera obscura, 61, 73, 124, 125-27, 205-6, 212

Cartesianism. See Descartes, René

Caterus, 32-33, 62, 215

causal relations (or causality), 18, 19, 21, 22, 24, 30, 31, 36, 39, 41, 43, 47, 48, 49, 64, 96, 101, 147, 193, 216, 217: language of, 56

cause, 122, 162, 195, 201, 210, 211, 212: concept of, 110; and effect, 167,

171-74, 175, 177, 179, 194; of the formal reality of objects, 33; God as, 55; of ideas, 31, 32, 35, 89, 131; of impressions, 150; natural, 60; of perceptions, 63; physical, 23, 124, 217, 218, 220; second, 42, 54; of sensations, 23, 27; of things, 118

Chambers, Ephraim, 40, 109, 183

Chanet, Pierre, 60-61, 69, 73, 205

Cheyne, George, 129

Clarke, Samuel, 77-79, 81, 82, 84, 86

Clayton, Robert, 83

Clerselier, Claude, 35

Cohen, Murray, 211

Coke, Zachary, 113

Collier, Arthur, 76, 127-28, 140-41, 148, 206

Collins, Anthony, 183

Cook, Monte, 74

Crousaz, Jean Pierre de, 115-17, 166, 212

Cudworth, Ralph, 28-29, 30, 129, 145, 214, 220

Cumberland, Richard, 114

Dalbiez, –, 8, 16

Danto, Arthur C., 216-18

deism, 129

Deleule, D., 164

della Porta, Giambattista, 125

Descartes, René: his account of perceptual acquaintance, 15, 16, 18-41; and the camera obscura, 125; Cartesianism, 13, 84, 86, 97, 100, 106, 107, 110, 112-14, 122, 136, 142, 153, 217; and degrees of reality, 217-18; and direct realism, 70-73; and knowledge, 212; Malebranche's interpretation and use of his doctrines, 45, 47, 48, 67, 78; and natural signs, 130, 220; his optical theories, 10; his physiology, 183, 220; Price's comment on, 84; Reid's interpretation of, 98, 182; and representation, 52, 58, 61, 65, 68-69; and science, 210; his use of scholastic doctrines, 89, 117, 207; his use of the term 'idea', 4, 5, 7, 13, 70, 79, 108, 109, 115, 202, 221. See also objective reality; signs, natural

Desgabets, Robert, 74

Ditton, Humphrey, 17, 124

Doddridge, Philip, 83-84, 87

Drummond, William, 87

Duchesneau, François, 218-20, 223
Duggan, T., 203, 222
Duncan, William, 113, 117-18, 122
Durand of St. Pourçain, 8

Ellis, J., 98
Ellis, Welborne, 84
Encyclopaedia Britannica, 122
entity (entities), 37, 48, 101, 115, 208,
209: concepts as, 8; ideas as, see ideas;
images as, 120; not involved in sensation,
20, 39; mental, 14, 57, 107, 109, 120,
209, 210; psychic, 11; scholastic, 8;
species as, 61; the term, 41
Epicureans, 59, 106
essence(s), 52, 53, 57, 58, 71, 78, 95, 106,
108, 110; of God, 92, 95; real, 210
existence: double, 4, 12, 86, 124, 128,
132-40, 141-43, 147-64, 173, 174-75,
176, 178, 209; extension essential for,
81, 197; single, 12, 86, 124, 127, 132,
134, 141, 142, 143, 147-64, 173, 182,
209, 213
extension: and colored points, 168; essential
for existence, 81, 197; God's use of, 50,
67; idea of, 52, 54, 67, 80, 101, 138,
151, 156, 157, 184, 190-92, 198, 203;
intelligible, 51, 53, 56, 72, 212; and
matter, 42, 45, 55, 199; and its parts,
155; as quality of objects, 133, 206; and
the soul, 84, 92; of space, 15, 92, 103

faculty (faculties) of the mind, 8, 16, 19,
22, 29, 44, 49, 60, 105, 106, 111, 113,
123, 131, 166, 179, 194, 195, 196:
apprehensive, 9; cognitive, 19, 21;
intellectual, 119; sensible, 10
Fedé, René, 74
form(s): ideas as, 33; images as, 25, 40;
intelligible, 95; of objects, 34, 39, 71;
physical, 20; sensible, 7; substantial,
151-52, 176, 177-78; of thought, 115
formal reality, 13, 31, 32, 33, 36, 38, 39,
41, 62, 68, 100-101, 107, 215
Foucault, Michel, 211, 223
Foucher, Simon, 68-69, 74

Garin, Pierre, 16
Gassendi, Pierre, 35, 215
Gaukroger, Stephen, 40
Gérando, J. M. de, 99-100, 104

Gerdil, Giacinto Sigismondo, Cardinal,
"Père Barnabite," 94-98, 103, 123
Gilson, Etienne, 16, 34, 41, 58
Ginsberg, Morris, 69-70
Glanvill, Joseph, 27-28
God, 38, 42, 44, 47, 57, 63-66, 74, 89, 91,
96, 106, 128, 145, 148: as cause of the
idea of God, 32, 49, 50, 89, 102; and
created things, 145, 164, 210; his
essence, 80, 92, 95, 103, 108; his
existence, 19, 31, 81; idea of, 32, 35,
36, 37, 41, 119; his ideas, 67, 68, 92,
95, 146, 221; his knowledge, 53-54; our
knowledge of, 63; his language, 13; his
laws, 43; his mind, 43, 44, 67, 90, 159,
163, 220; mind created by, 30; his
nature, 51, 53; his perception, 51; and
the power of thought, 85; his presence
or omnipresence, 72, 77-79, 81, 82, 86,
91, 92, 97; space as his sensorium, 78-
79; his substance, 86, 97, 145, 146; his
will, 55, 80
Gregory, David, 77
Grove, Henry, 127-28, 140, 145, 148, 159,
206

Hacking, Ian, 210, 222-23
Haldane, E. S., 39
Hall, T. S., 39
Hamilton, Sir William, 74
Hartley, David, 183
Hobbes, Thomas, 11, 17, 89, 112, 130-32,
145, 147, 169, 210
Hooke, Robert, 125-27, 134, 144, 159, 183,
184, 205
Hooker, Michael, 223
Howell, W. S., 122
Hume, David, 147-64; on awareness, 41,
222; on belief, 182; and bodies, 136; his
cognitive psychology, 184, 196, 220,
221; and idealism, 131; on the
imagination, 165-80; his logic, 120, 201;
and the nature of ideas, 59, 181-203,
207, 210, 215; and objects as
perceptions, 142-43; and physiology,
183; and real causes, 56, 210; and the
representative theory, 4-5, 121, 207; on
single and double existence, 86, 132,
147-64. See also points (colored,
mathematical, physical); presence to the
mind

idea(s): as acts of perception or thought, 9, 14, 16, 37, 45, 61-65, 70, 74, 83, 90, 94, 97, 104, 120, 162-63; association of, 167, 170; as corporeal or extended, 127, 164, 184; as forms, 108, 115, 117, 119; in God's mind, 51, 54, 55, 67, 95, 97; as images, 98, 110, 116, 129, 149; innate, 106-8; intellectual, 49; intelligible, 95, 97; as interpretations of motion, 26; as meanings, 4, 13, 109; in the memory, 154; as mental events, 35, 36, 37, 195; as modes of mind, 13, 31, 68, 109, 202, 207, 210, 218; as objects or entities, 4, 5, 14, 34-38, 49, 55, 58, 62-64, 68-70, 73, 76, 99, 100-104, 117, 136, 182, 208, 210, 212, 221; pure, 49; representative function of, 26, 31, 32, 45, 219; as representing objects, 32, 36, 38, 45, 98, 109; sensible, 29, 41, 49, 212; and signs, 22-31, 122, 212, 213; as signs, 24, 101, 220; simple, 94, 118, 129, 138, 197; as source of knowledge of body, 73; space as the place of, 79; terminology or language of, 4, 44, 100, 105, 106, 112, 131; and things, 137-38, 199, 207, 212; two concepts of, 4, 88-103, 208; veil of, 5, 140, 221; way of, 4, 5, 14, 15, 16, 76, 94, 98, 100, 102, 105, 110, 112, 115, 142, 182, 185, 195, 205, 206, 207, 208, 216, 220, 221, 222
idealism, 87, 130
identity and difference: numerical, 10, 102, 121, 148-52, 162, 163, 199, 207, 209; specific, 121, 142, 148-52, 161, 163, 169, 199, 200, 207, 211, 215
image(s), 22, 29, 35, 39, 78, 109, 114-17, 128-32, 136, 144, 148, 149, 154-55, 157, 171, 185-87, 188-89: appearing to the mind, 172; of body, 21; in the brain, 2, 27, 29, 45, 49, 77, 78, 106, 201; in a camera obscura, 73, 125-27; as coming from objects, 25; corporeal, 49; on the eye, 96; in the fancy, 155, 171; as figured light, 130; intelligible, 95; intentional, 8; as internal objects, 116; language of, 10; location of, 5-8, 11, 14, 130, 132, 182; as means of knowing, 8; mirror, 16, 60, 64, 128; not needed for thought, 117; of objects, 54, 59, 61, 67-69, 83, 119; in optics, 5, 128; on the pineal gland, 40; present to the soul or

mind, 79, 100, 107; representative, 33, 128, 168, 207; retinal, 11, 46, 92, 96; as things, 136; of things, 141; visual, 147. See also representation of images
imagination: as cognitive, 22; distinguished from understanding, 109-12; Hobbes on, 131-32; Hume's account of, 152, 155, 157-58, 160, 165-80, 188, 190, 198; and ideas, 23, 87, 108, 110; and knowledge of objects, 19, 45; located on the pineal gland, 40; Mayne on, 109-12, 121; as part of the body, 20, 107, 114, 122, 183
immaterialists and immaterialism, 159-60, 196, 222
impressions: bodily, 28; brain, 25, 26, 28, 126, 127, 199, 202, 206, 207, 212; on the cognitive power, 20; of colored points, 156; corporeal, 116; extended, 183; and ideas, 59, 139, 141, 149, 159, 197; or images, 168; of light, 23, 143; material, 97, 108; and matter, 77; mental, 99, 100, 120, 150; from objects, 40, 148, 200; perceptions as, 161; sense, 10, 45, 53, 90, 118, 153, 155, 167, 174, 187, 189, 192, 195; on wax, 19, 135

Jackson, John, 81-82
Jessop, T. E., 146, 208
judgment, 47, 54, 113-18 passim, 122, 128, 131, 143, 144, 155, 156, 166, 192, 195

Kames, Henry Home, Lord, 161
Kant, Immanuel, 164
Kenney, W. H., 122
Kenny, A. J. P., 41
Kepler, Johannes, 11, 125, 146
Keynes, John Maynard, 164
King, James T., 164, 202
King, William, 79
Knight, William, 87
knowledge, 14, 59, 60, 106, 132, 164, 186: and belief, 193; of body, 5, 15, 21, 26, 49, 51, 54, 76; concept or nature of, 18, 44, 50, 52, 70, 76, 113, 122, 202; deductive, 210; direct, 64; of essences, 53, 212; and experience, 161; as identical with its object, 7, 69; indirect, 6; of matter, 67; of objects, 3, 7, 13, 20, 34, 40, 103, 111, 116, 208, 215; of particulars, 8; and perception, 94, 110,

147-48, 222; problem of, 5, 73; as
representation, 4; scientific, 43, 213; and
sensation, 65; sensitive, 9, 220; of things,
19, 68, 208; and truth, 54; and
universals, 43, 118; of the world, 4, 18,
102, 181, 219

La Chambre, Marin Cureau de, 58-60
Laird, John, 69-70, 74
La Mettrie, Julien O. de, 145
Larmore, Charles, 40
Law, Edmund, 79-80, 81
laws: connate, 144; of motion, 210; of
nature, 43, 211
Layton, Henry, 108-09
LeClerc, Jean, 40, 115, 122
Lee, Henry, 128-29
Le Grand, Antoine, 107
Leibniz, Gottfried Wilhelm von, 77-79, 86,
87
Lennon, Thomas M., 17, 40, 41, 55, 104
Livingston, Donald W., 164, 202
Locke, Don, 222
Locke, John, 187, 193, 200: his cognitive
psychology, 16, 39; his critique of
Malebranche, 88-94; and existence in the
mind, 89, 153, 218, 220; on ideas, 15,
90, 93-94, 96, 99-102, 107-8, 110-14,
120, 127-29, 138, 147, 182, 212-13,
220; his influence on British logics, 117-
19; and knowledge, 56, 162, 164, 202,
210, 219; as a logician, 122-23; his
optical language, 125, 202; and
physiology, 92, 93, 127; and reflection,
116; and the representative theory, 4-5,
38, 99, 145; and sensible qualities, 151;
on signs, 211; and thinking matter, 85,
146; on thought and motion, 87; his
view of matter, 163
logic, 122, 123, 166, 193, 201: artificial,
166, 182; epistemic, 194; natural, 114,
166, 172-73, 182; new, 112-19; Port
Royal, 27, 105, 112-14, 115, 166
Lovejoy, A. O., 69-70, 74
Luce, A. A., 135, 146

Mackie, J. L., 101, 104, 145
McRae, R. F., 104
Malebranche, Nicolas: Alquié's study of,
72-73; and brain traces, 40, 56; the
exchange with Arnauld, 8-10, 14, 35,
53, 55, 56, 62-68, 72-73, 164, 192; his
doctrine of ideas, 13, 14, 15, 38-39, 41,
44-45, 46, 48, 54, 55, 69, 74, 76, 97,
103, 105-6, 108, 109, 122, 136, 146,
163, 164, 221; Leibniz's comments on,
78; Locke's critique of, 88-94; and
optics, 54, 56; and physiology, 45, 50,
127; on presence to mind, 78, 82, 84,
86, 91-92, 95, 144, 159; and science,
43-44, 55; on secondary qualities, 83;
his theory of knowledge, 43, 44, 49-52,
54, 58, 212, 220; his theory of
perception, 12, 42-55, 145, 158
Marin, Louis, 27, 30, 40, 75
Martin, C. B., 104
materialists and materialism, 84-85, 93, 130,
134, 146, 183, 196, 198, 199, 200, 201,
205, 207, 208. See also immaterialists
and immaterialism
matter, 70, 74, 77, 80, 81, 84, 87, 92, 106,
131, 140, 142, 146, 151, 161, 206:
corpuscular, 163, 188; divisibility of,
156; and form of objects, 6, 48; and
motion, 27, 196; nature of, 51, 55, 67;
particles of, 134; philosopher's, 137;
theory of, 42, 83, 150; and thought, 15,
83, 94, 124, 196, 202
Maull, Nancy L., 40
Maurin, Paul-Marie, 17, 130, 145
Maurolico, Francesco, 11
Maxwell, John, 122
Mayne, Zachary, 109-12, 120, 121-22, 212
meaning: carried by ideas, 107, 109, 184,
187, 196, 202, 212; concept of, 211,
219; epistemic, 219; of figures and
sounds, 27; linguistic, 219; of material
impressions, 28; of objects, 35, 75; in
perceptual acquaintance, 13-16, 25, 86,
207, 217, 220-21; and understanding,
13-16, 110, 114; of words, 184, 193; of
the world, 38
memory, 19, 21, 90, 108, 126, 131, 154,
167, 170, 180, 193, 214
metaphor, 18, 26, 51, 58, 72, 76, 92, 96,
97, 98, 99, 102, 103, 125, 147, 211,
221: of ideas in the mind, 14; optical,
220; spatial, 14, 60, 71
Mill, J. S., 17, 223
mind: as active, 7, 71, 85, 129; affected by
sensation, 24, 64; anatomy of, 181, 221;
as cause of ideas, 31, 108; as conscious,

111; as extended, 184; as form of the body, 44; as it forms ideas, 19, 30; God's presence to, 72; as a heap of perceptions, 153; history of, 118; as knowing, 26; knowledge of, 63; operations and workings of, 112, 114, 148, 173, 182, 188, 192-95, 196, 201, 202, 204, 207, 221; its relation to body, 22, 49, 68; its relation to objects, 15, 16, 59, 143; the senses as windows for, 61; walking, 14, 47, 48, 59-60, 66, 82, 89, 144. *See also* faculty (faculties) of the mind; presence to or with the mind

Molyneux, William, 133
Monboddo, James Burnett, Lord, 84-85, 87
Morgan, Thomas, 141
Motte, Andrew, 86

natures, simple, 21, 50
Newton, Isaac, 10, 40, 77, 78, 82, 85, 144, 210
Nicole, Pierre, 112
Nidditch, Peter H., 164
Noel, L., 16
Norris, John, 85, 86, 94, 98, 103, 108, 145
Nouvelles de la république des lettres, 103

objective reality, 6, 12, 13, 18, 19, 25, 30-34, 36, 39, 41, 48, 60, 61, 62, 63, 67, 68, 69, 73, 89, 100-101, 107, 117, 135, 136, 207, 215, 221
objects: external, 3, 9, 12, 13, 39, 49, 57, 58, 60, 61, 63, 65, 83, 88, 90, 95, 103, 111, 116-18, 120, 125, 129, 149, 154-57, 159, 161, 162, 164, 175, 197, 204, 207, 214; form of, 6, 7; geometrical, 95; immediate, 3; knowledge of, 3; material, 9, 28; outward, 5; physical, 4, 32, 46, 134; real, 12; representative, 6; sensible, 28, 52, 141. *See also* ideas; presence to or with the mind
occasionalists and occasionalism, 19, 22, 32, 56
Ockham, William of, 104
Olscamp, Paul J., 17, 40, 55
O'Neil, Brian E., 34-35, 41, 70-72
opinion. *See* belief(s)
optics, 5, 14, 44, 54, 55, 86, 96, 124-46, 147, 155-56, 181, 206, 222: language of, 10-12, 13, 86, 198, 205, 212

Paracelsus, 211
phantasms, 7, 8, 11, 12, 14, 28, 29, 59, 89, 110, 130, 131, 138, 145
physiology: of the body, 13, 50, 90; of the brain, 39, 45, 93, 195, 205; Descartes's, 18-24; Hume's use of, 183, 195, 202; of perception, 15, 29-30, 85, 124, 127, 199, 217-18; of thinking, 201; of vision, 54
Picard, Gabriel, 8-10, 16, 56
pineal gland, 25, 30, 40, 182
Plato (or platonic), 3, 8, 38, 97, 103
Plotinus, 74
points: colored, 10, 17, 156, 168, 190-92; mathematical, 10, 156, 190, 192; physical, 10; on the retina, 10, 125, 126, 156; system of, 11; visible, 10
Pope, Alexander, 181, 201
Popkin, Richard, 141-42, 146
Porterfield, William, 82-83, 85, 87, 111, 143-44, 148, 155, 159
power: cognitive, 20-21; motive, 20
Preceptor, The, 122
presence to or with the mind, 12, 15, 61-75, 76, 84, 100, 103, 133, 135, 139, 143, 152-57, 158, 163, 165, 166, 167, 182, 187, 204: cognitive, 32, 89; essences as, 71; Hume's use of, 13-14; ideas as, 4, 91, 127, 136; language of, 94, 111, 220; literal, 32, 58; and no action at a distance, 77; objects as, 6, 32, 33, 37, 38, 48, 58, 61, 64-75, 85, 86, 89, 95, 120, 157, 162; principle of, 83, 88, 134, 147, 149, 205
Price, Richard, 84
Priestley, Joseph, 84, 87, 183, 197-98, 202
psychology, 22, 105-10, 120, 194: cognitive, 16, 184, 196, 222; of perception, 18-22

qualities, 87, 174, 197, 200; coexisting, 152, 212-13; of objects, 26, 150; occult, 176; perceived, 151; primary, 88, 96, 98, 127, 142, 150, 160, 177, 208, 213, 219; secondary, 83, 96, 98, 141, 142, 150, 151, 160, 177, 208, 213, 219; sensible, 47, 50, 130, 157, 190, 215, 220

Radner, Daisie, 74
Ramus, Peter (Pierre de la Ramée), 114
realism, 101: commonsense, 142; direct, 6,

15, 34, 41, 61, 69, 71, 102, 120-21, 126, 136, 142, 199; illusory, 165; indirect, 72, 73, 102; representative, 41, 102, 120-21, 136, 221

reality. *See* formal reality; objective reality

Reid, Thomas, 3, 5, 13, 15, 85, 98-99, 100, 119-21, 169, 182, 183, 201, 202-3, 204-9, 211, 213-15, 216, 220, 221, 222

representation of images, 83, 186, 188, 189, 190, 193, 201: and knowledge, 65; psychological, 11, 196; and signifying, 24, 88

representationalism, 8, 9, 16, 26, 33, 34, 52, 61, 62, 67, 68-70, 93, 96, 98, 100, 106, 108-10, 116, 117, 120, 126, 128, 129, 164, 217

representative relations, 25

representative theory, 4, 5, 15, 74, 101, 120, 145, 221

Rescher, N., 17

resemblance, 25, 30, 95, 96, 128, 142, 147, 148, 149, 150, 157, 167, 170-71, 174, 175, 179; of ideas, 13, 38, 61, 125

retina, 25, 46, 54, 92, 96, 126, 127, 129, 144, 155, 156

Robson, John M., 17

Rodis-Lewis, Geneviève, 17, 26-27, 30, 55, 57, 74

Ronchi, Vasco, 11-12, 130, 145, 146

Rorty, Richard, 5, 16, 222, 223

Ross, G. R. T., 39

Rothstein, Eric, 165, 180

Royal Society, 145, 162

Ryle, G., 101, 104

Sanderson, Robert, 113-14

Scheibler, Christopher, 145

scholasticism: terms in, 36, 207; theory of, 6-10, 12, 14; 15, 30, 34, 38, 39, 48, 61, 69, 102, 108, 215, 216; writers on, 5, 16, 22, 33, 59, 60, 97, 113, 142

science, 18, 40, 43-44, 48, 55, 87, 208: of human nature, 166, 185, 194; of nature, 210; of signs, 219

Scotus, Duns, 8

Selby-Bigge, L. A., 164

semantic argument, 219

semantic interpretation, 38

semantic relation, 19, 30, 33, 37, 41, 61, 216, 217, 220

sensation(s), 25, 26, 30, 43, 44, 51-53, 60, 64, 70, 87, 97, 100, 117, 119, 125, 129, 144, 152, 156, 157, 183-86 *passim*, 195, 196, 202, 208, 213: and their causes, 23, 137; feelings as, 47, 49, 107, 133; and ideas, 22, 24, 30, 66, 98, 116-18, 139; as knowing, 45; as modes of mind, 67; organs of, 78, 220; as perceptions or thoughts, 138, 143; physiology of, 90; as properties of the brain, 141; reified, 136, 208; and resemblance, 96; of the soul, 77

Sergeant, John, 89

Sherlock, William, 103

signs, 13, 18, 22-31, 39, 88, 104, 116, 122, 193, 194, 202, 211, 213, 219, 223: artificial, 29; of the book of nature, 211; language of, 40, 212; natural, 22, 23, 24, 25, 27, 29-30, 39, 40, 75, 130, 213-15, 218, 223; unconscious, 215, 220; universal, 211

Simon, Jules, 55

Singer, B. R., 144-45

skepticists and skepticism, 4, 5, 15, 32, 125, 128, 140, 141, 148, 151, 157, 160, 162, 165, 175, 177, 180, 199, 205, 210, 211, 216, 221

Smith, N. Kemp, 74

soul, 23, 47, 48, 50, 70, 72, 74, 77, 78, 79, 80-84 *passim*, 91, 92, 93, 104, 105, 108, 127, 135, 144, 187, 206: action of objects on, 129; capable of receiving form of objects, 7; images present to, 7; and instinct, 121; magical faculty of, 168; nature of, 159, 178, 184, 196, 198; powers of, 60, 119; its role in the formation of ideas, 126; sees objects, 40, 205; thinking part of, 7, 28, 29

space, 197: and body, 145; our conception of, 156; empty, 156; and extension, 15, 184, 188, 191, 197; external, 134; and God, 78, 79, 80; idea of, 169; intelligible, 51, 56; material, 55; parts of, 192; and soul or mind, 15, 80, 82, 84, 85; and time, 31, 81, 140, 157, 167, 168, 175, 188, 190

species, 61, 72: expressed, 9, 40; intelligible, 7, 8, 33, 51, 56, 69, 71; intentional, 8, 16, 22, 216; material, 55; representative, 60

Spectator, The, 86, 87

Spinoza, Benedictus de, 159-60

Sraffa, Piero, 164
Starobinsky, Jean, 165
Stewart, Dugald, 77
Stewart, M. A., 104
Stillingfleet, Edward, Bishop, 88
Stocks, J. L., 104
Suarez, F. (and Suarezian), 8, 9, 16
substance(s): and accidents, 160, 216; categories of, 212; and causation, 22; created, 19, 82; of God, 77-79, 81; Hume's rejection of, 176-78, 187, 203; ideas as, 93, 97, 106, 108, 120, 136, 215; immaterial or incorporeal, 38, 102, 159, 218; material, 110, 150, 151, 152; metaphysical, 41; mind as, 61; objects as, 163; and power, 85; and quality, 197; spiritual, 135; thinking, 81, 196

Tacquet, André, 10
Tannéry, Paul, 39
Thackray, Arnold, 86
Thomas Aquinas, Saint, 6, 7-8, 9, 16, 33-34, 58, 67, 71, 89, 95, 103, 220
Tipton, Ian C., 135-37, 207-10, 222

Tolet, François, 8, 9
truth(s), 18, 19, 21, 40, 54, 67, 105, 107, 119, 122, 171, 217: inner, 55; logical, 114; metaphysical, 40; moral, 51; scientific, 40, 43; about the world, 53
Turbayne, Colin, 146

understanding (faculty of), 19, 21, 22, 36, 39, 44, 59, 60, 121, 129, 170, 174, 180, 191, 194, 205: act of, 101-7, 201; as a camera obscura, 124-25, 127; distinguished from imagination, 109-12; as intellectual seeing, 44, 45; objects in the, 32-34, 36, 48

vibrations (of nerves), 42, 124, 183
Vieussens, M., 122
Voltaire, F. M. A. de, 96, 121, 122, 201

Watts, Isaac, 80, 86, 113, 117, 118, 159
Wilkins, John, 113, 122, 211
Witty, John, 129
Wright, John P., 202

John Yolton is professor of philosophy and dean of
Rutgers College at Rutgers University. *Perceptual
Acquaintance* and a companion volume, *Thinking
Matter,* grow out of years of research in seventeenth-
and eighteenth-century thought. His earlier titles
include *John Locke and the Way of Ideas* and *Locke
and the Compass of Human Understanding*; he edited
The Locke Reader and the Everyman edition of
Locke's *Essay Concerning Human Understanding.*
Yolton also serves on the editorial board of the
journal *Eighteenth-Century Studies.*